$3.50

FULL PRODUCTION WITHOUT WAR

At a time when production is one of America's most pressing problems, this vigorous analysis of the reasons for non-production in our economy is of first importance. Mr. Loeb's point of departure is the business procedure known as "monopolistic competition." He demonstrates that our economy, far from being based on pure competition, is geared to expectant sales at predetermined prices rather than true demand.

Our economists have said much recently of the cyclic trends of national and international economy, warning that we are getting past the safety point on these oscillations. Mr. Loeb submits reasons to indicate that the amplitude of these swings is apt to increase if corrective measures are not soon taken. He devotes the latter part of his book to a consideration of ways and means of reducing the amplitude of business cycles so that demand and production can be sustained at a high level, and the various producers released to fulfill the potentialities of their concerns.

Mr. Loeb insists that full production without war is not just a dream but a very real possibility and hope. His thesis is a provocative one, which will be of keen interest to students of modern economic trends.

Full Production
Without War

Full Production Without War

By Harold Loeb

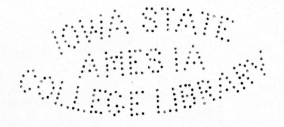

PRINCETON
PRINCETON UNIVERSITY PRESS
1946

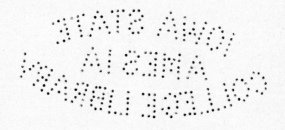

To the Memory of My Mother
whose faith did not flag

Preface

IN the land of the Mentawei, rice cannot be cultivated nor milk cows tended because there are so many feast days during which no work is performed. As a result, the people of this region do not live as well as do their neighbors.

In parts of Europe, America and other places where technology has reached an advanced stage, commodities which could be produced are not produced because of unemployment. When this occurs, the people of these lands are deprived of needed goods and services, and at the same time support would-be workers in idleness.

The irrationality of this latter conjunction impressed me as far back as I can remember. In 1920 and 1921 we used to discuss it—Stuart Chase, Howard Scott, myself and others who glimpsed the potentialities for general well being contained in modern scientific procedures. However, I did not think much about the matter until 1929.

In that year, many of my acquaintances had to curtail their standard of living, though no earthquake, plague or other physical disaster had arrested the production of wealth or lowered the productivity of society. Apparently the phase of contemporary living that related to the production and distribution of goods and services was subject to other than physical restrictions. With this thought in mind, I indulged in a fantasy which attempted to envisage what conditions would be like were men, machines, resources and knowledge fully utilized along the lines suggested by Howard Scott. Since I did not share the technocratic conviction that a dictatorship was required in order to sustain production, nor trouble at that time to delve either into statistical relationships or economic theories, the sketch paralleled in many ways the earlier forecast of Bellamy which I had not previously read.

Shortly afterwards, technocracy blazed across the horizon and exploded. I concluded:

1. Technocracy's primary tenet—that the manpower, resources and knowledge existing in the United States were sufficient to

provide an ample living for the total population—was probably sound.

2. The idea had captured the imagination of the public at a time of unsettled thinking because it based a promise of plenty and security on a foundation putatively scientific.

3. The exposure of the fact that technocracy rested on a mystic [1] pedestal although it had been put forward as the product of scientific research, had made it seem ridiculous and caused it to fade out quickly.

I decided to check the primary tenet by whatever data were available. Could the technical feasibility of abundant provisioning be demonstrated, its realization might be brought nearer. At any rate, such a check seemed the best approach or first step to the problem of unemployment and nonproduction.

The Civil Works Administration in 1934 gave me the facilities, a corps of experts, a staff, and access to government data, for conducting a survey of capacity, the NSPPC as we called it. The task was completed in 1935 and the *Chart of Plenty* [2] and the report of the *National Survey of Potential Product Capacity* [3] were duly published. Meanwhile the Brookings Institution had also conducted, completed and published a survey of productive capacity [4] using a different procedure and putting the question differently. Both studies indicated that the production and consumption of goods and services in the United States could be vastly increased by putting unemployed men and machines to work.

Notwithstanding this double substantiation of the "abundance" hypothesis, society continued to lack goods and to support the unemployed in idleness. And it continued to do so not because informed opinion doubted the possibility of producing more wealth. On the contrary, it turned out that many bankers, industrialists and business men—as well as economists, statisticians and Bellamites—had been aware all along that many

---

[1] "Mystic" is used in the sense of "directly apprehended" without going through the steps, logical and factual, associated with "scientific procedures."

[2] Viking Press, New York, 1935.

[3] New York City Housing Authority, 1935.

[4] *America's Capacity to Produce*, Nourse and Associates.

more goods and services could be provided. But it continued to do so chiefly because no one knew how to put the unemployed to work creating needed goods without wrecking the elaborate structure of customs and institutions which regulated the economic life of society—or how to correct the condition even by wrecking the structure, for that matter.

An investigation of economic procedures seemed in order. With insight into what made the motor run, so to speak, it might be possible to discover why one or two of the cylinders usually missed. So blithely I started on the study which follows.

As I proceeded, certain of my prejudices and predilections were dissolved. At the start I had tended to overrate the function of engineers and other blueprint planners and to underrate the function of the complicated business procedures by which prices and wages are set and resources are allocated. Gradually, the importance of this latter or economic [5] function impressed itself upon me. The procedures had been evolved by trial and error during many ages and could not be discarded without disaster before substitute procedures had been worked out. But no substitute procedure for a peacetime economy had been worked out even on paper, though this fact was not always faced.[6] Essentially the problem was to discover and to understand the factors which prevented our system of "production for sale on the market" from operating effectively. Then measures might be devised to correct or neutralize the inhibiting factors thereby evading the probably impossible task of devising and instituting a new system.

As the study tediously pursued its end, events occurred in the larger world which affected the situation. Other societies faced by unemployment and nonproduction found a means to put their manpower to work. It is evident that a society which fully utilized its manpower and resources would be richer, as the tribes adjacent to the Mentawei, or stronger, than another society which utilized only a fraction of its manpower, other things being equal. And although in the world of yesterday

[5] The word "economic" will be used broadly to mean "the effective shaping of means to ends." In its narrower application, "economic" will be used to mean "an optimum disposal or utilization of scarce means."

[6] This statement is supported on pp. 10 ff.

the societies which released their full productive power were not as well endowed in either resources or skill (technology) as the societies which used to limp along with part of their productive power operating sporadically, yet the advantage the former derived from full production was so great that it more than neutralized these deficiencies for a while. And the societies which realized their full strength by using all their manpower, applied the wealth and power thus made available to the conquest and exploitation of their neighbors in order to impose on the rest of the world a servile order.

Thus putting the unemployed to work, which originally had been desired in order to eliminate the waste and demoralization of nonproduction and thereby to release the potentialities of the American people, had become necessary so that the United States might continue to be a free political entity. What had once been thought of as a step forward in social self-realization had become essential for national survival.

The work was approaching completion in 1941. The rising tension of that period suggested that a study of the causes of unemployment, despite its importance for the future, had become academic for the time being. Consequently, in the spring of that year, I put these pages to one side and went to Washington to contribute what I could to the preparation effort. Now the problem of peacetime unemployment has again come to the fore. It has seemed timely, therefore, to review the discarded thesis and to revise those paragraphs affected by subsequent events.

This study is submitted in the hope that its interpretation of our working procedure will assist us to surmount the threat to well-being which the stopping of military production and civilian reconstruction is likely to bring, so that we may continue marching toward the ideal, envisaged by the founders of our nation, of a society so designed that each of its citizens enjoys the freedom to be and to become whatever, within his capacities, he desires.

HAROLD LOEB

Washington, D. C.
March, 1944

Introduction

TO produce a good or to render a service requires action. In a money economy this action is accompanied usually by transactions of a financial character. Money is exchanged for manhours and materials, rent is paid over to the owners of property, and interest to the owners of debt. Profits may be distributed or losses allocated. The first process, production, makes wealth available for human use. The second process puts money, a human invention which usually gives the holder the power to acquire goods and services, into people's pockets. The wealth made available by the first process may be called "the available supply." The buying power released by the second process constitutes "effective demand."

The money issued in the productive process,[1] which consists of the cost of production plus a profit or minus a loss, must equal the money value [2] of the goods which are sold.[3] It is therefore evident that the supply which is sold equals the effective demand (profit or loss being included) issued in the process of producing the goods which are sold. This truism is usually called Say's law. It is sometimes stated as "supply creates its own demand."

A further deduction would seem plausible. Since more wealth is desired by all societies, and since supply creates its own demand, it seems as if a rational society in the ordinary course of events would produce all the wealth that it could.

Although we know from observation that this latter deduction is unsound, it has probably had a great deal to do with the direction which economic thinking has taken. Since the time of Ricardo,[4] economists have been largely concerned with the dis-

[1] Distributive activities are considered to be part of the productive process.

[2] The metaphysical concept of a "real" value other than exchange value (price times quantity) is irrelevant to this discussion. Value will be used as if it were synonymous with selling price times quantity, however the selling price may have been established.

[3] Not all goods would necessarily be sold. This and other complications will be taken up in due course.

[4] In a letter to Malthus, Ricardo wrote: "Political economy, you think, is an enquiry into the nature and causes of wealth; I think it should rather be called an enquiry into the laws which determine the division of the produce of industry among the classes which concur in its formation." (Letters to Malthus, page 175.) In the Preface to his *Principles*, he wrote: "To determine the laws which regulate this distribution, is the principal problem of Political Economy."

tribution of income and only to a minor extent with its creation. As a result, the possibility that less wealth might be produced than could be produced because demand [5] was deficient received little attention until recently.   As Keynes puts it, "The idea that we can safely neglect the aggregate demand function is fundamental to the Ricardian economics, which underlie what we have been taught for more than a century.   Malthus, indeed, had vehemently opposed Ricardo's doctrine that it was impossible for effective demand to be deficient; but vainly.   For, since Malthus was unable to explain clearly (apart from an appeal to the facts of common observation) how and why effective demand could be deficient or excessive, he failed to furnish an alternative construction, and Ricardo conquered. Ricardo conquered England as completely as the Holy Inquisition conquered Spain.   Not only was his theory accepted by the City, by statesmen and by the academic world, but controversy ceased; the other point of view completely disappeared; it ceased to be discussed.   The great puzzle of Effective Demand with which Malthus had wrestled, vanished from economic literature.   You will not find it mentioned even once in the whole works of Marshall, Edgeworth and Professor Pigou, from whose hands the classical theory has received its most mature embodiment.   It could only live on furtively below the surface in the underworlds of Karl Marx, Silvio Gesell or Major Douglas." [6]

The study which follows will be concerned with the "puzzle" referred to in our quotation.   It will seek to discover why the effective demand released in the productive process commands a supply less than the supply which could feasibly be produced, a problem akin to the problem which Malthus envisaged.   The difficulty, as we shall see, does not lie in the release of a demand less than the value of the supply which *is produced*, but in the release of a demand less than the value of the supply which *could be produced*, an important distinction.

In pursuing this inquiry, the question of income distribution is relevant.   But in the analysis which follows, the problem of

---

[5] The qualifying adjective "effective" is to be understood whenever the expression "demand" is used, unless it is otherwise stated.

[6] *The General Theory of Employment, Interest and Money*, John Maynard Keynes, Harcourt Brace & Howe, p. 32.

distribution is subordinated to the problem of nonproduction. It is touched upon only because it affects indirectly the quantity of wealth produced.

The analysis starts in Chapter II with the consideration of the nature of competition. The discussion will distinguish pure or price competition, in which production governs demand, from monopolistic competition, in which demand to a large extent governs production.

In Chapter III, a framework will be presented which will enable us to envisage the effect of changes in the various factors which constitute demand and supply upon the over-all equilibrium adjustment.[7] This framework will enable us *to translate* the *procedures* of *monopolistic competition into terms* of the *total economy*, thereby revealing the bearing of these procedures upon the over-all equilibrium adjustment.

Nonproduction is accounted for in Chapter IV by showing how the procedures of monopolistic competition, in which demand largely governs production, result in cyclic up and down surges and thereby in nonproduction.

In Chapter V the factors controlling the amplitude and limits of the business cycle are considered.

In Chapters VI and VII, suggestions are made concerning how an economy of monopolistic competition might be released to fulfill its potentialities, since the institution of an economy of pure or price competition is not feasible.

Several economic concepts are described and defined in Chapter I. This task is particularly necessary in an economic discussion because of the difference, sometimes wide, between the meaning of many economic expressions as used by economists and as used by laymen. An attempt is made to create a verbal frame of reference in which the reader and writer can meet, so that the reader can better check the line of the subsequent argument.

In certain of the footnotes and appendices, the relations described in the text are represented in mathematical terms. Some readers may find it desirable to skip these digressions on first reading in order to follow the line of the argument without interruption.

[7] Defined on p. 5.

Contents

CHAPTER I

The Problem is Defined

1. THE NATIONAL INCOME, CAPITAL, MONEY, AND OTHER ECONOMIC
CONCEPTS ARE DEFINED AND EXAMINED.

THE sum of the finished goods and services actually produced in any year constitutes the gross national product.[1] Though diverse goods and services cannot be added up unless a common denominator is provided, their sum might be calculated by totalling the values of the various goods and services made available during the year, that is to say, by adding up the various goods and services multiplied by their prices. However, the national income is usually estimated by totalling all the money paid out during the year in the process of production plus or minus undistributed profits and losses. Such an estimate is relatively easy to make since the money paid out consists in the main of wages, profits, interest, rent, royalties and pensions, about which more or less reliable statistics are gathered. Since money paid out in the process of production equals the price received for the goods produced, as was noted in the introduction, the national income estimated in this way should be reasonably accurate, especially as changes in inventory carryover and other factors which sometimes cause money paid out to be more or less than the value of the goods and services produced can be incorporated. Income tabulations, however estimated, permit the comparison of one year's income with that of another when an adjustment is made to take into account changes in the price level.

The national income can be divided into capital goods and consumer goods.

Capital [2] will be used in this study to mean such more or less

[1] National income and gross national product need not be distinguished in this study, since the depreciation of plant and the subtraction of business taxes have no bearing on the discussion. For general purposes the more familiar phrase "national income" will be used when reference is made to the annual production of wealth.

[2] The only exception will be our use of the word "capital" in "capital gains."

1

durable man-made goods as implements, tools, machines, industrial buildings, railroad tracks, power houses and other concrete material instruments which aid men in the process of production. Land, therefore, will not be considered capital, but, like ore or falling water, a natural resource.

Capital goods, like other goods, require manhours for their production. Money commands (i.e., purchases) manhours as well as other things. *Money* therefore can be translated into capital but is not capital until it is so translated. Consequently, money is distinguished from capital and *will not be called by the latter term.*

Money may be defined as the means of payment and the medium of exchange. It is also used for storing command over commodities but has been largely superseded in this role by stocks, bonds, time deposits and other certificates of ownership and debt.

Sea shells, beads, cattle, gold, silver and other articles of utility or fancy have been used for money. In the days when physical commodities such as gold and silver were employed, a deficiency in demand due to a lack of money was supposed to be countered by prices falling until the deficiency was eliminated. However, the operation seldom worked satisfactorily for very long. Wealth, because of an advance in efficiency or other cause, has often increased faster than the supply of money. Prices sometimes would fall but seldom enough to restore the equality of demand and supply. The resulting deficiency which used to show up as a lack of money has harassed individuals and hampered enterprise in many times and places.

We need not concern ourselves with this former difficulty, since money has long been divorced (though still paying alimony) from the physical commodity which is supposed in the United States to stand behind it. The tie between money and its commodity base was weakened in the 18th and 19th centuries by the introduction of currency or paper interchangeable with the metal and issued usually against gold or silver reserves. Since the ratio of metal to paper was fixed arbitrarily and subject to change, the supply of money could be expanded regardless of the supply of metal on hand so long as confidence in its purchasing power was not undermined.

Latterly, a new form of money, the supply of which is even more elastic, has largely superseded the older forms, although both gold and currency are still used for money. Let us call this new variety *debit money* since it is issued against an acknowledgment of debt.

The method by which this money is created is of the simplest. A would-be borrower goes to a bank, requests and receives a loan which he deposits to his account. When the banker does not use for that purpose money received because someone else has paid up on a similar loan, but creates the money by giving the depositor a credit, the effective demand (and the supply of money, since money was defined as command over commodities) is increased by the amount of the new credit.

This commonplace procedure has long been employed to finance producers (i.e., commercial loans). When used for this purpose, the loan is usually repaid when the goods are produced and sold. As a result, the effect on over-all demand may be ephemeral.

However, the practice has been extended to assist would-be buyers of private securities such as stocks and bonds, as well as of public securities such as government bonds. A bank can loan its surplus funds to the government by purchasing bonds, on which in turn money can be borrowed and loaned out to the public. Since both the government and the public will presumably spend the funds thus received,[3] the volume of deposits and thereby of money would be increased by the double transaction. In short, the banking system by buying securities and borrowing money against them can extend the volume of deposits with the result that debit money can be created in large amounts.

The debit money outstanding varies from year to year. Its totals are included in Table V [4] where the total of all money outstanding, currency plus debit money, is given.

Theoretically, a limit exists in respect to the amount of debit money that may be issued. The limit is based on the amount

---

[3] Currency sometimes is held idle for periods of time. Debit money, however, is usually spent quickly since if not needed it would be repaid, to save the interest.

[4] p. 135.

of gold buried in the vaults of the United States. However, since the organization of the Federal Reserve system in 1914, and the reduction in the required reserves,[5] the limit has become of little practical effect. It was approached, it is true, in the spring of 1920. But since 1929, gold reserves have increased so much that the limit may not be approached again in peace-time. And were it approached, certain laws or regulations in respect to reserves could be changed [6] or gold devaluated and the limit raised. Thus for practical purposes the physical limit on the creation of money has been removed.

It is important to distinguish debit money (as defined) from ordinary debt.

Mr. A borrows $100 from Mr. B, let us say, either directly or through a bank. The amount of money outstanding is un-changed. Over-all demand is unchanged. Mr. A's demand or buying power is $100 greater, Mr. B's $100 less. Some day Mr. A returns the $100 to Mr. B. Again over-all demand is unaffected. Mr. A's demand or buying power is reduced, Mr. B's increased. Society presumably is unconcerned. Transactions of this nature will be referred to as debt and have little bearing on our argument.

Let us suppose, however, that Mr. A went to a bank and borrowed the money and that the banker handed over a check regardless of the fact that *no* Mr. B had deposited $100. In this case, as noted above, both the supply of money and over-all demand would be increased by $100. Should Mr. A repay this advance some day and should the banker not reissue it by lend-ing it to someone else, then both the supply of money and the effective demand for goods would be reduced by $100. We are calling money of this kind *debit money* and are submitting an estimate of its dimensions.

Owing to the elastic nature of contemporary money brought

---

[5] "The Formation of Capital," Brookings Institution, p. 89. By virtue of a concentration of reserves in Federal Reserve Banks, to which each member bank would have access in time of need, it became possible to reduce the amount of reserves which each class of member banks should hold. They were legally reduced to 13 per cent for the banks of the central reserve cities, 10 per cent for those of the reserve cities, and only 7 per cent for the county banks. An enormous expansion of credit was made possible.

[6] Such a change was made in the spring of 1945 to take care of war needs.

out above, it will be assumed in this study that society need not endure nonproduction because of the lack of money, i.e., the medium of exchange.

2. PRICE REFLECTS BOTH CHANGES IN EFFICIENCY AND CHANGES IN CONSUMER DESIRES. THE IMPORTANCE OF THIS FUNCTION IS EMPHASIZED.

As noted in the introduction, demand is released in the process of providing supply, and the two quantities, the demand released and the supply made available, are of necessity equal, because the difference, when there is any, between the cost of production and the price received is made up by the realization of profit or the acceptance of loss. Thus cost plus profit or minus loss must equal selling price, and the demand released must equal the supply produced and sold.

The relationship between supply and demand will be called the over-all equilibrium [7] adjustment when the over-all or total net [8] demand and the over-all total net supply for a year is meant. However, when a time period is set, demand may not equal supply within the period owing to the possibility that certain potential buyers might refrain from buying, or certain potential sellers might hold goods off the market, that is to say, might refrain from selling during the period.

The relationship, nevertheless, constitutes what may be called an equilibrium, owing to the fact that an excess of either quantity for the above or other reason sets up a reaction, such as a price or production drop when supply exceeds demand and a price or production rise in the opposite situation, which tends to restore equality.

Demand it was noted consists in the main of the money paid out in the process of production. Usually it is thought of as consisting of the supply of money, M, multiplied by its velocity V, that is to say, its rate of passing from person to person. Demand then could be represented by MV. For our purpose,

---

[7] The word "equilibrium" is used to indicate a condition in which variations from the price, quantity or whatever is being discussed, would not stand.

[8] The net demand comprises the demand for finished goods, and the net supply the supply of finished goods.

let us think of demand in terms of payments, costs payments plus profits and minus losses.

Cost includes not only the cost of the manhours which are embodied in the finished product, but also the cost of equipment (embodied manhours) and a charge for the use of such natural resources as are required.[9] These latter costs are known as interest, amortization and rent. *Interest* is the stipend paid the owner of money for the use of it. *Amortization* is a method of purchasing capital on the installment plan by which capital costs are spread over a period. *Rent* is a stipend paid the owner of a scarce resource for the use of it.

Were profit and loss eliminated, the price or value of the goods produced would exactly equal the cost of production. Although profits are realized, they are held within certain limits, when competition is effective (as will be described) and may be considered either the return or reward of the enterpriser, or part of the cost of management.

Rent, when competition is effective, serves to equalize the differences between natural resources. Thus price (despite the fact that it includes profit and rent) reflects the cost of production, which in turn reflects the effort and risk required to make a good available for consumption.

Since consumers prefer lower priced goods to higher priced goods, other things being equal, lower priced goods are easier to sell in most lines of effort than higher priced goods of the same quality. And price as described above reflects relative efforts. Thus the market system stimulates the production of the goods requiring less effort per quantity produced, and discourages the production of the goods requiring more effort per quantity produced. In other words, the competition of the market fosters *efficiency* (which may be defined in this connection as the ratio of manhour input or effort to quantity output).

Price also reacts to scarcity and abundance. When a commodity is provided in excess of the demand at the current price, price or production is likely to fall. When a commodity is pro-

---

[9] Raw materials, semi-processed goods and tools are purchased by most processors from other processors or suppliers. Since the price of such goods can be broken down into wages, interest, rent and profit, as described, all prices would consist of wages, interest, rent and profit, were costs traced back far enough.

vided in a quantity less than the quantity demanded at the current price, price or production is likely to rise. A change in consumers' desires affects demand. Thus price reflects demand in relation to supply as well as the cost of production and relative efficiencies, thereby tending to induce an *economic allocation of resources* inclusive of manhours. This property of price by which it simultaneously reflects both efficiency and desires will be called its *parametric function*.

A concrete example may make this clearer. Let us suppose that silk stockings have been selling at a dollar a pair, a price which covered the cost of production plus the minimum of profit [10] needed to keep the enterpriser in business. Let us further suppose that at some point in time the supply produced was insufficient to satisfy the demand for stockings at the dollar price, either because more people demanded stockings or the same people demanded more stockings. In such a situation, the price would be likely to rise, since the seller would quickly realize that he could feasibly obtain more than a dollar for his stockings. At the higher price, greater profits would be realized. The profit increment, sometimes known as surplus profit,[11] would either tempt new enterprisers into the field or would induce the existing enterprisers to hire additional men and to allocate additional resources (i.e., silk, etc.) and additional capital to the production of stockings. As a result, production would be increased. But the higher price would curtail demand.

Eventually production might be stabilized at a new production rate and a new price which reflected both the changed demand for stockings and the increase or decrease in the costs of production resulting from the altered operating rate. Thus the free play of price on the market interprets changing techniques and changing tastes so that satisfactions tend to be maximized and resources economically allocated.

The nature of the operation which enables prices to reflect simultaneously both relative efficiencies and relative desires has been analyzed by the economists. A price is established by the

[10] Unless a profit equal to current wages were included, the enterpriser would be likely to desert his calling and take a job.

[11] Surplus profit may be defined as profit greater than that minimum profit required to keep the enterpriser in business.

interaction of the bids of the buyers and the offers of the sellers on the market, or otherwise.[12]   Operations are then adjusted to the price established on the principle that it will pay the producer to turn out goods so long as the producer can recover his costs at the price established.   Should cost increase as production increased, the condition known as *increasing costs*, each price would determine the quantity which would be produced since the producer would cease to turn out goods when the cost of the last item produced equalled the price established on the market.

This principle applies both to an atomic field in which numerous producers compete to satisfy the demand, and to a restricted field, in which but few producers compete to supply the demand. In the first case, the price would determine how many producers would operate.   Certain producers, known as marginal producers, would be forced to close down whenever price dropped. And certain producers would be enabled to start operations whenever price rose.   Were but few producers involved, they all might continue to operate over a price range, but they would probably step production up and down as price rose and fell.

Assumedly the free flow of enterprisers from less profitable to more profitable fields would result in approximately equal marginal returns (i.e., the return of the last producer who considered it worth while to produce) over the whole field of enterprise. Since practical difficulties are involved in changing from one process to another, this ideal is far from being realized.

The price of labor, that is to say, wages, is subject to the same kind of reaction.   Employers are likely to choose to employ additional men at any wage the worker will accept so long as the product of the last man employed, the marginal product, can be sold without a loss.   The employer would not hire more men for he would lose money by so doing.   Nor would he usually hire fewer men because he would lose the chance to make more money by so doing.   Thus it is said that the wage *tends* to equal *the marginal product of labor*, which means that "the wage of an

[12] A market on which prices are set by bids and offers may be observed in a relatively pure form in the wheat pits and the stock exchanges.   Even when bids and offers are intermittent, as let us say in real estate dealings, much the same result is supposed to be attained.

employed person is equal to the value which would be lost if employment were to be reduced by one unit." [13]

Since production tends to rise until profit is reduced to a minimum,[14] and the minimum profit is established by the wage an enterpriser could obtain should he desert his calling and take a job, competition in a market economy would tend, were competition perfect, to induce approximately equal marginal returns not only between the profits of one industry and that of another, as was noted above, but also between the profit of the marginal producer and the current wage.

This tendency does not apply to returns from property, that is to say, from the ownership of going concerns, capital, money, or natural resources (rent). The reason is that one individual can acquire a greater quantity of any of these forms of property than another, a concentration often increased by inheritance, etc. However, society reduces the resulting income disparity by means of graduated income taxes.

The inequality resulting from ownership is sometimes defended even on economic [15] grounds. For example, von Mises writes:

"When we call a capitalist society a consumers' democracy, we mean that the power to dispose of the means of production, which belongs to the entrepreneurs and capitalists, can only be acquired by means of the consumers' ballot, held daily in the market-place. Every child who prefers one toy to another puts its voting paper in the ballot box, which eventually decides who shall be elected captain of industry. True, there is no equality of vote in this democracy; some have plural votes. But the greater voting power which the disposal of a greater income implies can only be acquired and maintained by the test of election. That the consumption of the rich weighs more heavily in the balance than the consumption of the poor . . . is in itself an 'election result,' since in a capitalist society, wealth can be acquired and maintained only by a response corresponding to the consumers' *requirements*. Thus, the wealth of successful business men is always the result of a consumers' plebiscite, and once acquired, this wealth can be retained only if it is employed in the way regarded by the consumers as most beneficial to them." [16]

[13] Keynes, *op. cit.*, p. 5. The tendencies referred to are often frustrated as will be indicated.

[14] Market reactions are analyzed in Chapter II.

[15] Sociological, technical and other reasons in defense of income disparity could be cited. They would seem, however, irrelevant to this analysis.

[16] Ludwig von Mises, *Socialism*, p. 21, Macmillan Co., New York.

In short, the market system tends to promote efficiency, and to translate consumer wants into satisfactions according to the urgency of the wants and the scarcities of the means. Furthermore, the variations in individual returns (excepting these from ownership) tend to reflect individual competencies, since the efficient enterpriser is enabled to realize greater returns than the inefficient (marginal) enterpriser and the skilled (scarce) worker a higher wage than the unskilled.

The contemporary economy does not fully realize the ideal sketched in above as will be brought out as we proceed. It does, however, succeed in getting more wealth produced and a more generous distribution, at any rate in the United States, than it succeeded in doing at any of its earlier stages. In fact, if non-production were eliminated so much wealth would be made available, that a high standard of living could hardly be avoided unless war, pyramid building or other wealth consuming device was instituted.

Our search is for the flaw or imperfection that induces non-production. It will be important to bear in mind that the economic system, in order to realize its potentialities, that is to say, in order to make available the most wealth possible in the proportions desired by the consumer, needs to allocate resources economically. This allocation is obtained today, imperfectly it may be, but obtained none the less, by the ability of price to reflect changes in efficiency and changes in desires, as described above. Measures which impaired this ability by interfering with the parametric function of price might fail of their purpose because an optimum production of wealth depends not only upon the full utilization of the available resources, but also upon their economic utilization.

This caution is important because no other procedure for allocating resources economically in a changing world has as yet been devised. It is true many commentators have convinced themselves of the feasibility of some other procedure for producing and distributing wealth. But none of the proposals seem to withstand scrutiny. Let us take a moment to consider the most favored.

It is often maintained that production would be greater and

distribution "more just" were goods priced according to labor input. Consumer good demand could be issued in the form of wages, so much per manhour, and capital goods created by some engineering procedure administered by the state or other social agency.

Such a system could be instituted, it may be supposed, at some moment of time were any set of existing prices crystallized on the assumption that they represented manhour inputs.[17]

The producers would seek to satisfy the demand elicited at the prices set. Let us now suppose that after a while an invention reduced the manhour input needed to produce silk stockings. The price of stockings would therefore be reduced to reflect the reduction in manhour input. As a result, the demand for stockings would increase and the managers of the silk stocking industry would step up production to meet the increased demand.

The question then arises as to what effect the increased production of silk stockings would have upon the manhour input required to produce them. Should it happen that manhour input per stocking increased as production rose, would the engineers in charge raise the price, thereby curtailing the demand? And to the production of what other commodity would the men released by the invention be assigned? Furthermore, if the men had to be recalled in order to increase stocking production as the price was reduced and demand rose, from what production would they be drawn?

The above paragraph was intended merely to suggest [18] the difficulty involved in superseding market procedures. Literally millions of decisions of the kind suggested above are made daily by the free play of market forces as enterprisers and workers seek to buy cheap and to sell dear. Many of the decisions are unsound. But unsound decisions are self-corrective in a market system. That is to say, overproduction is corrected by a price

[17] The direct calculation of manhour input by measurement would be statistically difficult owing to the practical impossibility of breaking down the input of embodied manhours (i.e., capital costs) as well as the difficulty involved in accounting for the different availabilities of the various natural resources roughly equalized in the contemporary economy by the institution of rent.

[18] Perhaps the clearest statement of the nature of the problem which the market mechanism resolves is given in von Hayek's article: "The Use of Knowledge in Society." The *American Economic Review*, September 1945.

fall or reduced production. Too high a price results in unsold
goods and falling prices. Too low a price results in a shortage
of goods, which causes prices to rise or production to be increased, etc. The net effect of the continuous actions and reactions along the above lines results in goods being produced and
distributed and resources being allocated in ratios that tend to
approach optimum ratios.

Were these adjustments effected by an overhead planning
board, assuming it to be possible, errors would not be self-
corrective. Prices too low would result in empty shelves. Prices
too high in overladen shelves, etc. And before these conditions
could be corrected, the central planning board would have to
act. And they would have no means of computing [19] the dimensions of the necessary corrective action.

The gist of the matter may be stated as follows:

Necessary manhour input for most goods and services cannot
be determined until the quantity demanded is known. The
quantity demanded cannot be determined by reference to consumers' desires until the manhour input or cost is known.
Consequently a procedure which attempted to set prices on the
basis of manhour input or costs, and production on the basis of
consumer demand, would incur accounting difficulties whenever
technology or taste changed. Were prices and production rates
crystallized by fiat, then goods would be produced that would
not be demanded, and demands that could be satisfied would be
frustrated, just as soon as either technology or taste changed.
And both are changing all the time.

This argument is not intended to refute the possibility of
socialism defined as state ownership of the means of production.
A socialist society could direct its state employed managers to
charge and to pay interest and rent and to administer prices so
as to maximize profit. However, just what could be gained by
state ownership were the procedures of private ownership mim-
icked is somewhat uncertain. Much would probably be lost in
the way of efficiency.[20] And the more equal distribution of

---

[19] See von Mises' *Socialism* or von Hayek's *Collectivism* for a more extensive discussion of the problem involved.

[20] The variety of efficiency referred to is the efficiency resulting from the de-
centralization of responsibility feasible under private ownership. Theoretically,

returns which might be attained could be realized under private ownership by the manipulation of income, inheritance and other taxes, should this be desired. Therefore, the above paragraphs are intended merely to indicate the infeasibility of scheduling prices and production rates from a central office in the long run.[21]

The relevance of this condition to our study is apparent. We are seeking the cause of nonproduction in order to suggest how it might be eliminated. Since no effective method of adjusting production to changes in technology and changes in consumers' desires is known, except the market procedures which have gradually been evolved by trial and error over the ages, and since consumer control and advancing technology (or material progress) are desired by the majority of the American people, our study will attempt to discover and to correct the flaws in these procedures within the framework of these procedures.

Before leaving the subject, it may be relevant to note that the desirability of utilizing market procedures for pricing goods and services does *not* mean that the production and distribution of *all* goods and services need to be subject to the market. On the contrary, when a framework of prices is established by market procedures, certain goods and services can be produced and priced and are today produced and priced by other means.

New York City's water department, for example, has little difficulty calculating how much water will be needed and how economically to construct dams and reservoirs in order to secure the needed supply. The demand is figured on the basis of universal provisioning and the cost is calculable in advance, since the prices of various factors of production are established on the outside market. As a result, the engineers of the water department can elect that production technique which promises to perform the needed service at the least cost. If the engineers did not have the prices of tools, human and natural power, land, etc., on which to base their calculations, they would not know

---

responsibility could be decentralized even were ownership centralized. In practice, however, this consummation seems difficult to realize.

[21] The experience of Soviet Russia would seem to substantiate the above opinion. The U.S.S.R. tried twice to eliminate the market and both times had to return to the mimicking of private ownership procedures. Lenin's retreat is known as NEP; Stalin's more gradual reintroduction of the market is still going on.

how to proceed. With costs (which are dependent on prices) unknown, every procedure which promised to supply water would seem about as good as every other.

Provisioning by social action independent of market procedures is often useful. Its utility may derive from the fact that goods produced in this way can be distributed at any price that is desired or even given away to part of the population. Thus second-class mailing service is sold at less than its cost and elementary education is given to those who do not pay taxes. There may be other situations in which society would be served by production and distribution independent of the market.

It will therefore be assumed in this study:

1. That a market procedure which enables prices to reflect changes in efficiency and in consumer desires is an essential feature of an economy designed to realize consumers' desires and to allocate resources economically on the basis of these desires.

2. That goods and services can be produced and distributed by other procedures so long as the market is extensive enough to provide a framework of prices on which the other (probably engineering) procedure can be based.

3. FULL EMPLOYMENT WOULD NOT NECESSARILY MAXIMIZE CONSUMER SATISFACTIONS.

The over-all equilibrium adjustment [22] results in an aggregate income which ranged, before the war, between $40 and $83 billion.[23] The factors which cause this adjustment to balance itself at productions far short of possible production, will be scrutinized. Our problem, however, would not be solved by determining why production has fallen short of the production of full employment, or even by discovering ways and means of maintaining full employment. Ways and means are already known. The Egyptians sustained employment by building pyramids, the Germans by manufacturing munitions. The United States, too, could maintain full employment, as the war years have shown, by undertaking military or other public works on a

[22] p. 5.
[23] Table II, p. 132.

vast enough scale. Instead of confining the problem to the employment phase, it will be advisable to consider if consumer satisfactions can be maximized and employment sustained at the same time, since full employment alone would not necessarily maximize or even raise the living standard.

Thus production rose to full shortly after Pearl Harbor. But the consumer received little more in the way of goods and service than he had been getting previously. A more significant example can be drawn from our peacetime experience. All but some two million workers were employed in 1929. If we assume these two million had been enabled to produce $3,000 worth of wealth each, an over-generous assumption, since most of these workers were shifting jobs and many were incompetent, the national income would have approached only $90 billion. Yet the National Survey of Potential Product Capacity [24] indicated that a slightly greater working force (52 million workers at 1929 working hours) could have produced, after a short tuning up period, 135 billion 1929 dollars worth of desired goods and services, and our war experience suggests that some ten years later goods and services worth nearly 200 billion 1944 dollars [25] could be produced with 11 million men more or less out of production.

One of the reasons that full production would not necessarily maximize consumer satisfactions and the general welfare is the possibility that the proportion of effort diverted to capital formation might be excessive. In each branch of industry, the state of technology establishes an optimum ratio between capital and production. Were capital formation such that the capital plant was increased more than needed, this optimum ratio would not be realized. In other words, should more effort be allocated to capital formation than was needed to maintain and improve the plant required to provide the consumer goods demanded at full employment, and should less effort, as a result, be allocated to the production of consumer goods than was technically feasible,

[24] *op. cit.*, p. 201.
[25] The gross national product at the late 1943 rate of production. Overtime work and the services of several million housewives and others who would not usually work are included in the total.

society would be deprived of a certain quantity of consumer goods unnecessarily, and of the satisfaction to be derived from them.

Although this relationship would seem self-evident, it is sometimes ignored, because of the prevalence of the illusion, inherited from the days when capital was habitually deficient, that capital cannot be overbuilt.[26] However, reference to any branch of industry brings out clearly the possibility of excess capitalization. If, for example, the demand for ice cream in some locality would not exceed 100 tons at cost prices even when employment was full, only a certain number of ice cream freezers, containers and all the other pieces of equipment, etc., required to produce and distribute ice cream, would be called for in order to satisfy this maximum demand at the smallest manhour input. Equipment above this amount (an amount which includes spare parts, extra machines, etc., in order to take care of breakdowns and other emergencies) would not increase social satisfaction. In fact, equipment above this amount would reduce the net satisfaction of society, if we assume the manhours required to fabricate this surplus equipment would otherwise have been utilized to provide something which would have satisfied some need or want, as would be the case were employment full, as postulated.

The above possibility does not rule out the desirability of capital expansion. As production and productivity increased, more capital might be needed to supply the demand. In fact, at any time efficiency could be increased by installing additional capital.[27] But this potentiality does not conflict with the proposition that technology establishes an economic ratio between capital and production in each field of effort and that an excess formation of capital in any field would have to be accompanied by a complementary deficiency of consumer goods production were employment full.

It is true that such an excess and deficiency in one time period might be corrected by forming less capital and producing additional consumer goods in a subsequent period. But such a

[26] Starting with p. 34, the competitive procedures which result in the production of excess capital are discussed, and on p. 159, the effect of this practice on the over-all adjustment is considered.

[27] Footnote, p. 158.

correction *cannot be accomplished* under existing institutional procedures. On the contrary, a reduction in consumer goods demand and production accompanies today a reduction in capital formation. This relation will be examined in a later chapter.[28] At this point, it is necessary only to bring out the *possibility* of excess capital formation in a particular time period.

Capital is useful in that it facilitates the production of consumer goods or other capital goods. Since excess capital formation might occur in one locality in respect to one kind of equipment such as ice cream freezers, it is reasonable to suppose it might occur in a large economic entity such as the United States in respect to capital in general.

Thus, even had full production been attained in 1929, or some other year of peace, consumer satisfactions would not have been maximized if in that year an excess of effort had been allocated to capital formation.

There is another situation in which full production would not maximize satisfactions. Should income distribution be such that a fraction of society commanded so much wealth that this fraction was hard put, under existing mores, to maintain a consumption that did justice to its income, even though its members allocated whatever fraction of their income was needed to maintain and expand the capital plant by the amount that was technically desirable; and another fraction of society commanded so little wealth that they were incapable of procuring a part of the consumer goods which the economy was capable of providing, then too, consumer satisfactions would not be maximized, even though full production was maintained. Evidently this situation is closely related to the previous one in that, in the situation just cited, full production would be maintained only if those with high incomes engaged in excess capital formation, unsatisfactory consumption or other devices for expending effort uselessly.

The canons on which the above judgments are based are technical and not moral, aesthetic or psychological.[29] It is not

---

[28] pp. 83 ff.

[29] Consumer satisfaction would not be maximized in a society in which income varied widely, owing to the psychological probability that additional goods for those who consume much, provide less satisfaction than additional goods for those

being stated that income disparity beyond a certain point is unjust, unedifying or unsatisfying. It is simply being maintained that income disparity beyond a certain point might lead to a consumer goods production less than the production which could be accomplished with the existing resources and technology.

Because of the possibilities cited above, two different "possible" productions will be referred to in the balance of this study.

The first, which will be called *full production*, will be synonymous with full employment. It will signify the wealth that would be produced were every would-be worker (willing to work for the marginal product [30] of labor) employed with a normal margin for job shifting, slippage, etc.

The second, which will be called *capacity production*, also requires full employment. But capacity production will signify that production of wealth which could be provided were production limited only by physical and technical factors. Thus, if consumer goods production could be increased by altering in some indicated way income distribution or the proportion of effort allocated to capital formation, the possibility of such an alteration will be investigated, even though the necessary alteration could not be effected without changing certain of the prevailing institutional procedures.

Perhaps the distinction between these two definitions can be made clearer by referring briefly to the two studies of possible production referred to in the preface, one of which assumed the persistence of prevailing institutional procedures and the other did not.

Brookings Institution [31] estimated the extent of the unused facilities of a large sampling of industries, checked the unused facilities against the available labor supply to ascertain whether labor was available, took a weighted average of the individual nonproductions, on the assumption that the various industries could operate at capacity insofar as the available manpower permitted, and came out with an estimated possible percentage increase of production.

who consume little. However, relations of this character, no matter how plausible, are outside the scope of this study and are irrelevant to the argument.

[30] Defined on p. 8.

[31] *America's Capacity to Produce, op. cit.*

According to this method, the full use of productive facilities would induce an expansion of both capital goods production and consumer goods production, amounting to some 19 per cent, supposedly in about the same proportions as these goods were produced in 1929. (The writer suspects that more of the unused facilities were found to reside in the capital goods industries than in the consumer goods industries.)

The National Survey, on the other hand, projected a budget of desired goods and services by referring to the expenditures of families in the middle income brackets and then checked the limiting factors, the plant capacity, the labor supply and the natural resources, in order to discover how much of this budget could be provided for the whole population without reducing the consumer goods expenditures of those who had more to spend.

It is evident that this method of estimating possible production disregards existing institutional procedures which establish the ratio of capital formation to consumer goods production at the various production levels. Thus, the estimate of the National Survey of Potential Product Capacity was based on the assumption that the capital formation of 1929 was sufficient to expand the productive plant at the optimum rate and that the total of productive facilities which were not used in 1929 could therefore be allocated to consumer goods production.

It is not our thought to defend at this point either of these procedures for assessing possible production, and certainly not to defend the conclusions of either survey, both of which have been rendered obsolete by the history of the war period. Furthermore, the *dimensions* of nonproduction have little bearing on this study. It is important, however, that the distinction between *full* production—which the Brookings study tried to estimate—and *capacity* production—which the National Survey tried to estimate—should be kept in mind.

The results of the two studies varied widely. The Brookings study concluded that goods and services worth some 95 billion 1929 dollars might have been produced in 1929. The National Survey concluded that goods and services could be produced sufficient to provide every family in the land with an income equivalent to that which $4,000 purchased in 1929 without reducing the expenditures of those who had more in 1929, or curtailing the capital formation of 1929.   Such an income would have amounted, as noted above, to goods and services worth some 135 billion 1929 dollars.

Our search is for the cause of the irrational procedure we are calling nonproduction.   It will be indicated that unless continuous war or other device for voiding wealth is posited, the maintenance of full employment depends on an increasing demand for consumer goods to an extent which would not be achieved under recent peacetime procedures even though every one willing to work for the marginal product of labor were continuously employed.   Consequently, in order to eliminate nonproduction without resort to war, pyramids, or similar diversions, it would be necessary to approach capacity production.   Therefore it is convenient at the start of our inquiry to distinguish full production, which involves the employment of every would-be worker, from capacity production, which is predicated upon the maximum production of consumer goods and services consonant with the maintenance and improvement of the plant.

4. THOUGH FULL PRODUCTION COULD BE ACHIEVED BY EXPORTING MORE GOODS THAN ARE IMPORTED, THE RESULTING NATIONAL INCOME WOULD NOT MAXIMIZE SATISFACTIONS AND THE PRODUCTION COULD NOT BE SUSTAINED INDEFINITELY.

It was indicated in the last section that full production achieved by excess capital formation would be unsatisfactory. Similarly, full production achieved by excess exports would fail to maximize satisfactions and would lack stability.   Though this conclusion may be self-evident, it had better be scrutinized owing to the fact that certain theorists see in a so-called "favorable balance of trade" the panacea for many economic ills including nonproduction.[32]   The basis for this opinion is a delusion that shipping wealth abroad in exchange for promises to

[32] Mr. Maffry has recently presented the case "for an outflow of capital supporting an excess of exports" (p. 6, "Foreign Trade in the Post War Economy, Current Business," U. S. Dept. of Commerce, Nov. 1944).   However, even he envisages foreign investment as an interim measure "at least unless and until other solutions to the savings-investment problem are found" (p. 11).   The writer concedes its probable utility as an interim measure.

pay necessarily enriches a community, notwithstanding the fact that fulfillment of the promises by shipping back at some future date more goods than the United States would send out may not be feasible. Were this the situation, such promises would eventually go by default. Thus the United States has in recent decades shipped out more wealth than it has received in return.

The delusion that exchanging goods for promises increases the wealth of the community springs from the general acceptance of the benefits to be derived from trade. The classic economists pointed out that the exchange of a relatively scarce commodity for a relatively abundant one enriched both parties to the transaction. Furthermore, trade renders the division of labor increasingly feasible, since it permits labor units to concentrate on fractional processes. The division of labor, by splitting productive effort into many simple motions, has enabled several societies to substitute natural energy for muscular energy in large sections of the productive process. The resulting increase in efficiency and the consequent reduction in manhour input necessary to produce a unit of wealth has made possible the increase of material well-being which distinguishes the present era from previous ones. However, trade of this kind is reciprocal. One-sided trade in which wealth is exchanged for promises is another matter.

Nevertheless, even this practice has had a utility of a kind. Owing to the prevalence of nonproduction, demand and supply in the United States have been less than possible demand and possible supply, as was indicated in the previous section. When this condition exists, an increase in demand from any cause whatsoever enables society to produce and distribute a greater supply than otherwise could feasibly be distributed. Paying wages to men to produce wealth destined to be given to foreign countries in exchange for promises, increases the domestic effective demand, since men receive wages who otherwise would be unemployed. A greater supply as a result is produced domestically to meet the increased demand. Thus the American people obtain more wealth to consume when they generously ship out a greater value of goods than they accept in return.

Much the same thing, it is true, might be said of colonization,

foreign military ventures, etc.   In fact, the latter forms of voiding wealth are in some ways more satisfactory than surplus
exports, because of the fact that colonization and war provide
additional high salaried jobs.   John Stuart Mill is said to have
described colonies as "a vast system of outdoor relief for the
upper classes."   However, the United States did not develop
this latter method of voiding wealth to a great extent, possibly
because it had plenty of empty spaces nearer home into which
to pour effort.

On the other hand, the United States has developed unrecip-
rocal foreign trade probably to the highest point that has ever
been attained.   After the first World War, it sent not only goods,
but also money abroad in return for IOUs, the money to be used
in part to pay for the excess of exports over imports.

The matter is relevant to this study for the following reason:
A certain amount of foreign trade is helpful as suggested above
even for a community so large and so well endowed by nature
as the United States.   But such trade has no effect on the over-
all equilibrium adjustment.   That is to say, were $5 billion
worth of goods exported and $5 billion worth imported, the
equality or inequality of demand and supply would be the same
as if the trade had not occurred.   The transactions, in other
words, would balance each other out.   However, were $10
billion worth of goods exported and only $5 billion worth im-
ported, the demand supply equation would be unbalanced by
the addition of $5 billion to the demand side.   Probably, addi-
tional goods would be provided to satisfy this demand if facilities
were available, which they would be were production less than
full.   In producing these additional goods, more money would
be paid out . . . and so on, conceivably until full production
was attained.

This solution is adjudged unsatisfactory in the first place because consumer satisfactions would not be maximized.   It is
evident that the American people would be depriving themselves
of the $5 billion worth of excess exports.   In the second place,
the procedure could not be sustained indefinitely.   Sooner or
later the cumulative interest on the rising supply of bonds floated
to loan money to the foreign buyers to enable them to purchase

American goods without shipping wealth back in return could not, as noted above, be met. When this occurred, the market for foreign loans would dry up and exporting would collapse. In short, the experience of the 1920's and 1930's would be repeated.

Our search is for a solution that need not end in a calamity, sooner or later.

CHAPTER II

Price and Monopolistic Competition

1. PRICE COMPETITION IS DISTINGUISHED FROM MONOPOLISTIC COMPETITION.

OUR preliminary discussion indicated that the physical act of production, which makes the supply "available," and the financial act of paying out money, which renders the demand for goods "effective," have resulted in an over-all demand-supply adjustment or balance. Although over-all demand and supply approach equality for the reasons noted, the demand for and supply of any particular good is equal only by accident, because individuals choose freely between the available commodities. Consequently, the demand for any particular good is likely to be more or less than the supply.

As was suggested in Chapter I,[1] market procedures have been developed which serve in practice to equate the demand and supply of each commodity. Let us therefore review these procedures in order to indicate to what degree they are responsible for the flaw in the system we are calling nonproduction. Fortunately market procedures have been scrutinized by many capable analysts so that we need merely summarize certain well recognized aspects which bear upon our larger inquiry. In doing so, we shall draw upon the brilliant study of Edward Chamberlin,[2] since in general, our study envisages the effect of the prevailing form of competition, which we shall follow Chamberlin in calling "monopolistic competition," [3] upon the over-all equilibrium adjustment.

[1] pp. 7 to 9.

[2] *The Theory of Monopolistic Competition*, Harvard University Press, 1933.

[3] The term "monopoly" usually means "one seller." However, "monopolistic competition" as defined in the text, in no way limits the number of sellers and should not be confused with "monopoly." "Monopolistic" is used to describe the competition in question for lack of a better adjective. Sometimes the competition in question is called "imperfect" but this expression is even more misleading since monopolistic competition can be and often is as perfect as pure or price competition.

24

It is convenient to divide competition into two inclusive categories—*price*, or pure,[4] competition, and *monopolistic* competition. *Price competition* may be defined as competition unalloyed with monopolistic elements. Other forms of competition then constitute *monopolistic competition*.

The sole requisite of price competition, therefore, is the absence of monopolistic elements. However, in order for such elements to be absent, two conditions are necessary:

"In the first place, there must be a large number of buyers and sellers, so that the influence of any one or of several in combination is negligible. There is no need that their numbers be infinite . . . but they must be large enough so that even though any single individual has, in fact, a slight influence upon the price, he does not exercise it because it is not worth his while. If the individual seller produces on the assumption that his entire output can be disposed of at the prevailing or market price, and withholds none of it, there is pure—(or price)—competition so far as numbers are concerned, no matter at what price he actually disposes of it, and how much influence he actually exerts.

"Secondly, control over price is completely eliminated only when all producers are producing the identical good and selling it in the identical market." [5]

In short, the conditions necessary for price competition consists of (1) "a relatively large number of buyers and sellers," and (2) "a perfectly standardized product." The first (1) "diminishes the influence of anyone in the general market situation to negligibility" and thereby prohibits control or interference in the movement of prices by changing the rate of production; the second (2) "by identifying completely the product of a single seller with those of his competitors, denies him any measure of control over his price as distinct from the general market price, which control might exist by reason of buyers' preference for one variety of good over another." [6]

[4] Mr. Chamberlin uses the adjective "pure" since his emphasis is upon the absence of monopolistic elements. We are using the adjective "price" since our emphasis is upon the fact that in price competition changes in factors such as the cost of production or consumers' taste are reflected directly by changes in price. In monopolistic competition, price tends to be lethargic and changes in the factors are reflected variously as will be brought out as we proceed.

[5] Chamberlin, *op. cit.*, p. 7.

[6] Chamberlin, *op. cit.*, p. 16.

Because most prices involve monopolistic elements, "it is monopolistic competition that most people think of in connection with the simple word 'competition.'" [7]

Monopoly is never absolute in the economy since in every case some substitute commodity exists, although control in some instances is so nearly complete, as in the case of a portrait painter possessing both a private income and a public reputation, that it may be considered absolute. Thus the phrase monopolistic competition, used to describe competition alloyed with monopolistic elements, includes all forms of competition that cannot be described as pure or price competition.

Business is done in the actual world by innumerable combinations of competitive and monopolistic practices. Only a small percentage of business is accomplished under conditions approximating either "price competition" or "unregulated monopoly." The individual farmer selling to the elevator which sets its price to accord with the latest market quotations, cannot influence the market by withholding his supplies. He is too small a unit to affect appreciably the "available supply" and his product is undifferentiated from that of millions of others. In his case a condition very near to price competition existed before the war.

On the other hand, the owner of a valuable patent enjoys for a time an almost unregulated monopoly. In every case, the patent can be somehow evaded. But if it is a "valuable" patent, the substitute process or product will be so much more expensive or less desirable than that owned by the patentee, that the patentee may reasonably be considered to control supply and therefore price.

Probably the most familiar method by which price competition is evaded, is by "the differentiation of the product." Whenever one product is differentiated from another, either in reality or in fancy, the similarity of products necessary for price competition is broken down. Instead of any seller being able to pair off with any buyer, as is true in an open market such as the wheat pit, sellers will pair off with buyers, not by chance and at random, but according to individual preference. Thus along with patented features we may include trade marks, trade names,

[7] Chamberlin, *op. cit.*, p. 10.

peculiarities of package or of container, singularity in quality, design, color or style, as definite though not absolute limitations on the market.

Differentiation may also exist with respect to the conditions surrounding the sale of an article. "In retail trade, to take only one instance, these conditions include such factors as the convenience of the seller's location, the general tone or character of his establishment, his way of doing business, his reputation for fair dealing, courtesy, efficiency, and all the personal links which attach his customers either to himself or to those employed by him. Insofar as these and other intangible factors vary from seller to seller, the 'product' in each case is different, for buyers take them into account, more or less, and may be regarded as purchasing them along with the commodity itself. When these two aspects of differentiation are held in mind, it is evident that virtually all products are differentiated, at least slightly, and that over a wide range of economic activity differentiation is of considerable importance." [8]

Obviously, the above differentiations, all of which subvert price competition to a greater or lesser extent, are not novel. Goods were differentiated to an even greater extent before the industrial revolution. But the industrial revolution fostered standardization. And the identity of products which resulted made the extension of price competition into wider fields technically feasible. This latter possibility, however, has been contravened by deliberately reintroducing the differentiations which the machine tended to iron out.

Selling effort, especially advertising, must be included as a monopolistic practice. By means of advertising and other forms of selling effort, the market is distorted. Instead of the sale going to the lowest cost producer, it often goes to a higher cost producer who has diverted part of his income to reiterated protestations of virtue.

Finally, a nexus of practices has been devised by which small units have been integrated into larger concerns. By this means, the number of competing units has in many cases been so reduced that one or more of them, by withholding or reducing

[8] Chamberlin, *op. cit.*, pp. 56–57.

their supplies, can affect price. This condition may be called oligopoly when the sellers are reduced to a few. In this situation price is usually set by the leading going concern in concert with the others, or otherwise, and the dominating unit or units penalize a price cut on the part of a competitor by "meeting its competition" in the territory of the competitor so effectively that the rival has to come to terms. The need of this strategy was recognized by Congress and permission to adjust price "to meet competition" (in "good faith" to be sure) was inserted in the Clayton Act.

It is apparent that price competition is exceptional. No large field of enterprise other than that of farming seems to be unalloyed with one or more monopolistic practices, and farming of late is increasingly regulated by the government. Even the non-farm extractive industries, mining and lumbering, in which the product is undifferentiated and many enterprisers compete, are seldom operated on price competition lines. Somehow or other a degree of control over the market has been obtained. Furthermore, where private enterprise has failed to coordinate the producers, the government has in certain cases come to the rescue, as in bituminous coal mining, and in certain branches of farming.

The same observation applies to labor. A great deal of labor is undifferentiated. The sellers of manhours number millions. Despite these conditions labor, by generations of struggle, has obtained in many fields a degree of control over the supply and thereby over the price (wage). And where labor has been unsuccessful, the government has stepped in to assist it by fostering collective bargaining, by setting minimum wages, by relief payments, etc.

Nevertheless, it is important to scrutinize price competition for the following and other reasons:

1. Many commentators assume that the economy is one of price competition marred by imperfections. This assumption would seem unsound. Monopolistic competition cannot validly be described as imperfect competition, since it has other characteristics than those that would be expected from this nomenclature.

2. In branches of farming in which the government has not yet intervened in peacetime to control the supply and maintain the price, poultry raising, for example, and in a few other areas, price competition largely prevails. In reviewing the economy as a whole, this exceptional procedure needs to be taken into account.

· 2. IN PRICE COMPETITION, DEMAND FOR THE PRODUCT OF THE INDIVIDUAL PRODUCER IS UNLIMITED AT THE PRICE PREVAILING. AS A RESULT, IT IS TO THE INTEREST OF EACH PRODUCER TO OPERATE AT HIS MOST EFFICIENT OR HIGHER SCALE, AND TO REFRAIN FROM AVOIDABLE SELLING EXPENDITURES OR OTHER EXTRANEOUS COSTS.

When demand is deficient on the wheat pit or the stock exchange, the price of the commodity falls until a price is reached at which transactions can be consummated. An order to sell "at the market" is always filled except during rare national emergencies. Thus, a deficient demand is corrected by a drop in price which lowers the value of the supply, and vice versa.

Since the commodities being dealt with are standardized, each share of stock and each bushel of wheat being practically identical with every other of the same grade, and since there are usually so many buyers that the influence of any one of them, or of any combination of them is negligible,[9] the procedure conducted on these markets fulfills the conditions defined in the last section as those of pure or price competition.

It is evident that the price at which transactions are consummated equates demand and supply, since an excess of either quantity would induce a price change. However, were the conditions of price competition absent, should one seller for example obtain control of all the wheat fields, and should this seller hold his wheat for the price which would return him the greatest profit, demand and supply would still be equated because the monopolist would either organize matters so that a greater supply was not produced, or he would destroy the supply in excess of that demanded, as the Brazilian Government used to do with excess coffee.

[9] When enough buyers or sellers get together so that their influence is not negligible, the competition is not considered "pure."

Thus the concept of a price which equates demand and supply is seen to be somewhat meaningless except in the case of price competition.   In other situations, supply and demand would still be equated but often by adjusting the supply instead of the price.   When this occurred, supply would represent the output which the producer or producers made available in order to meet the demand at the price established.   Let us call such a price the "administered price."   When price is administered, the producer usually *gears production to meet the demand evoked by his price.*

As might be expected, an administered price tends to be more stable than the price of price competition.   In fact, the price of commodities in fields of price competition is likely to fluctuate violently owing to the fact that purchasers tend to buy when they think prices are about to rise, and sellers tend to sell when they think prices are about to fall.   They do not attempt to buy or to sell at the price which equates demand and supply.   As a result, the price at which transactions are consummated may range quite widely above and below the equilibrium price at which the quantities are equated, as the actions of the stock and grain markets indicate.

In order to illustrate [10] the nature of the operation which is being studied, schedules or curves are often employed, since a curve may be used to represent any series of numbers.   However, instead of representing a cross-cut of time, such as the demand-supply adjustment of any moment, let us recognize that supply is not something fixed but is usually in the process of becoming.   This conceptual shift can be accomplished by making use of a cost schedule.   Were a commodity such as wheat under consideration, the cost per unit would rise from the low cost at which only the best fields were cultivated to the high cost incurred when all possible fields were cultivated, the less fertile as well as the more fertile.   This condition, known as "increasing costs," [11] is represented by Curve *CC* in Figure I.[12]   It is evident

[10] The curves are submitted for illustrative purposes. Chamberlin uses them for purposes of demonstration. The reader desiring proof of these preliminary, generally accepted observations, should refer to Chamberlin's study.

[11] p. 8.

[12] p. 33.

that all commodities are subject either to increasing, decreasing or constant costs.[13]

Demand usually increases as price falls. Consequently, demand must be represented by a falling curve as in Figure I.

Under the conditions represented by the curves, the distance *PA* between the point at which the curves intersect and the X-axis would mark the equilibrium price at which production and demand would be equated. The distance *OA* between the point of intersection and the Y-axis would mark the production which could be sold at the equilibrium price without loss. The reason the intersection marks the equilibrium price is because lower or higher prices would not stand. Thus a price higher than the equilibrium price would permit the realization of surplus profits [14] and thereby draw additional higher cost producers into the field. Their activity would increase supply above quantity *OA* and force the price down. On the other hand, a lower price, a price below costs, would force the marginal producers out of business, thereby reducing supplies and eventually raising the price.[15]

The demand curve *DD* which represents the aggregate demand of all buyers for the product of the industry, curves downward as noted above since each drop in price would permit more people to purchase the commodity and would permit each would-be buyer to purchase more of the commodity, thereby increasing the quantity demanded. However, the demand curve for the product of each *individual* seller, unlike the demand curve for the total product, would be *horizontal*, for the reason which follows:

[13] The analysis which follows indicates that the condition of increasing costs is likely to exist in fields of price competition, decreasing costs in fields of monopolistic competition.

[14] Defined on p. 7.

[15] The latter reaction sometimes does not eventuate in the actual economy. The price of farm produce often fails to cover the costs of the less efficient producers who continue none-the-less to produce. In part this may be accounted for by the fact that government agencies have been supporting prices in many price competition fields, thereby encouraging producers to hold on. In the main, however, this phenomenon is the result of over-all nonproduction. When unemployment exists—as in the actual peacetime economy—the channels of escape are blocked. Unemployment thus tends to keep unsuccessful enterprisers to their enterprises even when they are unable to earn a wage earner's pay check.

Price competition, as defined, involves (1) a large number of buyers and sellers, (2) a perfectly standardized product. As a result, the product of the single seller would be very small in relation to total production. In fact, the offerings of each individual seller would be so small a fraction of the total offerings that they would have no appreciable effect on price. The market, on the other hand, is so large that it can easily absorb the total product of any one producer. The individual seller, being well aware of these facts, does not seek to control the market. He sells or refrains from selling on calculations based upon price, and not upon the possibility of influencing price. Demand to him is unlimited. His problem consists in deciding whether to sell today, next week or next month. At each price he can dispose of his total product. To represent this condition, the individual supplier's demand curve must be drawn horizontal, since a horizontal curve signifies that demand is capable of taking the total supply at the prevailing price. Thus the farmer can dispose of his total output by bringing it to market when price competition prevails.

The lines d_1d_1, d_2d_2 and d_3d_3 are drawn to represent this condition. d_2d_2 represents the demand for the product of a single seller when the price is at the equilibrium price. d_1d_1 would represent the demand at a price above the equilibrium price, and d_3d_3 at a price below the equilibrium price. d_1d_1 and d_3d_3 are broken to signify that they are hypothetical, since at the prevailing price, assumed to be the equilibrium price, the demand for the product of all sellers (who are offering the standardized product) would be at the same level or price.

It is evident that at price PA, all producers whose costs were PA or less would recover their costs, a cost, by the way, which is supposed to include "profits just sufficient to cover the minimum necessary to attract capital and business ability into the field." [16] Those whose costs were less would realize surplus profits.

Thus the price which is determined in price competition by the shapes of the cost curve and the demand curve determines in its turn the level or price of the individual demand curves and

[16] Chamberlin, *op. cit.*, p. 22.

thereby who can produce profitably and who would be forced
to close down.

From these relations, so sketchily suggested above but accepted by the consensus of economists, certain conclusions may

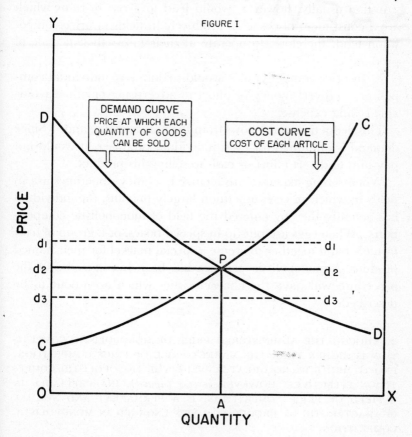

be drawn which bear upon our enquiry.   Let us sum them up
briefly.

1. In price competition, the interest of the individual producer acting on his own would be served best by operating at
his most efficient scale.

This deduction derives from the fact that demand for the
product of an individual producer is unlimited at the prevailing
price.   As a result, nothing would be gained, and something

would be lost were an individual producer to operate at less than his most efficient scale. Operations higher than his most efficient scale might be profitable if his cost curve rose but gradually and if the prevailing price permitted surplus profit. Such a situation usually, however, would lead to a rise in rents which are a constituent of costs.[17]   Producers in fields of price competition tend, therefore, to operate at their most efficient scale of production.

2. In price competition, it would seldom pay individual competitors to divert money or effort to advertising or other avoidable selling expense.

This deduction also follows from the nature of demand.   Since demand is unlimited for each individual producer, it would not pay him to divert effort or cash to selling his product.

When selling expenses are incurred, as they sometimes are in fields in which price competition largely prevails, the individual has actually thereby entered the field of monopolistic competition.   When eggs are put up in special boxes, or a group of fruit farmers band together to create a special market for their named product, a monopolistic practice has been introduced and the procedure will have the characteristics which are about to be described.

3. THOUGH THE ADMINISTERED PRICE OF MONOPOLISTIC COMPETITION IS HIGHER THAN THE MARKET PRICE OF PRICE COMPETITION, PROFIT MIGHT BE NO GREATER WERE THE MONOPOLISTIC COMPETITION EFFECTIVE.   HOWEVER, *excess capacity*, INAPPRECIABLE IN A FIELD OF PRICE COMPETITION, IS A PERMANENT AND NORMAL CHARACTERISTIC OF PRODUCING UNITS ENGAGED IN MONOPOLISTIC COMPETITION.

In order to describe the market procedures of monopolistic competition, we must turn from the general field involving a commodity, as represented by Figure I, to the particular field involving a commodity produced by one producer among a

[17] Intramarginal producers would have the same unit costs as the marginal producer if rents were counted in and rents must be included in a field of price competition since they are imposed by the competition of rivals for the property. However, rent changes tend to lag somewhat behind price changes, particularly when prices are volatile.

few or many competitors producing similar but not identical products.[18] This frame is necessary because product differentiation, and the other monopolistic controls or interferences, alter the nature of the demand. Instead of buyers being willing to accept any unit of the commodity, as with wheat, eggs (of the same grade), Government bonds, etc., they are given a basis of preference and will therefore pair off with sellers according to these preferences.[19] To understand the basis of these actions, we must therefore deal with the individual producer and not with the group as a whole.

It does not matter whether the monopolistic factor consists of tacit or explicit agreements in regard to price, rate of production or what-not, between the leading going concerns; or whether the monopolistic factor derives from the condition that the vendor's place of business is in a particular location, or his product bears the imprint of his name; in either case, the vendor is able to influence demand by his policy. And this ability is the mark of monopolistic competition.

As Mr. Chamberlin puts it: "Under pure (price) competition, the individual seller's market being completely merged with the general one, he can sell as much as he pleases at the going price. Under monopolistic competition, however, his market being separate to a degree from those of his rivals, his sales are limited and defined by three new factors: (1) his price, (2) the nature of his product, and (3) his advertising outlays." [20]

The competitor, aware of these possibilities, designs his product, regulates his selling effort, and administers his price, governing his rate of production by the response his actions elicit. In short, he *orders or designs the product, sets the price*, and *gears production to the response received.*

These actions alter the nature of demand. Instead of demand for the product of the individual producer being unlimited, as

[18] This definition holds good when monopolistic competition exists by virtue of product differentiation, selling effort, etc. When monopolistic controls are effected by oligopoly, etc., the product might be and often is standardized, as are steel rails, but the competitors are so limited in number that they are enabled to affect demand by varying their price.

[19] Chamberlin, *op. cit.*, p. 69.

[20] Chamberlin, *op. cit.*, p. 71.

in price competition, demand in monopolistic competition varies with changes in the product, the selling effort and the price.

For example, if the price per pair of trademarked shoes had been $5 and the producer decided to raise it to $6, he would not lose all his customers, as he would if he were selling bushels of wheat and raised his price above the market price. He would lose only some of his customers. If he lowered his price to $4, he would gain additional customers, but not necessarily enough additional customers to sell out all his shoes. Some buyers would still prefer other brands. Demand for the product of such a producer may therefore be considered to range from a low demand at a high price to a high demand at a low price, thus differing from the unlimited demand for the product of the individual producer in price competition.

The fact that demand for the product of the individual producer is altered by changes in price and other factors has important consequences. It means that the seller can seek that price, to limit our discussion to one of the possible variations, which maximizes profit. This price, as noted above, will fall somewhere between the high price, at which demand would be too low to permit him to operate efficiently, and the price which failed to cover costs. Somewhere between these extremes would be the price which maximized returns.[21] Such a price would be the equilibrium price were the seller a pure monopolist, because a monopolist who had found the price which maximized his returns would not persevere in a higher or lower price even should he try one out, except for special reasons—to put a newcomer out of business, for example.

But we are *not* dealing with pure monopoly. We are *not*

---

[21] Joan Robinson in "The Economics of Imperfect Competition," Macmillan, states it as follows: "It is assumed to be the aim of the producer to fix that price at which the excess of gross receipts or *revenue* over costs will be at a maximum.

"He will achieve this if he regulates output in such a way that the addition to his total revenue from selling an additional unit is exactly equal to the addition to his costs caused by producing that unit. If he sold one unit less, he would lose more of revenue than he saved of cost, and if he produced one unit more, he would incur more of cost than he gained of revenue.

"The addition to total revenue produced by selling an additional unit of output is *marginal revenue*. The seller is assumed always to equate marginal revenue to marginal cost. He may be conceived to do this either by estimating the demand price and the cost of various outputs, or by a process of trial and error."

supposing that the producer or producers possess essential patents, resources, or other means of holding the field closed. We are supposing merely that the product is differentiated.[22] Consequently, should a producer succeed in establishing a price and a production that permitted substantial net returns, it may be assumed that additional enterprisers tempted by the surplus profits would enter the field. As a result, capacity would be increased and the market divided among the new and old units, thereby reducing the individual producer's scale of production below his most efficient scale.

Furthermore, since there is seldom a shortage of would-be enterprisers, credit, labor or capital in the United States in times of peace, it may be supposed that newcomers would continue breaking into the field or old timers would continue expanding their capacity until surplus profits were no longer realized, either because the market had been subdivided among so many producers, or because price had been reduced in the heat of competition, or because of a combination of these two events. Thus prices in the steel industry before the war were held at a level which would secure generous profits were the industry operating at capacity. However, when it ran at 50 per cent of capacity in April, 1939, profits were probably no higher than they would have been under price competition, and in years when the rate dropped below 40 per cent no net profits were realized.

The price resulting from the behavior cited, a price permitting just enough profit to justify the producer's staying in business, would also mark an equilibrium, because neither a lower nor a higher price would increase returns. A lower price by definition would fail to provide the necessary minimum profit and a higher price would reduce demand below the operating level which permitted the competitor to make ends meet.[23]

This result does not mean that surplus profits are never realized in monopolistic competition. On the contrary, surplus profits are realized whenever demand increases faster than capacity as is usual in the early stages of a production upsurge.[24]

---

[22] Were the control due to the smallness of the field, as with steel rail producers, the situation would be similar were ingress into the field free, as is postulated.

[23] See Appendix, p. 40, for a geometrical demonstration of this detail.

However, the above condition does mean that prices are held above [25] the price of price competition even when no agreement, tacit or explicit, restrains the competitors.   As Mr. Chamberlin puts it: "The outcome (higher prices) involves no combination—not even a tacit agreement—among the sellers.   It is the result of each seeking independently his maximum profit.   The idea of conspiring (even tacitly) with his rivals may not enter the head of the man who takes it as a matter of course that he deals with his own customers and charges enough to make a good profit."   (A good profit presumably only if he gets enough customers.)   "But it is fortified in actuality by formal or tacit agreements, open price associations, trade association activities in building up an esprit de corps, price maintenance, the imposition of uniform prices on dealers by manufacturers, and excessive differentiation of product in the attempt to turn attention away from price.   Business or professional 'ethics' are another factor.   It has long been considered unethical in the professions to compete on the basis of price.   There is, therefore, no reason whatever why the supply of doctors or lawyers cannot multiply with economic impunity" [26] until, we suppose, they lose enough by the subdividing of the market to eliminate the profits that otherwise would accrue to them from their high prices.

The importance of this situation for our inquiry does not lie in the limitation on surplus profit (in monopolistic competition when effective) or that price in a field of monopolistic competition is *higher* than price in price competition, but in the fact that production in monopolistic competition, because of the subdividing of the market and the reduction of each participating producer's production, *would not be at the most efficient scale* except in the rare instances, which exist at times, as for example, during a war, when the demand for the product continues to increase faster than capacity is expanded by the ingress of newcomers or otherwise.   When this eventuality occurs, the total product capacity is used and production can be maintained at the most efficient or higher scale.

[24] This event is considered in Chapter V.
[25] See Appendix, p. 40, for a graphic demonstration of this detail.
[26] *op. cit.*, p. 106.

Since production at other times is conducted at less than the *most efficient scale*, a *proportion* of the *product capacity* of the *producer* is not utilized. Thus *monopolistic competition fosters* the *creation* and *perpetuation* of *excess capacity*. As a result, whenever product differentiation (real or fictive), trademark, selling effort, location, or other monopolistic feature, gives each producer a market more or less closely bound to his product, idle capital is normal and permanent.

The existence of excess capacity and idle plant which the statistical data referred to in Chapter I conclusively demonstrated [27] has now been given a theoretical standing, and the nonproduction of the individual producer has been accounted for, since an operating rate less than the most efficient operating rate is another way of saying nonproduction. To this extent our search has been furthered.

But over-all nonproduction *has not been accounted for*. On the contrary, the theory of monopolistic competition permits the free ingress of new competitors as did the theory of price competition. And if newcomers entered fields of effort until the unemployed were absorbed, production would be full. It is true if the market had been so divided that the sales of each competitor had been reduced to the point where surplus profit had disappeared, the prospect for a newcomer would not be tempting. On the other hand, an aspirant for business would possess certain advantages in such a field which he would not possess if entering a field of price competition. Because of the possibility of manipulating the product, the price or the selling appeal, a newcomer might succeed in taking away the market of a competitor without producing more efficiently than the competitor. The above discussion, therefore, does not explain over-all nonproduction, the non-use of capital and men, but only excess capacity, the non-use of capital. And idle capital alone does not constitute nonproduction, since the idle capital could not be operated were there no unemployed.

[27] Should further supporting evidence be desired, reference could be made to the Census of Manufactures' report on unused capacity for the years 1922 and 1923. The data are tabulated in Brookings' *Capacity to Produce, op. cit.*, pp. 561–9. Also the doubling of production between 1939 and 1943, while plant capacity for peace time products was increased by much less, indicates that the excess capacity persisted up to the war.

Thus the analysis given above seems to account for part of the difference between full production and capacity production as defined in Chapter I, although it does not account for over-all nonproduction and unemployment.

APPENDIX TO 3.   THE FOREGOING DISCUSSION IS RECAPITULATED IN GEOMETRICAL TERMS.

To analyze the situation of a competitor producing a commodity similar but not identical to the products of his competitors, it is helpful to represent his cost schedule or curve.   With exceptions, discussed in the appendix to this chapter,[28] the cost curves of individual producing units possess certain well-understood characteristics.   In nearly every case the cost of production falls from the high cost of low production to the low cost of optimum production when the unit is running at its most efficient scale, and then rises again as the plant, farm, mine, machine or man is overextended.   These characteristics apply to all kinds of producers.

CC_1 in Figure II is drawn to represent the unit cost of such a single producer dropping from the high unit costs of low production to the low unit cost, KM, of maximum efficiency, and then rising again as the plant is overextended and more effort is required to obtain an additional unit of output.

K_1K_1 would then be the equivalent of d_2d_2 in Figure I and would represent the demand for the producer's product were the field one of price competition.   The producer in such a field could not obtain a higher price than KM for the reasons given in section 2.   However, he could sell all his product at price KM and would produce therefore OM goods, since only by producing OM goods, the quantity resulting from production at the most efficient scale, could he recover his costs.[29]

Were the producer turning out a differentiated product, in other words, were monopolistic instead of price competition in question, then the demand curve for the producer would not be K_1K_1.   The reason is that the individual producer's market would be separate to some degree from that of his competitors if his product was differentiated from that of his competitors.

In other words, the demand for the product would vary, as noted in the foregoing section, from a low demand at a high price to a high demand at a low price.   To represent this condition, the demand curve would have to be drawn on a slant in order to show that each

[28] p. 57.
[29] It is assumed that rent would equalize the cost of intramarginal producers. See footnote, p. 34.

change in the price would alter the demand for the product.[30]   Let
the slanted curve DD_1 represent such a demand.

The slope of the curve shows the increase in sales which one producer of the group could realize "by cutting price, provided others

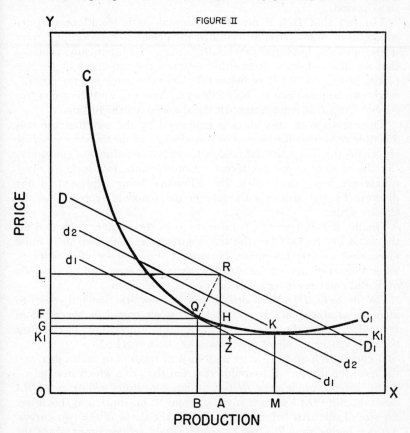

FIGURE II

did not cut theirs; and conversely, it shows the falling off in sales which
would attend an increase in price, provided other prices did not also
increase." [31]   In short, DD_1 shows the effect of price changes for one
producer on the assumption that all producers but the one in question
maintain the price at which they had been selling their goods.

For DD_1 to be established, we have to make the further unrealistic
assumption that all other prices and products in the total economy are

[30] To simplify our exposition, we will confine ourselves to the possibility of
varying the price.   Mr. Chamberlin has extended his argument to cover other
possible variations.

[31] Chamberlin, *op. cit.,* p. 90.

fixed, since a drop, for example, in the price of cement, might reduce the demand for structural steel. Although this assumption is unrealistic, its unrealism is not consequential. The changes in other prices and products may reasonably be assumed to even out for some short period.

The fact that DD_1 is neither horizontal, as it would be in price competition, nor vertical as would be the demand curve for air [32] were it monopolized, has important consequences. Geometrically, it means that the demand curve must either intersect the cost curve CC_1 in two places, be tangent to CC_1 or below CC_1. (In the latter case the product might not be produced.) This follows because CC_1 must be a concave curve. And DD_1 must approach the shape of a straight line.

The variation in curvatures is explained by the fact that the cost schedule represents the costs of one producer and the demand schedule represents the composite demand of hundreds or millions of consumers (for the product of one producer). Consequently, two scales of magnitude are being dealt with, the difference being expressed in our diagram by the greater curvature of the schedule representing the smaller scale.

Finally, if DD_1 cuts CC_1 it must do so in the manner indicated for the following reason: On the left, demand becomes zero at a finite price, and a fairly low price, because of the presence of substitutes, while costs rise toward infinity because of the necessity of covering overhead costs, however small the rate of production.

On the right, DD_1 must drop below CC_1 because demand ceases to increase as abundance is approached,[33] while costs can never fall to zero but must, in the case of an individual producer, start to rise after the most efficient scale of production has been reached.

If curves DD_1 and CC_1 were as shown in relation to each other and the axis, the distance RA would represent the price which maximized profit, for the profit area $RHGL$, which constitutes selling price RA times quantity OA less costs $HAOG$, would be maximized at this price, the size of this area being determined by the shape of the two curves. A price higher than RA, for example, would reduce profit, since the reduction in quantity would more than neutralize the increase in price. Similarly, a price below RA would reduce profit, since the reduction in price would more than neutralize the increase in quantity. Thus price RA maximizes profit under the conditions and would be the equilibrium price were we dealing with pure monopoly, the price to which the monopolist would return should he deviate from it by acci-

[32] The demand for ordinary, undifferentiated air would not vary appreciably at different prices if we assume a minimum per capita income sufficient to purchase the air required for life.

[33] Were everyone's want of a good satisfied, a further increase in production could not be sold.

dent or for some other reason. But pure monopoly is not in question. As noted in the foregoing section, it must be supposed that newcomers, tempted by the surplus profit, would break into the field and subdivide the market, thereby reducing the demand for the product of those vendors already in the field.

This result can be shown on the diagram by moving the demand curve to the left since such a move, while keeping the same slope, signifies that the demand at every price is equally reduced, a fair deduction, because there is no reason to believe that the slope of the demand curve would be altered by newcomers entering the field with additional goods for sale. Each enterpriser, however, would have to content himself with a smaller share of the total market. In order to maximize profit as demand DD_1 dropped down toward d_1d_1, price or production or both would have to be dropped.

If costs CC_1 were unchanged, prices lower than RA and individual productions lower than OA would successively be found.[34] Profit areas, similar to but smaller than $RHGL$, would continue to be maximized. (Prices which did not maximize profit would no doubt be tried out, but they would not stand, since an enterpriser would gain by varying his price along the successive demand curves DD_1, d_2d_2, d_1d_1 until he reached the point, such as R on demand curve DD_1, which would maximize profit.)

The end of the process would be reached when the demand curve was tangent to the cost curve. At this point, Q on the diagram, surplus profit would be wiped out. For the surplus profit area, i.e., price QB less cost QB times quantity OB, would be zero.

Furthermore, price QB would mark an equilibrium,[35] since no producer could better his condition by raising or lowering his price. As the diagram indicates, a price higher or lower than QB would result in unit costs higher than unit prices. Thereafter newcomers would not be tempted into the field by the existence of surplus profits. The analysis indicates that despite prices higher than those of price competition (QB is higher than KM) profits in monopolistic competition are not necessarily higher than the profits of price competition.

Since production OB, the equilibrium production under monopolistic competition, is lower than production OM, the equilibrium production under price competition, the production of a particular manufacturer would be lower in monopolistic competition than in price competition and would be at a level less than the level of optimum efficiency. This result would be due, as the discussion has indicated,

---

[34] This conclusion is supplemented in Chapter IV where further factors are introduced. For example, when demand falls below the demand which calls for the equilibrium production OB, it is more likely to be met by a reduction in production than by a reduction in price.

[35] Qualified in Chapter IV when cyclic movements are taken into account.

to the subdividing of the market so that demand called for a quantity which failed fully to utilize the productive plant.

Furthermore, this result could not be avoided by the actions of the individuals involved. Let us suppose, for example, that a producer has become a zealous convert to a low price policy. Let us further suppose that his price had been stabilized at QB, the equilibrium price, and his production at OB. On being converted, he throws caution out of the door and orders full speed ahead. Quantity OM is produced and offered for sale. If he offers his goods at price KM, he would get orders only for K_1Z products, since the demand for his particular product would be increased only to K_1Z at price KM. As a result, ZK products would be left unsold. If, however, he dropped his price below KM in order to sell OM goods, he would probably lose money even faster.

It may be supposed that he would consign theorists to their cloisters and would mark up his prices and come to terms with his competitors. He would not acquire demand for his entire product at price KM (as he would have in price competition) in part because in monopolistic competition, customers maintan varying degrees of allegiance to the name, trademark, package or what-not of each individual firm, and resist the allure of lower prices with varying degrees of fortitude and faith. These varying degrees are represented by the *slope of the demand curve;* in our example DD_1, d_1d_1, etc.

4. PRICE COMPETITION AND MONOPOLISTIC COMPETITION HAVE ADVANTAGES AND DISADVANTAGES THAT ARE IN SOME WAYS OPPOSITE.

Let us summarize the content of the preceding sections by citing briefly some of the advantages and disadvantages inherent in the two forms of competition.

Excess capacity. Price competition, in which the producer cannot influence price or profit appreciably by varying the scale of production, fosters operations at the most efficient scale. As a result, excess plant capacity is held within narrow limits and capital tends to be fully utilized.

Monopolistic competition in which price is administered and production geared to the resulting demand, results in excess capacity and in operations at less than the most efficient scale.

Selling expenses. Since the vendor can sell his total product in price competition, the diversion of effort to advertising, salesmanship, research, etc., is inhibited or held within narrow limits.

In monopolistic competition, the vendor can seldom sell at

the administered price the quantity of goods which he would produce were he operating at his most efficient scale. Consequently, it usually pays the vendor to divert effort to selling and advertising, activities of dubious utility when carried beyond a certain point.

Similar factors stimulate the diversion of effort to research and promotion, which activities have been largely responsible for the technological progress of recent decades.

Price stability. Price competition results in wide price swings.[36] As a result, economic calculations are made uncertain and large scale promotions difficult.

Monopolistic competition in which a change in demand is seldom reflected immediately by a change in price but more usually by a change in production [37] results in relatively lethargic prices. The association of the producer with his product and his product with its publicized price also tends to hold prices steady. As a result, calculations in respect to the future are more feasible than in price competition. Also, the association of the producers with his product serves to maintain quality since a defective product can often be traced back to the producer.

Size of production units. Price competition requires that every field of effort shall be divided into many competing entities in order that no producer can influence price. In certain fields, this atomic structure would reduce efficiency, as in automobile production, in others it would be infeasible, as in railroading. Also, products must be standardized so that the buyer has no choice between the product of one producer and that of another. Thus art, handicraft, fashion [38] and novelties could not be provided by price competition.

Since a large field of producers is not essential for monopolistic competition, the size of industrial units is not limited. As a result, organizations capable of handling the traffic of a continent and of developing the economies of mass production, have scope for development.

[36] p. 30.
[37] pp. 118 ff.
[38] In the sense the word is used above, a good is "fashionable" only so long as it is exclusive. Thus, the latest fashion could not be standardized and remain fashionable.

Higgling, planning and efficiency. The smaller the producing units, the greater the scope for higgling and the smaller the scope for planning. Efficiency is probably furthered by maximizing planning within the limits needed for price to function parametrically.[39] Thus efficiency would probably be held down in an economy of price competition by the inability to plan as far ahead.

By organizing industries vertically, as have certain steel corporations, and horizontally, as have department stores and mail order houses, higgling has been largely eliminated within controlled spheres in the industries engaged in monopolistic competition, and the scope for planning has been increased. Efficiency, as a result, has been fostered.

The parametric function of price. When price competition is effective, changes in supply or demand are reflected immediately by changes in price. As a result, relative costs (efficiency) and relative desires (scarcity) are interpreted by the price of goods and services, economic decisions are rendered feasible, and resources are effectively allocated.

In monopolistic competition, as in price competition, price reflects changes in costs and desires as described in Section 3. However, the reflection of changed conditions is neither so immediate nor so pure as in price competition.

The lethargy of price is probably more advantageous than otherwise. (See price stability above.) The impurity or distortion, however, is probably harmful.

Price in monopolistic competition reflects the cost of production just as accurately (perhaps more accurately since price swings are minimized) as does price in price competition. But it is not the same cost. It is *not* the cost of production at the *most efficient scale of operation.* Price in monopolistic competition reflects the cost of production at the scale of production to which the industry is committed by the conditions summarized in Section 3. This cost is higher than the per unit cost at the most efficient scale of production, since the cost of carrying excess capital is usually included as well as that of selling effort, research, etc. Consequently, economic decisions based upon the

[39] p. 7.

prices established by monopolistic competition are distorted to some extent by the fact that it is not the minimum cost which is being reflected.

Furthermore, the excess overhead due to excess capital lowers the share of labor and enterprise since labor and enterprise share the gross returns with other income recipients and necessarily receive a smaller share (percentage of the total) when the owners of capital receive a larger share. As a result, wages and profit are held down in monopolistic competition below the level they would attain were the capital fully utilized.[40]

Because most of industry is engaged in monopolistic competition, the price distortion, due to higher than necessary costs, is nearly ubiquitous. As a result, economic choices can still be made between alternatives and resources effectively allocated.[41]

In other words, price still functions parametrically in monopolistic competition and the main effect of prices higher than those of price competition is the allocation of a greater proportion of

[40] This self-evident deduction is not disproved by the fact that wages and profits in monopolistic competition range higher than wages and profits in price competition, a result probably due largely to the greater efficiency, for reasons suggested above, of most industries engaged in monopolistic competition.

[41] Miss Barbara Wooton, *Lament for Economics*, pp. 165, 166, Farrar & Rinehart, New York, questions the consumer's ability to distribute his resources rationally when prices are interfered with by monopolistic controls. She writes: "If, for example, the price of houses is kept up, and the supply restricted by a builders' monopoly, then this distortion will enter into and bias every subsequent market influence in which the cost of housing appears as datum; and owing to the elaborate interconnections of markets, this single imperfection of the market process may mean distortion over a very wide field indeed. For high cost houses mean high rents, and the level of rentals may affect wages, etc."

Our impression is that Miss Wooton is comparing an economy with a fault, to a perfect economy. Obviously, an imperfect price in an interacting system eventually distorts every other price. But if nearly every price is distorted by monopolistic controls to some extent, which would seem to be a realistic description of the actual state of affairs, and if the distortions tend to be in the same direction (namely, upward) the total effect might well be a price structure which would permit the consumer to approximate a rational disposal of his scarce means.

An over-all distortion remains: that between prices in the price competition industries and prices in the monopolistic competition industries. This distortion may not, however, be very important, since it may be neutralized or more than neutralized by the greater efficiency of the industries which administer prices. Thus our impression is that the ratio between the value of beans and Buicks, let us say, would not be altered much if both beans and Buicks were produced and distributed in a system of price competition or in a system of monopolistic competition. Obviously, this is only an impression, since we cannot refer to the actual world for verification.

the total income to property owners.[42] The consequence may have been helpful in the early days of the United States when savings were habitually less than requirements. It is probably detrimental today, as the subsequent discussion will indicate.

Structural and cyclical price flexibility. A further distinction between the two forms of competition can best be presented by making use of two familiar concepts, that of structural price flexibility and that of cyclic price flexibility.

Structural price flexibility refers to the ability of prices to reflect relative efficiencies and scarcities—or the relationship of one or more products to other products. It is concerned not with the level of prices but with the interrelationship of prices. The successful accomplishment of this function, the parametric function, permits the economic allocation of resources as described in Chapter I.

Cyclical flexibility, on the other hand, refers to the ability of prices to reflect the relationship of over-all supply and over-all demand. It has to do therefore with the so-called business cycle.

In price competition, demand and supply are equated, as we saw, at an equilibrium price which reflects both demand and supply. This condition holds good not only for a single product, but would hold good for the total product, were a total economy of price competition feasible, because a deficiency in demand for any cause would result in a fall in price. Consequently, price would be perfectly sensitive, deficiencies in demand would be eliminated as fast as they appeared,[43] and nonproduction, should it occur, would be the result of some other cause.[44] Thus price competition possesses both structural and cyclical price flexibility.

In monopolistic competition, a deficiency in demand would

[42] If resources are allocated as effectively in monopolistic competition as in price competition, then the direct effect of costs higher because of excess capital than those of price competition would, as noted above, be a decreased share of income to wages and profits, and an increased share to interest payments.

[43] This probability is considered more fully on p. 67.

[44] Certain theorists suppose that nonproduction is due to labor demanding a wage greater than the marginal product of labor. Though nonproduction from such a cause would seem possible, it apparently is not the cause of nonproduction in the United States, since labor, as the analysis will explain, would be entitled to higher returns were production stepped up. However, labor could not hold out for a higher wage successfully in an economy of price competition, since wages, like other prices, would be subject to the market.

not be automatically corrected by a drop in price, but would probably result in a drop in production or in a combination of the two as in Figure II.   Thus price in monopolistic competition has little cyclical flexibility [45] although, as indicated in the last section, it has structural flexibility.

This lack does not account for nonproduction. It does not, as was noted in the last section, indicate why new enterprisers do not pour into the more profitable fields whenever men are released by enterprisers reducing their operating scales or installing a labor saving device. But it does give us a clue to nonproduction, which we shall shortly follow up.

The above summary suggests that an economy of monopolistic competition might be more effective than an economy of price competition could excess capital and nonproduction be kept within narrow limits.   However, let us put this possibility to one side for the time being and consider another relevant aspect of competitive procedures.

5. IN FIELDS OF MONOPOLISTIC COMPETITION, PRODUCTION IS USUALLY SUBJECT TO DECREASING COSTS.   AS A RESULT, AN IN-CREASE IN OVER-ALL PRODUCTION USUALLY PERMITS HIGHER PROFITS AND WAGES.

Our analysis indicated that producers in fields of price competition tend to operate at their most efficient scale of production, and that producers in fields of monopolistic competition tend to operate at less than their most efficient scale of production.   As a result, price competition is usually subject to increasing costs,[46] and monopolistic competition to decreasing costs.   This conclusion may be deduced as follows:

Should every producer in a field of effort operate at his most efficient scale, an increase in production would be accomplished in one of two ways: either the existing producers could operate on a scale greater than their most efficient scale and incur thereby higher per unit costs; or new competitors could start producing.

---

[45] The data given in Table I, page 98, substantiate this deduction. The reaction of a concern faced by a deficiency of demand in a field of monopolistic competition is considered in Chapter IV, pp. 106 ff.

[46] p. 31.

In a field of price competition such as farming, the most convenient sites and resources would already have been preempted. The new competitors, therefore, would have to utilize less convenient sites and more expensive resources (resources requiring more effort to make available). Consequently, per unit costs would increase were production stepped up by either or both methods.

When wheat cultivation, for example, is extended, less fertile fields have to be cultivated. As a result, cost per bushel is likely to be greater. (The fact that this condition has been neutralized and more than neutralized in many periods by the advance in technology and other factors does not negate the conclusion, though it qualifies it. The factor of advancing technology will be brought into the general picture in the next chapter.)

The above relationship, sometimes known as the law of diminishing returns, is akin to a natural law, since it is dependent on certain objective facts such as the tendency of men and other free agents to browse first in the richer fields. Its applicability, however, often is over-extended. Thus the "law" is sometimes supposed to pertain to all economic activities. Should it do so, an increase in over-all production would necessarily result in higher costs per unit, and lower profits per unit.

As a matter of fact, the "law," though applicable to fields of effort in which price competition prevails, since site and resource happen to be important factors in such fields, does not pertain most of the time to fields of monopolistic competition. In this area, the "natural law" is usually superseded by an institutional relationship which might be called "the monopolistic competition principle of decreasing costs."[47]

Thus, if competitors in a field of effort should be operating at a scale less than their most efficient scale, as is usual in fields of monopolistic competition in times of peace for the reasons cited in Section 3, stepping up production would increase efficiency.

---

[47] Many economists question the prevalence of decreasing costs. Since they acknowledge that "lumpiness" in one or more factors of production—such as management or equipment—creates an area in which costs fall as production increases, their objection does not disqualify our argument. If the possibility of expanding or improving the plant is excluded, the area of decreasing costs would be limited on the up side by the production of maximum efficiency.

Efficiency was defined as the ratio of manhour input to quantity output. An increase in efficiency, therefore, would lower manhour input per unit output, or cost per unit.

The natural law of increasing costs is superseded in fields of monopolistic competition by this institutional relationship in part because "site and resource" are unimportant in most processing and servicing activities. Even when the activity involves refining a natural resource such as ore, so many sites of comparable convenience are available, that the efficiency of the smelter and refinery is likely to depend more on the design of the capital equipment than on the location of the site.

Thus an increase in production in a field of monopolistic competition usually lowers per unit costs until plant capacity is reached, a level rarely sustained in the United States except under the stimulus of war or preparation thereof.

The statistical evidence supports this conclusion. The following table,[48] which was part of the testimony of the United States Steel Corporation before the T.N.E.C., and could be duplicated by data from nearly every other industry, indicated the following cost per ton of average steel products shipped:

Per Cent of Capacity Operated	Cost Per Ton Under 1938 Conditions
20	$99.40
40	79.70
60	72.30
80	68.30
100	65.90

It is evident that in the steel industry per unit costs decrease as production is stepped up—up to 100 per cent of capacity.

In general, therefore, it is true that (1) farming and other fields subject to price competition incur increased costs as production is stepped up, unless the advance in technology, or other factors neutralizes this condition, and that (2) processing, servicing and other activities in which monopolistic competition prevails, incur decreased costs as production is stepped up, at least until plant capacity is approached.

[48] From government publication, *Analysis of Steel Prices, Volume and Costs, Controlling Limitations on Price Reduction*, p. 35.

(Even this limit on the condition of decreasing costs is largely theoretical, for the reason that new plants, except in certain industries in which technology is static if there are such, are usually more efficient than the plants being superseded. Thus the point of maximum efficiency is a moving point which may advance in time.) [49]

The value of farm produce, the only important field of price competition, constitutes but a small fraction of the value of the total product, some $10 or $12 billion worth out of a total of $50 to $80 billions in the prewar economy, and the per unit cost of farm produce would probably not increase much [50] were farm production stepped up to meet the demands of a fully employed population.[51] On the other hand, the decrease in costs in the bulk of industry would be considerable were production stepped up to full if the condition prevailing in the steel, cement, railroad and other industries submitting profit and loss estimates periodically, are typical. As a result, an *over-all increase* in production would be subject to decreasing costs as such times as production in general was appreciably less than practical plant capacity and unemployed men were available.

This condition suggests that profit could usually be increased by stepping up production, other things being equal. And this deduction too has been substantiated by recent events. As production increased from the low level of the late Thirties to nearly $200 billion worth in the war years, both profits and wages rose (real as well as monetary). Thus, the widely held belief that

[49] For further comment on this detail, see pp. 204–7.

[50] This supposition is supported by the National Resources Committee (*Technological Trends and National Policy*, National Resources Committee, p. 104). The report states: "It is probable that this group [the half of the farmers who produce some 90 per cent of the product] could, by utilizing some available technologies and with some increase in area of land for tillage, produce 10 per cent to 11 per cent more—thus accounting for all products sold or traded." And thus releasing, though this is not stated, the other half of the farmers, many of whom are sub-marginal, their land and equipment, to satisfy further needs and wants of the population. The war record of the farmer bears out this supposition.

[51] The NSPPC estimated that demand for food and clothes at capacity production would call for a 20 per cent increase in farm produce. Actually farm production under the stimulus of war demand increased 25 per cent between 1939 and 1944, notwithstanding a net decline in farm employment and only a 6 per cent increase in acreage (*Current Business*, February 1945, p. 10).

production is held down in order to augment profits evidently is
erroneous. Holding down production has the opposite result.
Self-interest would be served best by increasing production whenever production was short of plant capacity and workers were
available.

The over-all condition of decreasing costs stressed above may
seem to conflict with the analysis of monopolistic competition
submitted in Section 3. It is necessary, therefore, to indicate
why the conflict is only apparent; that is to say, why an over-all
increase in production would reduce costs and increase profits,
though an individual unit's increase of production, unaccompanied by a general increase in production, would usually cause
an enterpriser to incur loss, as concluded on p. 43.

In Section 3, demand was assumed to be independent of
supply. This assumption is legitimate when the demand for a
single product or the demand for the product of a single producer is in question because the demand for a single product is
affected so slightly by changes in the production or supply of
that product, that the effect is inappreciable. Even in the case
of a great motor car company, the effect upon demand of a
change in the company's production, and therefore, in the money
paid out in the productive process, would be too small to increase
or decrease appreciably the sale of the automobile. The reason
is that the money paid out by any one concern is divided by the
recipients among so many goods and services, that the share
that is returned to the concern by way of sales would not be
appreciable.

Thus, a single producer who stepped up production from a
position of equilibrium (such as price QB, production OB, in
Figure II), would increase the supply of *his* product and the
demand for *all* products. The increase in demand would not
balance the increase in his supply. On the contrary, the increase in demand would be divided among many goods and
services, including capital goods. A single producer, therefore,
could not count on diverting to his product an *appreciable* fraction
of the demand increment released by his increase in production.
All he could count on would be the diversion to his product of

that fraction of the total demand which his product normally enticed.

This fraction would be insufficient to increase net returns. In fact, if the enterpriser had determined his price accurately, an increase in his operating rate would, according to the logic of Section 3, diminish net revenue or profit, regardless of what price was elected. It was therefore maintained [52] that a management which increased production in an equilibrated field would be sacrificing its stockholders and violating its fiduciary relation, since profits would be curtailed by any variation in the rate of production despite the condition of decreasing costs.

However, were all of industry in question, then a change in production would materially affect demand. The mutual interdependence of production and demand was emphasized in the introduction where the two aspects of the productive process were described. Production not only makes goods available, but also releases the demand by which goods can be procured. And the two quantities, the supply made available and the demand made effective, would be equal were the goods sold. Thus our assumptions of an independent demand, of a demand independent of the supply, *is not permissible* when *over-all demand* and *over-all supply* are in question. On the contrary, when the over-all quantities are in question, an increase in supply results in an increase in demand. (This condition could be represented on a diagram by using one curve to represent both demand and supply, a curve rising from the low supply and demand of a low scale of production to the high supply and demand of a high scale of production.)

Should over-all production be increased, demand would increase as supply was increased. Since this event would be accompanied in fields of monopolistic competition by falling per unit costs, the increased supply could be sold under usual conditions [53] at a price which increased net return. Consequently, it would pay enterprisers to step up production when production was less than plant capacity, could men be found to operate the

[52] p. 44.
[53] The conditions which would not permit increased returns are studied in Chapter V.

idle equipment, and could enough producers act together appreciably to increase demand.

On the other hand, should an individual producer increase production acting alone, he would augment *his* supplies and *over-all* demand by about the same quantity. And the increase in over-all demand would be spread so thin, as noted above, that the fraction which returned to him (by way of increased sales) would be negligible.

Thus, the analysis of Chamberlin and the demand schedules represented in the diagrams were quite rightly based on the assumption that demand and costs were *mutually* independent; that an increase or decrease in a concern's production had no appreciable effect on demand; since this is nearly true *in the case of one producer*.

It therefore appears that (1) one or a few producers cannot step up production without reducing profit [54] in the ordinary course of events, despite the widespread condition of decreasing costs, (2) all, or nearly all producers could profitably increase production whenever the scale of production was less than the most efficient scale and men were available to operate the equipment at the increased scale.

6. A DIFFERENT APPROACH TO THE PROBLEM IS INDICATED: AN APPROACH WHICH TAKES INTO ACCOUNT THE RECIPROCAL RELATION OF OVER-ALL DEMAND AND OVER-ALL SUPPLY.

It was suggested in the last section that all or nearly all producers might profitably increase production could and should they act together because of the over-all condition of decreasing costs whenever production was less than that of the most efficient scale.

It is necessary to determine why such an increase is accomplished only at certain times even though additional labor has been available in all peace years, and why the stepping up of production when it has occurred in recent decades has not been continued until full employment was attained, except during war crises.

[54] Certain conditions which would permit greater profit to be realized at lower prices are discussed in the Appendix, p. 57.

Furthermore, it was suggested that this condition could not be investigated by means of the conventional demand and supply, or demand and cost schedules used in this chapter because demand is not independent of either the supply, or the money paid out as costs, when all of industry is in question. Since demand in any time period consists in the main of costs plus profit minus losses, the over-all demand curve as was noted above, tends to coincide with the over-all supply curve. As a result, neither the demand nor the cost curve would intersect the supply curve if all of industry were in question. In order, therefore, to segregate the factors which determine the scale of production—or, to put it in other words—in order to discover why nonproduction is practiced in the contemporary American economy, something other than the conventional demand and supply curves are evidently required. Let us therefore return to the proposition with which this study opened and represent in its simplest form the relation of over-all demand to over-all supply, the relation we decided to call "the over-all equilibrium adjustment."

This adjustment occurs, as we have seen, at various scales of production. Sometimes demand and supply are equated at a low production. Sometimes demand and supply are equated at a fairly high production.[55] A conspicuous feature of this adjustment is the fact that production is always shifting. Production is always increasing or decreasing.

It is convenient therefore to open our inquiry by considering the behavior of certain factors of the equilibrium adjustment. Since a change in any factor affects every other factor to some degree, reactions are complicated. However, our understanding will be aided by assuming single or isolated effects in certain cases.

Furthermore, let us introduce into the proposition a factor which is continually changing in one direction, irrespective of other economic events, that is to say, efficiency. And let us check our logic by using algebraic symbols to represent the

---

[55] The production record of the war years casts doubt on earlier statistical estimates of full production. Apparently 1929 production was a lesser fraction of full than even the N.S.P.P.C. estimated.

situations. Not only do symbols [56] divorced from actual quantities serve to segregate relationships and thereby expose errors in logic which often escape observation when tangled up with real things, but also relationships in mathematical form sometimes permit the observer to perceive implications which would otherwise escape him.

What we have to deal with is an automatic equilibrium similar in some respects to the equilibriums that are so frequent in nature. Somehow or other, as was suggested,[57] demand and supply are maintained in a kind of balance. A deviation of either quantity from equality sets up a corrective reaction. Although the two quantities are never exactly equal, in some years the inventory carryover is a little greater or a little less, the commodities unsold at the end of the year do not increase greatly in time.

When we have determined how this over-all equilibrium is maintained, then we can refer again to the nature of competition in order to show that the causes of nonproduction reside in the monopolistic procedures described in this chapter.

APPENDIX TO CHAPTER II. AN EXPLANATION IS OFFERED OF THE EXCEPTIONS TO THE RULE THAT CURRENT PRICES TEND TO MAXIMIZE PROFITS.

The fact that certain producers without introducing a technical improvement have successfully dropped their prices and increased thereby both production and profit, does not disqualify the reasoning presented in Section 3 since exceptions in the social sciences do not necessarily invalidate the rule. It does require explaining, however, if our logic is to be convincing.

Let us recognize, in the first place, that the typical cost and demand curves pictured in Section 3 assume many shapes. The cost curve of each productive process differs from the cost curve of every other productive process because the individual technical production problem differs. Sometimes these curves are not smooth. By that we mean that sometimes they do not change at a steady acceleration or deceleration. They may, for example, be wavy or jagged. Costs do not, in the actual world, drop consistently as production is increased. On the contrary, the cost curve may be more or less level for quite a

---

[56] The symbols will be introduced in the next chapter.
[57] p. 5.

span, then drop abruptly when the quantity required of the commodity is sufficient to justify the use of power machinery, and thereafter drop slowly up to the point where the equipment installed is fully utilized. There may be several such changes in direction, as various possible technical procedures are successively made available.

Furthermore, the demand curve may not drop consistently. The demand curve in Figure II was drawn to represent the increased demand for one product of one producer. As price drops, the quantity demand increases, since more and more income groups are able to indulge their desire for the article. Furthermore, as the price drops, the quantity demanded increases disproportionately (causing the curve to be concave) [58] owing to the fact that the various income groups *increase in size* as income drops. More families have $4,000 a year than $5,000; more families $3,000 than $4,000; and more families $2,000 than $3,000. It is not until the $1,000 a year mark is passed—or was passed, since our data, taken from *America's Capacity to Consume* (Brookings Institution) covers the year 1929—that the size of the income group diminishes. And families of four possessing less than $1,000 a year can purchase only the cheapest goods.

If the curve had been designed to represent the demand for bread, the curve would have been drawn close to the vertical, for in the case of universally consumed items (which necessarily are relatively cheap) a drop in price permits individuals to consume more without drawing additional economic classes into the market. In other words, a price drop would not permit individuals who otherwise would not have consumed the product, to consume it. Under these circumstances, the demand is said to be *inelastic*. Commodities of quite another kind, such as steel, are also relatively inelastic,[59] owing to the fact that demand for steel depends not only on price but also on other factors such as the amount of heavy construction under way, which may be greater when prices are high, as in 1929, than when prices are low, as in 1932.

Furthermore, the demand curve, like the cost curve, may be wavy or jagged, owing to the fact that demand may increase erratically as price is dropped. For example, in the early days of motoring, only the rich could indulge in motor cars. The price was lowered nevertheless as efficiency increased. But the first price drops did not cause demand to expand enough to permit of the economies of mass production because the expansion of the selling field from the million dollar class, let us say, increased the potential market relatively little.

However, as prices continued to drop, demand increased disproportionately. A new body of consumers came into the field as the men

[58] In Figure II, demand was represented by a straight line because the concavity was so slight in relation to the curvature of the cost curve.

[59] Demand inelasticity is considered in more detail on pp. 110–11.

in the higher salary brackets and the small property owners began to experiment with the new vehicle. As a result, the manufacturing of parts entered the mass production stage and manhour input per car was materially reduced.

The question arises as to what effect the wavy character of many cost and demand curves has upon the producer who is attempting to maximize profits.

Mrs. Robinson [60] has given thought to this situation. Her conclusion, which would seem indubitable, amounts to this. When either the cost schedule, or demand schedule, or both, is wavy or jagged, the price which maximized profit may not be discoverable by marginal (or small) trial and error variations, for there may be several prices which would appear to maximize profits. The enterpriser cannot tell by trying prices a little above or below the price which appears to maximize profits that a sharp price drop would unleash a greatly increased demand, and that the market thereby uncovered would be so much greater than the market he has been reaching, that production could be largely increased and great economies and profits thereby realized. Consequently, unless he is unusually daring, he is likely to stick to a price which is the most profitable within his limited range but which does not open up the great potentialities for profit of a price sharply lower.

We are now in a position to understand how certain producers, by lowering prices and increasing production, have in the past increased their net returns. Such a result might reasonably be expected, for example: (a) if the producer, through control over the ingress of newcomers,[61] has been maintaining prices above the prices that would maximize profits (certain observers claim this condition frequently exists); (b) if wavy demand or cost curves or both concealed the price that maximized profits.

Since these conditions are present, at least to some extent and at certain times, the propaganda in favor of lower prices would seem of occasional public benefit. However, if our argument is valid, this propaganda, even if it results in action, is of limited applicability. There is no reason to believe that an important fraction of industry has been subject to conditions (a) or (b). Consequently, there is no reason to believe that the advice to lower prices possesses more than a limited and particular relevance which pertains to so few going concerns that their action or nonaction along the lines indicated would have little general effect.

---

[60] *op. cit.*, Chapter III, Section 4.

[61] Ingress is so difficult in certain fields either because of the high initial cost of production or because of patents or other controls, that a condition resembling monopoly is approached.

However, Mrs. Robinson's analysis assists us to understand how our reasoning, which led us to conclude that prices by and large were adjusted to maximize profits, may still be sound, even though there have been specific cases in which a reduction in price induced so great an increase in demand that profit was greater at the lower price than it had been at the former level.

CHAPTER III

The Demand-Supply Adjustment

1. THE ADVANCE IN EFFICIENCY IS PERSISTENT AND LARGELY INDE-
PENDENT OF THE STATE OF THE ECONOMY. ITS ADVANCE MAKES
AVAILABLE INCREMENTS OF ADDITIONAL WEALTH.

MONEY is issued in the process of production as described
in Chapter I, the sum of the payments constituting the
"effective demand" [1] for goods and services. If we
represent goods and services by Q, price by P, and demand by E,
supply and demand could be represented by

$$E \gtreqless QP \ [2]$$

which tells us that the effective demand may be greater than,
equal to, or smaller than the available supply, a truism of no
significance.

However, supply, QP, tends to approach demand E, and vice
versa. [3] If, supply should happen to be greater than demand,

---

[1] The effective demand in any year consists of money paid out in the process of
production minus hoardings and plus dishoardings. The word "hoardings" is used
in preference to the word "savings" or "withholdings" because it is necessary to distinguish money withdrawn from circulation and left in stockings or under beds (i.e.
hoardings), from money deposited in a bank or used to purchase stocks, bonds, land,
etc. (i.e. "withholdings"). The latter kind of transaction as was indicated on page
4 does not affect the dimensions of the over-all or aggregate effective demand.
Money deposited in a bank or used to purchase stocks, land, etc. is merely transferred from a person or agent (such as banks and other going concerns) to another
person or agent, just as a personal loan transfers buying power from one person to
another. As a result, such transactions do not alter the total of money available for
purchases. Effective demand, therefore, consists of the money paid out in the
process of production including the *net new money increment* minus hoardings and plus
dishoardings. Since hoardings and dishoardings (as defined above) are very small
in the contemporary United States in respect to the total income, effective demand
is likely to approach closely the sum of money paid out in the process of production.

[2] To be exact, the formula should be written

$$E = Q_1P_1 + Q_2P_2 + Q_3P_3 \ldots \text{etc.} = \sum_1^n QP$$

to represent quantity of each item multiplied by the price of each. The validity
of the logic is not affected by our use of the simpler expression denoting the aggregate
quantities.

[3] If interested in determing how far short of equality E and QP fall in any year,
reference could be made to inventory carryover, since differences in the quantities

certain enterprisers as noted in Chapter I would either drop their prices or reduce their rate of production because piling up an unsalable surplus would cause them loss and other difficulties. Similarly, if supply should happen to be smaller than demand, certain enterprisers would either raise prices or step up production, since they would thereby increase their incomes (their buying and consuming power). Consequently, E and QP approach equality. The price at which they are equal we have called the *equilibrium price*, and the scale [4] of production at which they are equal, the *equilibrium production*. The proposition as a whole, that is to say, the over-all equilibrium adjustment may therefore be considered to approach the equation:

$$E = QP$$

The proposition does not represent all goods, because Q stands for *finished goods only* and not goods in process. Thus Q represents net goods and services and not a summation of goods in all their transformation. Similarly E represents income or buying power and not the summation of all the money transactions that occur during a year, In short, E represents monetary income, Q, real income, QP real income in monetary terms, and the proposition $E \lesseqgtr QP$ represents the relation of demand and supply.

Our manipulations will consist in the main of adding and subtracting increments,[5] ΔE, ΔQ, etc., and considering what effect such an event might have on the relationship.[6]

E and QP would appear as an increase or decrease in inventory. The largest variation in recent peacetime inventory carryover occurred in 1929 when due to exceptional circumstances (a sharp reduction in monetary income toward the end of the year) inventory carryover is estimated to have increased over the 1928 carryover by goods valued at some $1\frac{1}{2}$ billion dollars.

In calculating the difference between E and QP, such goods as are deliberately destroyed in any year should be counted in. Deliberate destruction is exceptional and the quantities actually destroyed have in all but a few years been inappreciable in relation to the total income.

[4] The phrase "scale" or "level of production" is being used when referring to the over-all economy to signify production in relation to full production or zero.

[5] An increment may be defined as the amount by which a varying quantity increases between two of its stages.

[6] Using the sum of sizeable increments involves an error. When the increment is not neutralized during the time period—when, let us say, ΔE, is not balanced within the time span by, for example, the increment ΔQ, so that the equation $E = QP$ is transformed into the equation: $E + \Delta E = (Q + \Delta Q)P$ but results instead in an upward or downward movement of indefinite duration (examples of which will

The over-all equilibrium adjustment is not static. Each of the quantities is subject to change. Real income as well as money income rises and falls. The price level as well as individual prices vary from year to year. One of the factors which causes the quantities to vary is efficiency which is established as was noted [7] by the ratio of work or labor to production. Since both the input (of manhours) and the output (of product) are measurable quantities, their ratio, efficiency, may be expressed in numerical terms. For example, if it formerly took four men to produce ten shoes an hour, and today four men produce twenty shoes an hour, the efficiency of shoemaking would have doubled, were other relevant factors constant. Such an increase would unbalance the over-all equilibrium adjustment if prices were constant since either demand, which varies with manhour input, or supply, or both, would necessarily be changed by this event.

Furthermore, efficiency, as was suggested in the last chapter, differs from most of the other relevant factors, in that it *advances* persistently. [8]

In fact, one of the few things definitely known about society is that efficiency has been increasing. We may suppose that ethics, politics, esthetics, philosophy, etc. have improved or retrograded; that man is happier or more miserable, more warlike or more peaceful today than in the past. But we cannot be certain, since we have no measuring rod, no way of comparing, if we exclude subjective evaluations, the painting for example of one period with that of another. Relative efficiencies, can on the other hand be measured.

Since efficiency is a function of technology, and since technology is an application of science, an advance in the field of scien-

occur in the following pages)—our symbolic representation does not succeed in perfectly representing the event. This methodological inadequacy does not, in our opinion, invalidate the logic.

[7] p. 6.

[8] The population has also increased persistently in the United States during the period under review. Its increase could be incorporated in our proposition by using the concept productivity—efficiency times the number of workers available—instead of the concept efficiency. However, it is simpler to disregard this factor since its presence does not affect our logic. Also the rate of increase has been falling. The fact that higher living standards lower the rate of population increase was not foreseen by early economists and led to the fear that the population would increase so much in relation to the land area that living standards would be reduced.

tific knowledge directly proportioned to the advance in efficiency, may be inferred, though the application of science (technology) doubtless lags somewhat behind the advance in knowledge (pure science).

Furthermore, the rate of increase is largely independent of financial or social factors. Thus in times of depression, efficiency is increased by the efforts of going concerns to survive; in times of prosperity, by the efforts of going concerns to augment their profits. And so in times of war, of peace, of hope and of despair, engineers, inventors, foremen, workers, and housewives devise new methods, and enterprisers find it to their interest to put them into effect. Endeavors to sabotage this process during times of stress has not in the recent past met with success, at least in the United States.

How much efficiency has increased in the production of any particular article can often be determined, though just how much efficiency as a whole has increased in the past hundred years is somewhat uncertain, in part because many of the commodities in use today were not in use a hundred years ago. Thus, the energy available per man has increased about thirty fold in the past hundred years. The invention of the cotton gin increased the laborer's output about 1500 times. Over a hundred years ago it required some nine farmers' families to supply one city family and themselves. Today, nine farmers' families supply over 27 city families plus themselves and some foreigners, and the farmer's family doesn't work as much as it used to work either in the field or in the house, preserving, etc., being done largely in factories. But these direct ratios cannot be accepted as measurements of efficiency, because some six million farmers, their four million farm hands and some help from their families could not supply 136 million people, plus many millions of foreigners, if thousands of other workers today were not fabricating agricultural machinery, refining petroleum, fixating nitrogen, processing food, etc. Consequently, on this basis, we would have to be satisfied with the roughest kind of guess in respect to the increase in efficiency.

There are, however, ways of estimating the increase of efficiency, one of which, submitted in Appendix 1 [9] of this chapter, indicates that efficiency has advanced between $1\frac{1}{2}$ and 3 per cent a year; an estimate which is quite close to other more recent calculations.

Since it does not matter for theoretical purposes whether the rate of increase has been as low as $1\frac{1}{2}$ per cent or as high as 3 per cent, the matter of its accurate statistical determination may be left to others.[10]   Our concern is with the effect of this increase upon the demand-supply equation.

Let us suppose, for example, that each manhour of labor produced twice the quantity of goods formerly produced in a period when employment, wages and other prices were constant.   It is evident [11] that in this situation demand would be insufficient to buy the supply, in fact demand could acquire only half the supply.   Society would be faced, in other words, by a deficiency of demand in respect to supply.   Four possible reactions to this situation will be considered in the next section.

2. THREE WAYS BY WHICH THE ECONOMY MIGHT RELEASE THE WEALTH INCREMENT MADE AVAILABLE BY THE ADVANCE IN EFFICIENCY ARE SUGGESTED, AS WELL AS A REACTION WHICH WOULD NOT RELEASE THE WEALTH INCREMENT.

Reasons were submitted to indicate that the over-all equilibrium adjustment is continually being unbalanced by the advance in efficiency.   This advance results in a potentially greater supply at no increase in costs, or necessary increase in demand because of the interdependence of the two latter quantities.   Let us

[9] p. 90.

[10] Dr. Clark Warburton has extended production trends into the future by drawing lines through the points of peak or normal production (years of high production excluding war years).   According to his estimate, value of delivered final products increased by 3.7 per year in total and by 2.2 per capita.   The latter figure should be close to our concept of the increase resulting from the advance in efficiency.   "Normal Production, Income & Employment, 1945–1965," Clark Warburton, *Southern Economic Journal*, January 1945.

[11] In mathematical terms, let $Q_1 = 2Q$.   Then, if $E = QP$ and if $Q_1 = 2Q$

$$E < Q_1P.$$

Or, if we use the symbol we shall use hereafter, if $E = QP$, and if, due to an advance in efficiency, Q is increased by ΔQ then:

$$E < (Q + \Delta Q)P$$

other things being equal.

consider four ways by which the economy might react to it.
(There are other reactions than the four which follow. But these
other reactions are subordinate, or so similar to the four basic
reactions that they need merely be cited in passing.)

It will be indicated that the wealth increment made available
at no increase in cost by an advance in efficiency (1) might be
released by lower prices, (2) might result in a reduced scale of
production and employment, (3) might be released by higher
wages, or (4) might be released by an increment of demand
resulting from the creation and distribution of new money. It
may be helpful to note before taking up these four possibilities in
detail that reaction (1) is compelled only in fields of price competition, reactions (2) and (4) are usual in fields of monopolistic
competition, and reaction (3), though prevailing in both forms of
competition, is seldom a primary reaction to an advance in efficiency and cannot be relied upon, under present conditions, to
release the wealth increment. Since monopolistic competition is
the dominant form in the current economy, the discussion subsequent to this chapter will be largely concerned with discovering
what is responsible for the choice between reactions (2) and (4),
one of which results in nonproduction, the other in the release of
the potential wealth increment, and usually in an increase in
employment.

CASE I

If demand equalled supply at any time, and if supply was
potentially increased by an advance in efficiency so that more
goods could be produced with the same manhour input, then, as
indicated in Section 1, demand would fall short of supply were
employment maintained and price held constant. To forestall
the resulting deficiency of demand, price might be dropped [12] so
that demand could acquire the increased supply.

Were the adjustment accomplished by this means, the prospective deficiency of demand in respect to supply would be forestalled without altering employment. Furthermore, such an ad-

---

[12] If $E = QP$ and Q is increased by an increment ΔQ, the resulting inequality $E < (Q + \Delta Q)P$ could be forestalled by dropping price to P_{-1} so that $E = (Q + \Delta Q)P_{-1}$. P_{-1} would have to equal $E/(Q + \Delta Q)$ to realize equality.

(In this and subsequent sections, in which certain factors are segregated for scrutiny, it will be assumed that other factors are constant even when it is not stated.)

justment not only would release the wealth increment made available by the advance in efficiency, but would distribute it widely since a drop in price permits all consumers to share in the benefit according to their relative buying power.

If the price of the various articles whose production had been facilitated by the efficiency advance, reflected fully the reductions in costs (the flexibility known as "structural"), individual productions would have to be adjusted since the lower price of certain articles would increase the demand for these articles and reduce the demand for other articles. If, however, a fall in the general price level reflected the sum of the efficiency advances (the flexibility known as "cyclical") individual prices would have to be adjusted since the items being produced more cheaply would realize surplus profits, and the other items which had not experienced the efficiency advance would incur losses at the lower price level. Presumably in either case, prices and productions which reflected the new conditions resulting from the efficiency advance would eventually be found by the procedures described in Chapter II.

It is along these lines that the economists have expected, or at least hoped, that the economy would take care of efficiency advances as well as other changes. As described in the last chapter, such an adjustment would be automatic [13] in an economy of price competition, because price would be perfectly flexible and would immediately reflect changes in other factors. Thus a deficiency in effective demand for any reason whatsoever was supposed to be translated into a corrective price reduction. Should this occur, the consumers would be able to purchase the supply made available, no matter what happened in the world of finance, technology or politics. Since the producers would each be operating at or close to his most efficient scale [14] and since the ingress of producers would be unrestricted, a maximum supply also would be probable. Since the millions of consumers would each be selecting from the multifarious wares presented for their approval those goods and services which most appealed to them,

---

[13] Automatic is used to characterize a "self-action" reaction; that is to say, a reaction which occurs without the intervention of social or other over-all authorities.

[14] p. 33.

an optimum supply could also be expected, the proportion of the various quantities demanded being governed, to be sure, by the income distribution which prevailed.

However, the actual economy is not one of price competition, and price reductions, it was indicated, do not automatically correct a deficiency of demand in fields of monopolistic competition.[15]

CASE II

When efficiency advances, demand would fall short of supply were price unchanged and the potential wealth increment produced, as indicated in Section 1. However, instead of producing the greater supply, production might be held down to the existing level of demand since producers engaged in monopolistic competition usually gear production to the demand evoked at the administered price. Were this the only reaction, equality would not be restored even though production would now meet the original demand, because holding production constant when efficiency has advanced throws men out of work. Disemployed men have less buying power than employed men, since they receive no wages. A reduction in buying power reduces the effective demand. Production might again be reduced to meet the reduction in demand, and so on. . . .[16] In short, a downsurge in production would be touched off.

The series would approach a point of equilibrium above the total arrest of production, because the value of the goods not produced would be greater than the curtailment in costs. The reason is that overhead costs can seldom be reduced in the same proportion as production and operating costs are reduced. In other words, most industries, as was noted in Chapter II, are subject to decreasing costs, and decreasing costs, when production is increased, denotes increasing costs when production is decreased. The value of production, as a result, would fall faster than costs and demand as production was lowered, with the result that the deficiency in demand would eventually be overcome and equality regained.

[15] A fuller discussion of this inability, is presented in Chapter IV, Section 3.

[16] If $E = QP$ and $E < (Q + \Delta Q)P$ and production was reduced by an increment $\Delta Q_2 = \Delta Q$, equality would not be restored because in reducing production, demand would be reduced by an increment, and $E - \Delta E < (Q - \Delta Q_2 + \Delta Q)P$ if $E = (Q - \Delta Q_2 + \Delta Q)P = QP$. The series is cumulative.

We may conclude therefore that a reduction in employment incurred in response to an increase in efficiency, though used to prevent the creation of the unvendible surplus which would be produced were prices maintained, results in a decrease in demand,[17] which in turn may cause a further decrease in production and so on, with the result that over-all nonproduction is increased.

CASE III

When efficiency advances and demand as a result falls short of the potential supply, the prospective deficiency might be avoided by a rise in the wage rate. Should total wages be increased thereby by an amount equal to the value of the wealth increment made available by the advance in efficiency, it is evident that the over-all adjustment would remain in balance.[18] Such an event would increase the national income by the value of the wealth increment without altering price, profit, rent, interest, employment or other factor but wages. Furthermore, the rise in wages would be likely to decrease income disparity since the wealth increment due to the efficiency advance would be diverted to labor by this arrangement.[19]

Thus Case III differs from Case I (price reduction) in that the benefit in Case I was distributed over all of society (the consumers) in the proportion in which the individual consumed. In Case III the *benefit is confined to the workers.*

[17] The problem of the producer faced by a deficiency of demand is considered on p. 118.

[18] Thus if income E be divided between wages W and other income sources R and if $W + R = QP$, so that $W + R < (Q + \Delta Q)P$, the prospective deficiency of demand could be avoided by raising wages by an increment $\Delta W = \Delta QP$, so that $W + \Delta W + R = (Q + \Delta Q)P$.

[19] It might be asked how wages, which are costs of production as well as a source of income, can be increased without reducing another income source, namely, the profit or net revenue of the enterpriser. Ricardo and others have associated wages and profits by supposing that when wages rise, profits fall, and vice versa. As a matter of fact, if efficiency, production and prices were constant, then an increase in wages would necessarily reduce profits, just as Ricardo supposed. (If $W + R = QP$, an increase in W would reduce R, other things being equal). Ricardo assumed that Q was constant. We are postulating that Q is increased by an advance in efficiency, thereby making available an increment of wealth which may be allocated to any consuming class insofar as mathematical logic alone is involved. Thus, if efficiency had increased so that $W + R < (Q + \Delta Q)P$, wages could be increased by the amount of the prospective deficiency without reducing R, or changing any factor.

There are, however, several complications involved in maintaining the over-all equation by way of raising wages. For instance there is no necessary correspondance between an advance in efficiency and a rise in wages. However, society might intervene through labor unions or otherwise and devise some procedure by which an increase in efficiency was translated into higher wages as a matter of course, although such a procedure would remove management's incentive to improve efficiency.

Besides the practical difficulty just suggested, there are theoretical objections to a procedure which would translate each improvement in a productive process into higher wages for those involved in the productive process.

Society requires information in respect to relative efficiencies and scarcities, as was emphasized in Chapter I, in order to allocate resources economically and to choose effectively between the various available goods and services. An increase in the efficiency of one or more processes reduces the manhour input needed to make available the goods which are produced by these processes. It does not reduce the manhour input required to produce other goods and services. But unless these changed relations were reflected by changed prices, prospective buyers could not take them into account.

If increased efficiencies were translated into higher wages, the increases would not be reflected by lower prices since the cost of production would not in this case be lowered. As a result, price would cease to reflect relative efficiencies and scarcities, and would instead be crystallized at the existing level. In other words, price would not function parametrically and the basis for effective choice between alternatives would be removed.

Furthermore, the increment of supply made available by the advance in efficiency would not be demanded unless the price were lowered, since society would continue to demand goods in about the same proportion as previously despite the fact that the efficiency of making certain products had been improved.

For example, if the automobile people had translated their technical improvements into higher pay for automobile workers, automobiles might still cost from two to five thousand dollars. As a result, the automobile workers, though possibly obtaining higher pay than they do today,[20] would be few in number. And society would be poorer by some millions of motor cars, not to mention secondary losses. Thus, raising wages pari passu with each advance in efficiency is infeasible on theoretical as well as on practical grounds.

The above objection, however, would not apply if the increase in efficiency was translated into higher pay for all workers, and not into higher pay for the workers involved in the improved productive process *only*. But this arrangement, too, would incur difficulties. The value at current prices of the wealth increment made available by the efficiency advance (a complicated calculation) would have to be divided among some forty to fifty million wage workers. In order to do this, wage rates would have to be administered, thereby arresting the freedom of wages to reflect conditions, an undesirable result for reasons frequently emphasized in these pages.

However, the possibilities suggested above are not all inclusive. Another possibility is suggested in Chapter VII.

CASE IV

When efficiency advances and demand as a result falls short of the potential supply, the prospective deficiency might be avoided by the spending of newly created debit money on consumer goods, capital formation, public works, relief, or anything else for that matter. The reason is that debit money, whose creation and cancellation was described in Chapter I, appears in the equilibrium adjustment as it is spent as an increment of demand. An individual, for example, might go to a bank and ask for the loan of a thousand dollars. Should the bank write a check for the money, a check representing a disbursement not balanced by an equal deposit and refrainment from spending on the part of somebody else, and lend it to the individual, he could proceed to buy a car with it. As a result, the over-all or aggregate effective

---

[20] The pay might not be higher because the economies of mass production could not have been instituted under the above conditions, since the market for motor cars would have remained very small. Any example of this kind is somewhat fantastic because most technical improvements are tied up with mass production and mass production cannot be instituted without mass consumption which depends, in turn, upon low prices.

demand would be increased by $1,000 and this $1,000 would be spent for a segment of the available supply,[21] without the money having appeared as anyone's individual income.   By this means the wealth increment made available by the advance in efficiency could be released without altering the price level or employment.

The new money, however, could enter demand by other than the direct route suggested above, and it is the other routes which are important, since money introduced along the lines suggested (consumer and other commercial loans) is usually paid back and thereby withdrawn [22] in a short time.   However, before investigating these more important routes, it is advisable to leave the line of our argument in order to consider certain aspects of profit, saving, and capital formation which bear upon the procedure by which wealth is released by the creation and spending of new money.

3. THE BEHAVIOR OF INDIVIDUAL PROFIT IS DISTINGUISHED FROM THAT OF NET OVER-ALL PROFIT AND THE INFEASIBILITY OF RELEASING A WEALTH INCREMENT BY AN INCREASE IN PROFIT WERE OTHER FACTORS CONSTANT, IS SUGGESTED.

The income division, profit,[23] like wages, is used to purchase goods and services and constitutes an important fraction of the effective demand.   The word *profit* in economics denotes the compensation of the enterpriser, to whom the difference between total costs and gross revenue is usually assigned.[24]   Essentially,

[21] If $E = QP$, and $E < (Q + \Delta Q)P$ due to an advance in efficiency, an addition to E of an increment ΔE, consisting of an injection of newly-created debit money, would restore the equality, if $\Delta E = \Delta QP$.

[22] The paying back would not, it is evident, cancel the sale.   But it would cancel the increase in demand by subtracting from the buying stream at the later date the amount of the previous increase.   It may be assumed were the time interval short that the deflationary effect of the latter event would roughly balance the inflationary or releasing (in the situation being discussed) effect of the former event.   As a result, this double event would not release the wealth increment in a short time period including the two events.   Were the period of appreciable duration the first event might have had a cumulative effect, as will be brought out.   Should this occur, the later reduction in demand would not cancel the full effect of the initial release.

[23] Rent and interest payments are also used to purchase goods and services.   It does not seem necessary to consider the release of wealth increments by an increase in these factors because their dimensions are established in most cases by contract for periods of time.   Consequently, their totals are not flexible in the same degree as are the other constituents of demand.

[24] Certain enterprisers do not charge up their time, or the rent of their farms when owned, nor interest on most of their capital, as cost items.   For this reason,

it is a means of recording relative efficiencies,[25] since the more efficient enterprisers realize greater profits than the less efficient enterprisers.[26] Furthermore, profit is an essential part of the pricing procedure. Prices which interpret relative efficiencies and scarcities are established, as described in Chapters I and II, by the producer selling at the highest obtainable price in order to maximize *profit* (price competition) or by the producer administering his price, etc. so as to maximize *profit* (monopolistic competition). The resulting prices serve to govern the allocation of resources to the end that an optimum production of wealth may be provided and satisfactions maximized (as modified by the prevailing distribution of income, to be sure).

No other feasible methods of establishing prices possessing this parametric function have been developed. If prices were set on the basis of each individual going concern's costs, each individual enterpriser would establish a different price (as do the sellers of houses, farms, etc.) and buyers would have to survey the field before consummating a transaction; the more efficient producers would be demoralized by a surfeit of orders; the less efficient by their scarcity, and chaos or a dictator would probably emerge from the resulting confusion.

profit is often defined as the difference between cost and gross revenue, with rent, interest and the time of the enterpriser figured in as part of the cost. In order, however, to keep in touch with our statistical data, we shall use profit in its looser connotation when referring to "entrepreneurial withdrawals," which includes the profit of farmers, shopkeepers and other individual enterprisers, since entrepreneurial withdrawals as recorded by the Department of Commerce apparently make no deduction for the time of the enterpriser, the rent of his farm when owned, etc. When referring, however, to corporation profits, the issued part of which is listed as "dividends," the stricter definition holds good. Corporations not only deduct the usual direct cost items (wages, interest and rent) from their gross revenue, but also depreciation and amortization charges, etc., before estimating net revenue or profit, from which dividends are usually drawn.

[25] Efficiency in this instance is used broadly to include efficiency in selling and bargaining. The enterpriser who buys his manhours cheaper than does his competitor makes more profit, just as if he utilized the same manhours more efficiently. In industries in which equal wages for every competitor were established by a labor union or otherwise, and the salesmanship of the several competitors was equally persuasive, and the price and availability of needed materials were the same for all producers, and rent was effective in evening up natural advantages, profit would rougly measure efficiency in its strict technical sense (the ratio of manhour input to quantity output).

[26] The question of ownership does not enter here. In a socialist system, the profit would accrue to society. In the USSR, for example, the profit of heavy industry, and other state enterprises, accrues to and is invested by social authorities.

If, however, prices were based on average costs, and we overlook the "operational" difficulty involved in this calculation [27]— profits and losses would result—profit for the more efficient, losses for the others. We may reasonably conclude therefore that profit (called "loss" when negative) will be a useful accounting device in any economic system which practices the division of labor and trade.

(It may not be out of place to recall that the distinction between pricing (1) by bids and offers on the market, and pricing (2) by administering the price, does not necessarily affect the dimensions of profit. For the individual firm, the first procedure would mean a higher operating rate and lower prices than the second. But profits in both cases would tend to be minimized if competition were effective.)

The factors which govern the profit of the individual enterpriser are different than those which control over-all net profit. The individual enterpriser can make a profit or not, a large profit or a small profit. For him profit is indeterminate. In price competition, his profit depends on his ability to produce more cheaply than his competitors. As noted elsewhere, all producers in price competition are supposed to make a profit except the submarginal producers, a profit dependent on each enterpriser's individual costs.

In monopolistic competition, each enterpriser has a somewhat individualized market and administers his price, orders his product, and regulates his production as described earlier. Presumably he or the industry acting together will adjust prices and production so as to maximize profit, as was illustrated by Figure II. In any case, the size of his profit is indefinite within certain limits and depends, in monopolistic competition, in large part on his ability to persuade enough customers into buying his product to permit him to operate at a so-called profitable scale of production.

In any case, the profit of the individual concern can be varied widely. It may be increased by operating efficiencies, by sales-

---

[27] The difficulty noted in Chapter I, ascribed to the fact that costs depend on the operating rate, and the operating rate depends on costs (prices), with the result that neither can be known unless the other is given.

manship, or by buying cheaper labor. It may be decreased by inefficiency, by the divisioning of the market, by buying labor dear, etc.

Over-all net profit, on the other hand, is subject to quite other factors. Instead of being indeterminate, it is established by the over-all quantities: gross revenue and total costs.[28] Thus the struggle for individual profits consists essentially of a struggle for a share of a quantity which is established by factors outside of the control of the individual participants. One producer, in practice increases his profit at the expense of another producer.

Profit, like wages, interest and rent, is a source of income, and appears in our demand-supply proposition as a component of demand on the left. However, it cannot be supposed that a wealth increment made available by an advance in efficiency would be released by an increase in profit, not only because profit in a competitive economy tends to be held down to a minimum, but also because profit, unlike the cost factors, is realized and usually issued after a commodity has been produced and sold.

It is true that insofar as mathematics are involved, a deficiency of demand due to an efficiency advance or other cause, could be forestalled by an increase in profit. However, because of the delay in realizing and issuing profit noted above,—a delay which in the case of corporations, is the nearly universal practice—it cannot be supposed that such a release would be effected in practice. This fact is indicated by the nature of the equilibrium adjustment. For example, in a year after a year in which no net profit was realized, demand, the sum of all costs, would approximate the value of the aggregate supply. Should efficiency advance so that supply was greater than demand, all the goods could not be sold. Should price be lowered or wages raised so that demand equalled supply, no profit would be realized in the subsequent year if the above statement was complete.[29] In short, no matter what changes occurred in efficiency, price or cost, profit would

[28] Over-all Profit $= QP$—Costs.

[29] If Costs, $C = QP$, then $C < (Q + \Delta Q)P$. Were the equation re-established by dropping P to P_{-1} so that $C = (Q + \Delta Q)P_{-1}$ no profit would be realized. Or if the goods were sold by raising wages concurrently with the efficiency advance so that costs were increased by an increment $\Delta C = \Delta QP$ and $C + \Delta C = (Q + \Delta Q)P$, again no profit would be realized.

be unchanged from one time period to another were the factors listed above the only factors. The reason is that a change in any of the above factors would have to be neutralized by a change in another factor before the equation could be re-established and the goods sold.

Thus, in a production-for-sale economy in which the supply of money and its velocity [30] were fixed, employment was constant, and no enterpriser took his profit in kind, or issued it in advance of sales, net profit would be predetermined by the net profit of the previous time period, at least roughly, if we allow for increments and decrements due to the overlapping of transactions in any time period.

Should we therefore conclude that over-all net profit tends to be less variable than the other factors in the equilibrium adjustment?

Such a conclusion would be flatly contradicted by the statistical evidence. Profit, instead of being the least variable prime factor, is probably the most variable. The data clearly indicates that variations in net profit have been wider than variations in wages, rents, interest or even quantity produced.[31]

It is therefore necessary to explain the technical means by which these disproportionate variations are effected.[32] However, before scrutinizing the relation of profit, production and money creation, it will be helpful to fit saving and investment into the equilibrium adjustment.

4. THE PRACTICE OF SAVING AND INVESTMENT AND ITS EFFECT UPON THE DEMAND-SUPPLY RELATIONSHIP ARE CONSIDERED.

In the four cases considered in this chapter, the effective demand for consumers' goods and for capital [33] were lumped together and represented by the symbol E. Likewise both consumer goods production and capital formation were lumped together and represented by the symbol QP. It is convenient in the subsequent argument sometimes to distinguish the demand

---

[30] Velocity is defined in Appendix II, p. 92.
[31] See Tables II, and IV, pp. 132 and 134.
[32] Section V.
[33] Defined on p. 1.

for consumer goods from the demand for capital, and the supply of consumer goods from what might be called the supply of capital. Let us therefore consider what is involved in the practice of saving and investing.

It is the custom of many individuals and going concerns to withhold money from consumption and to apply (i.e. invest) the withheld funds [34] to expanding the capital plant (capital formation). Money is withdrawn from the spending stream, the fraction *S*, let us say. This leaves the fraction, let us call it, *G*. Under these conditions, the fractions *G* and *S* always total 1.[35]

As a result, the effective demand, *E*, would be broken up into two parts, *GE* and *SE*, the first segment of which would be used for the purchase of consumer goods and services; the second segment of which, the withheld (saved) fraction, would be utilized for expanding the capital plant.

The other half of the proposition could be divided in the same manner. The available supply, represented by *QP* (quantity times price) could, if a fraction of income were withheld (saved) and invested, be divided into two parts: *GQP*, consumer goods, and *SQP* [36] capital goods. Consequently, in an economy in which withholding (saving) and investment occurred, supply and

[34] The money withheld may be invested directly by the individual who, for example, might hire men to construct a factory or apartment house, or indirectly by buying existing securities or by putting the money in a bank, insurance company, etc., which concern in its turn bought bonds or stocks, or invested the money directly in some enterprise. The directness or indirectness of the procedure does not affect our proposition, as long as the process is completed. Money withheld from consumption and used to purchase existing stocks, bonds, buildings, etc., merely pushes the problem of investing the money onto another person, the vendor who has sold the property. If the vendor should choose to purchase consumer goods with the proceeds, then the saving would be nullified by an equivalent dis-saving and our proposition would be unaffected, that is to say, the money would, in effect, not be saved and invested.

[35] If $S = 1/6$, then $G = 5/6$ and $S + G = 1/6 + 5/6 = 1$.

[36] The concept, the supply of capital goods, has little meaning—that is to say, it refers to nothing in particular in the actual world *before* the capital formation is effected. When men and knowledge are available, capital of some kind can always be created. For example, were metals deficient, dams and roads could be built of earth and rock. At all times there are possible capital formations which could be undertaken were the situation propitious. This condition does not disturb the mathematical logic of this section. Though *SQP* has no definite limits inherent in its nature, its dimensions are established by the money allocated to capital formation and the price of goods and manhours.

demand could be represented by the proposition:

$$E = GE + SE \lesseqgtr GQP + SQP = QP$$

in which G and S as stated above are fractions which always add up to 1.

Saving and investment may be considered to be equal. This assumption is self-evident, if we define income as:

Income = Value of Output = Consumption + Investment

and Savings = Income − Consumption

Then Savings = Investment [37]

Many theorists deny the equality of saving and investment. Any abstraction can be questioned, for an abstraction depends on the definition of terms. If saving or investment were defined in some other way they would not be equal. If, however, the above definition is accepted, then saving and investment [38] are equal, subject to the following elucidations:

1. As noted in Chapter I,[39] a part of the money supply is created by the banks. Some of the money, which we are calling debit money, is borrowed in order to create or form capital.[40] Thus the dimensions of investment are in practice subject to alteration by increments or decrements of debit money. As a result, the total of investment need not and seldom does correspond to the total of money withheld from consumption. But if saving is defined as above to include these increments of debit money (sometimes called involuntary savings) then saving and investment would be equal. Similarly, withheld money is often used to pay off a debt to a banker. Such a transaction, if the

[37] Quoted from *The General Theory of Employment, Interest and Money* by John Maynard Keynes, p. 63.

[38] For a discussion of other possible definitions of saving and investment, the reader might refer to Keynes, *op. cit.*, pp. 74–85 and to Gottfried Haberler, *Prosperity and Depression*, League of Nations Publication, Chapter 8.

[39] p. 3.

[40] It is sometimes supposed that debit money is used largely for commercial loans, and withholdings for loans of a permanent character, such as investments. However, so large a proportion of new flotations have been paid for by newly created money that the supposition would seem invalid. The fact that the new money is usually created only when the borrower has put up existing assets as security, does not alter the fact that the new capital is being paid for by new money.

banker does not reissue the money, amounts in effect to the cancellation of money. As a result, withholdings are sometimes greater than investments. If saving is defined to allow for these decrements, then the equality between saving and investment remains.[41]

2. Saved money may be applied to the purchase of existing assets. This pushes the spending of the saving onto the vendor as noted above. However, the buyer may purchase the asset at an enhanced price. The result is a profit [42] or capital gain. When this occurs, the increment, the difference between the saving of the buyer and the dis-saving of the seller, is reflected by the enhanced price of the security. Even though no capital formation occurs in this situation, since capital formation signifies a physical expansion of the capital plant, the equality of saving and investment is maintained, the increase in saving being accompanied by an equal increase in the investment, i.e. in the value of the capital plant.

The practice, therefore, does not result in saving being unequal to investment but it does result in saving being greater than capital formation at such times as security values are advancing. Thus security buying and selling may account for the wide gap that sometimes occurs between net saving and net capital formation.

Despite the absurdity of supposing that machinery and certificates can make use of dollar bills, or that bonds, stocks, dynamos or shoes can cancel or absorb buying power or money, certain commentators, in order to explain the gap cited above, suppose that the stock market absorbs money when it rises. Obviously, it does nothing of the kind. It merely translates one man's savings into another man's capital gains, leaving net buying power quite unchanged.

Perhaps the fact that the market does not absorb money may be made clearer by a simple analogy. Let us suppose that three individuals and a broker sit around a table, each individual with

---

[41] To include these events in our formula, SE will represent money withheld from consumption $\pm m$, money created or cancelled, and the expression $SE \pm m = SQP$ will represent the saving investment equation.

[42] Capital gains are not included in profit as defined by the Department of Commerce. (*National Income 1929–35*, Department of Commerce, p. 6.)

a million dollars in the bank, and bid up the price of an antique owned by one of them from $50 to one million and fifty dollars, at which price it is sold. This transaction is obviously accomplished without reducing the quantity of money in the bank accounts of the individuals and the broker, and without reducing the net buying power of the group involved. The antique has risen in price, that is all.

A rising stock market might increase the disparity of incomes but it can no more absorb money than a falling stock market can disgorge money. On the contrary, since rising security prices invite debit money creation, a rising stock market serves to *increase buying power usually*, although it may also reduce the propensity to consume, the ratio GE/SE.[43]

3. The value of the increment of capital formation does not depend upon saving (the amount of money withdrawn from the spending stream plus a debit money increment or decrement), because as soon as an investment is consummated, the capital formed or the asset purchased, the investment becomes worth what it will bring on the market. Moreover, the fact that capital ceases to equal savings *once* it is formed does not conflict with the fact that the amount withheld plus a debit money increment or decrement, equals the amount invested in any time period.

If it were desired to represent saving and capital formation sometime after the saving had been invested, variables V_1 and V_2 would have to be substituted for E and P in the factors representing saving and capital formation. Thus, as soon as the investment was consummated, the proposition

$$GE + SE \lesseqgtr GQP + SQP$$

would become $GE + SV_1 \lesseqgtr GQP + SQV_2$

owing to the shift from a money input measurement of capital to a market valuation.

SV_1 and SQV_2, though necessarily equal are not identical. V_2 like P is the price of tangible and intangible factors existing in the world of men and things. V_1 like E is merely a symbolic representation, with no physical standing, except for engraved

[43] Discussed on pp. 231 ff.

bits of paper. For V_2 has become the price of structures, going concerns, rights, etc., as established by V_1, the ownership and debt claims (stocks, bonds, etc.) representing these structures, going concerns, rights, etc. *Neither quantity is included in our proposition*:

$$E \gtreqless QP.$$

What we mean by this latter statement is that as soon as a fraction of buying power is invested and a fraction of materials and labor has been transformed into capital, the quantities cease to pertain to the demand-supply proposition. Thereafter, the two quantities lead a life of their own, maintaining their equality in value, affecting and being affected by the demand-supply proposition also, but in no sense a part of it. Neither the stocks, bonds, mortgages and other ownership and debt claims which represent the capital of the United States, nor their physical or institutional embodiments, going concerns, buildings, rights, good will, etc. are incorporated in demand or supply. As a result, the $SV_1 = SQV_2$ of any year is a kind of residuum cast off by the economic activities of that year. The sum of these residua, less depreciation or using up, represents the national capital wealth, calculable either by adding up claims SV_1 or the entities SQV_2.

In throwing out these residua, *society does not reduce its income.* The national income of the year after the year O is not less than the national income of the year O, because an increment of capital has been created by the efforts of man and added to the aggregate capital.

This fact is quite obvious as noted above in respect to demand. In purchasing timber for a barn, let us say, the money diverted to this purpose is returned just as surely to the buying stream as the money spent for bacon and eggs. Mines, factories, stocks and bonds can no more absorb money than hams, eggs, books and shaves. The buying power is merely passed on.

In respect to supply, a fraction of supply, a ham let us say, is not only removed from the total supply by purchase, but also it is forthwith destroyed, or consumed, as we put it. This is not true of a steel beam. The latter may become part of a bridge which lasts for an indefinite period. However, the difference is only relative. Even pyramids wear out in time. And certain consumer goods, diamonds for example, last for a long time. In general, capital lasts longer. But goods which have gone into consumption or capital formation are removed from our proposition; that is to say, the residua of goods are removed from the available supply which, like effective demand, is a recurrent phenomena, a running stream. As one lot of dollars or goods disappears, another lot comes up.[44]

By this we mean merely that money diverted to constructing a barn, let us say, is returned to the buying stream, as it is spent in the form of wages, interest, rent, profit, etc., although the barn remain as a monument or residuum of the transaction.

We may conclude, therefore, that the practice of saving and investing does not directly affect the nature of our demand-supply proposition, since neither demand nor supply are altered by the casting off of residua in the process of capital formation. Our formula, including Cases I to IV, need not be reconsidered in the light of this practice; the four cases need not be recast into spending (GE) and saving $(SE \pm m)$, consumer goods production and capital formation.

However, certain aspects of spending and saving bear on the over-all problem of nonproduction, as will be brought out. Consequently, it is convenient to provide spending and saving, consumer goods production and capital formation with a symbolic representation.

Since buying power is habitually divided between consumer goods spending (GE) and withholding (SE) as described above, it might be supposed that an increase in withholding would decrease consumer purchases. Furthermore, since men are needed to produce consumer goods and services as well as capital goods, employment, if the above supposition were sound, would be unaffected by variations in the proportions of money spent for consumer goods and money withheld and invested.

[44] The fact that certain raw materials are not recurrent does not affect the above statement. QP, like E, is recurrent even though certain of its elements should disappear from the earth, or become too expensive to use.

For example, should an individual choose to withhold and invest $1,000 of the $5,000 income which he formerly spent entirely on consumer goods, he would have to discharge, let us say, his cook [45] and hire, let us say, a carpenter. Were this the general rule, net employment would be unaffected by the proportion of purchasing power spent on consumer goods and the proportion withheld and invested. The carpenter's income would be increased by $1,000, the cook's decreased by $1,000. Total demand and total supply would be unaffected.

Actually, consumer goods production and capital formation, instead of varying inversely, as in the above example, vary directly. "Consumption and capital formation" as Dr. Moulton puts it, "do expand and contract together." [46] The records [47] show that capital formation and consumer goods production have been rising and falling together, the swings of the former being somewhat wider than the swings of the latter.

The apparent contradiction between our logical supposition of an inverse relationship and the observable fact that consumer goods production and capital formation increase and decrease together, may be resolved as follows:

Early theoretical economists as noted above envisaged the economic system as one in which production would approach full. Under these circumstances, any increase in capital formation would compel a decrease in consumer goods production and vice versa.

Today our economy does not, in times of peace, operate fully. But if the economy is not operating fully, then an increase in consumption need not be translated into a decrease in capital formation, or an increase in capital formation need not be translated into a decrease in consumption. On the contrary, either could be translated into an increase in production, and vice versa, insofar as the physical factors are involved.

The same condition holds good for the demand side of the equation. If new money should be created, loaned out and

---

[45] If we suppose the individual bought fewer clothes in order to hire the carpenter, the producers of clothing and the raw materials of which clothing is made, would be disemployed by the amount of the withholding.

[46] *The Formation of Capital* by Harold G. Moulton, p. 43.

[47] Chart II, p. 138.

spent on expanding the capital plant, it would reappear as income, wages, profits, interest and rent, as it was spent and therefore be available in the subsequent period for redivision between consumer good spending and withholding as usual. Consequently, saving and investment can be increased in any time period in which production is short of full without consumer spending being decreased. And in the subsequent period, the aggregate income, both withholding and spending, would be greater.

For example, if the individual who had been spending $5,000 a year and wanted to build a barn, should (instead of firing his cook and hiring a carpenter) go to the bank and borrow the $1,000, and if the bank should create this money instead of merely loaning the individual $1,000 which someone else had deposited, then not only would a barn be built without firing the cook, not only would unemployment be reduced by one carpenter, but the aggregate monetary income of society would be increased by $1,000, the carpenter's wage. Thus the elasticity of money permits an increase in either consumer spending or withholding without diminishing the other,[48] and the elasticity of production whenever production is less than full, permits an increase in either consumer goods production or capital formation without diminishing the other.

The further fact that all spending including that accomplished with created and withheld money returns to the main stream undiminished as soon as the money is spent, regardless of what residua have been cast forth into the world of capital and the claims against it, explains how an increase in capital formation by means of debit money and reemployment forthwith increases consumer spending and vice versa.

The above relationships are pretty well recognized by the average business man who realizes that increased consumer spending leads to increased investment, since the more goods that are consumed, the more capital can be profitably employed; and that increased capital formation results in increased monetary income, and greater consumer spending.

---

[48] Consumer goods spending is increased directly by debit money advances in the case of installment buying, etc.

5. WERE THE WEALTH INCREMENT RELEASED BY THE CREATION
AND SPENDING OF NEW MONEY, PROFITS WOULD BE INCREASED IN
RELATION TO WAGES AND AN UPSURGE IN PRODUCTION MIGHT BE
TOUCHED OFF.

CASE IV (CONTINUED)

It was indicated in our discussion of Case IV that a wealth
increment made available by the efficiency advance could be
released by a newly-created money increment. There the matter was dropped until saving and capital formation could be
explored, and profit defined, because it was evident that newly
created debit money might not be used to purchase consumer
goods, as in the instance cited,[49] but might be used for capital
formation; that is to say, to purchase such manhours, space, raw
and other materials as were needed to form an addition to the
capital plant. Should this occur, the release of the wealth increment would not be effected [50] by the first spending of the new
money, since supply, the supply of capital, would be increased as
well as demand by such a spending.

Nevertheless, the creation and spending of enough new money
would release the wealth increment for the following reason.
In the creation of an addition to the capital plant, the workers
employed and the vendors of the requisite materials would receive
the new money and in their turn spend it as noted in the previous
section. And they would spend some of this increment of demand for consumer goods. Consequently, the potential wealth
increment, which would result in a deficiency of demand were it
not released by a demand increment or lower prices, might be
released by the second or later spending of the new money, and
would be so released if the new money, in its second or subsequent
spending, created an increment of demand equal to the prospective deficiency.

Such a reaction may be counted on because as noted above an
injection of money, however it may be used in the first place,

---

[49] p. 71.

[50] Capital formation is included in the demand-supply equation. However, that
part of the wealth increment made available by the efficiency advance which per-
tained to capital would not cause an unbalance because of the shadowy nature of
"*SQP*," the available supply of capital, stressed in the previous section. The situation is more fully developed in Chapter V, pp. 144 ff.

eventually reappears unless withdrawn, as income, i.e., as wages, profit, interest or rent, and is then divided, as is any other money received as income, between consumer goods spending and withholding. The fact that a portion of the increment of new funds is often applied first to capital formation or to the purchase of capital assets, and in this case might serve to reduce a deficiency of demand in respect to supply only on its second or later appearance, does not alter the fact that eventually a sufficient injection of new money would release the wealth increment made available by an advance in efficiency unless it were withdrawn and cancelled first.

The involutions contained in the above explanation can be evaded by a simple change in statement which takes income velocity [51] into account.

Instead of stating that a wealth increment made available by an advance in efficiency would be released by a money increment equal to it in value (as given in our provisional statement of Case IV), let us clarify the proposition by stating that a wealth increment would be released by a money injection which *in its spending* increased *demand by the value* of the potential wealth increment.[52]

By so re-stating the proposition, we free ourselves from the unreality of assuming that a new money injection would necessarily be applied directly to the purchase of a part of the available supply. As a matter of fact, new money which is not issued for a definite time and then recalled (commercial and consumer loans for the most part) is applied usually either to the purchase of bonds, stocks, land, buildings or other assets,[53] or to capital formation. In these events, it serves to release the wealth increment only on its second and later spendings.

To summarize, an injection of new money, let us call it, m:

1. May be allocated directly to the purchase of consumer goods in which case demand is increased immediately in respect to supply by the increment, $m = \Delta E$.

[51] In Appendix 2 to Chapter III, p. 92, income velocity is discussed.

[52] Thus, if $E < (Q + \Delta Q)P$, equality would be restored by a money injection, which in its spending, created an increment of demand ΔE, equal to the wealth increment ΔQP made available by the advance in efficiency.

[53] Ownership and debt claims, stocks, bonds, etc. will hereafter be called "assets" for short.

2. Or it may be allocated to capital formation thereby increasing both demand and supply (the supply of capital) [54] and not increasing demand in respect to supply until a later spending.

3. Or it may be allocated to the purchase of assets, in which case demand would not be increased in respect to supply [55] until the second or later spending of the money.

The release of a wealth increment by a new money injection would usually [56] increase over-all net profit for the reason which follows. The demand increment resulting from the new money injection would permit vendors to sell the increment of supply made available by the advance in efficiency (or its equivalent) without lowering unit prices. But aggregate costs would not have increased since the wealth increment by definition was made available at no increase in costs, or to be exact, only by the interest on the new money which appears in the national balance sheet as a cost item and would be a charge against the borrowers. Consequently net return or profit would be increased by the value of the supply increment less the interest on the new money.[57]

Consequently, new money which in its first spending might have been used to put a fraction of the unemployed to work constructing a factory thereby adding to wages on the one side and capital on the other, would in its later spendings permit additional goods to be sold without reducing prices. Should these

[54] This increment of supply has no direct bearing since a new item of capital when completed, pertains as noted above, to that shadowy world represented in the last section by $SV_1 = SQV_2$ which coexists with, but does not interfere with, the basic demand-supply equilibrium. pp. 146 ff.

[55] The seller of the assets would have the spending of the new money. He or one of his successors would presumably spend it on consumer goods and capital formation unless he repaid a loan from a bank. In that case the money creation might be neutralized. Footnote page 72.

[56] The conditions under which the event would not increase profit are discussed in Chapter V, Section 3, p. 151.

[57] This result can be represented by splitting over-all demand into two components: Cost C and Profits D. Then if $C + D < (Q + \Delta Q)P$ and new money is borrowed which in its spending increases demand by an ΔE equal to ΔQP, so that $C + D + \Delta E = (Q + \Delta Q)P$, the increased supply could be sold as noted above. And net over-all profit would become $D + \Delta E$ less the interest on the new money. For

Supply	−	Former Cost	+	Interest on m	=	Former Profit	+	Demand increment	−	Interest on m
$(Q - \Delta Q)P$	−	C	+	Interest on m	=	D		$+ \Delta E$	−	Interest on m

additional goods have been made available by the efficiency advance at no increase in costs, profit would be increated by the event.

It may therefore be concluded that the introduction of a sufficient quantity of new money, no matter whether it is used first to buy existing consumer goods or used first to form capital or purchase assets, will serve, if not withdrawn and cancelled:

(a) To release a wealth increment made available by the efficiency advance or its equivalent.

(b) To permit the increased supply to be sold without a reduction in per unit prices thereby increasing net returns or over-all profit.

Thus the variations in net over-all profit, when the competitive nature of enterprise tends to reduce the profit of individual firms to a minimum norm, are in part the result of the injection and removal of quantities of money.[58]

Furthermore injections of new money depend, when privately sponsored, largely upon the expectation of profit.[59]   Thus the relation would seem reciprocal, and suggests another deduction.

Since money creation depends in part upon profit expectancy, and since profit may be increased by the creation and spending of new money, the release of a wealth increment by the method of new money creation might result in a cumulative upward movement.

The question of whether a wealth increment could be released by an increment of profit has therefore been answered.   Although the wealth increment could not be released directly by means of a profit increment for the reasons cited in Section 3, the wealth increment would be released and net over-all profit increased, were the requisite quota of new money created and spent.

---

[58] Because of the prevalence of decreasing costs, stressed in Chapter II, profit is likely to increase disproportionately also when production is increased and prices maintained.   However to sell the goods and thereby to realize the increased profit either the volume of money or its velocity would have to increase were prices maintained, as is evident from the formula.   In short production and *MV*, the volume of money times its velocity, are mutually dependent when prices are constant, as we know a priori because of the nature of the demand supply relationship.

[59] Chapter V, p. 145.

One other aspect of the situation had best be noted, an aspect which will be developed in Chapter V. If the demand increment resulting from the new money injection were greater than the wealth increment, an excess of demand over supply would result. Such an excess might be countered by increased production. The effect might be cumulative, since each increase in production would result in more money being paid out as income, which would increase effective demand, which in turn might induce increased production, so long as additional men, money, and productive facilities continued to be available.

Thus the injection of new money is likely to touch off an upsurge in production, either because of the interactions of profit, capital formation, and new money injections, or because more new money might be injected than was needed to create a demand increment equal to the wealth increment. In either case, a spiral upsurge in production would be initiated were other factors neutral or in balance. Case IV therefore in several respects is the opposite of Case II.

SUMMARY

The efficiency advance permits in every year an increment of wealth to be produced at no increase in costs. Were the increment produced supply would be increased and demand would be unchanged. As a result supply would be greater than demand and the increment could not be purchased. However:

Case I. The increment might be released for purchase by a drop in price.

Case II. The increment might not be produced. This reaction would cause men to be released from work and would touch off a cumulative downsurge of demand and production if other factors did not intervene.

Case III. The increment might be released by an advance in wages, although no method has yet been indicated by which a wage increase could be correlated with the advance in efficiency without disrupting the parametric function of price.

Case IV. The increment might be released by an injection of new money. This event might touch off a cumulative upsurge in demand and production: (a) Because of the reciprocal relationship of profit and new money injections, (b) Because an injection of new money greater than that required to create an increment of demand equal to the increment of wealth would result in an excess of demand over supply and a reaction akin to Case II in reverse.

APPENDIX 1 TO CHAPTER III. THE ADVANCE IN EFFICIENCY IS ESTIMATED.

The following table prepared by Dr. Mordecai Ezekiel is based on the then available statistics covering quantities produced and man-year inputs.[60]

Physical Productivity (Efficiency) [61] *Per Worker By Census Periods 1870 to 1930*
(1900 Productivity = 100)

CENSUS YEAR	AGRICULTURE	MANU-FACTURING	MINING
1870	58	64	36
1880	77	75	56
1890	82	93	84
1900	100	100	100
1910	100	117	104
1920	119	131	139
1930	141	163	147

It is evident that the rate of increase is uneven but persistently upward or forward and, though greatest in mining, most consistent in manufacturing. The figures, indicate an average increase of about four per cent per year for the three branches of industry included in the table.

Dr. Weintraub, in his survey of efficiency [62] found a 20 per cent overall increase in efficiency between 1929 and 1936. This estimate would indicate an average of something over 3 per cent per year. Though Dr. Weintraub emphasizes the shift from factory work to office work, he evidently assumed that the expanded office work indicates increased services to the public, since he includes the additional office workers as part of the necessary labor input. Although unquestionably some in-

[60] Reprinted from the *Annals of the American Academy of Political and Social Science*, Philadelphia, November 1936.

[61] Both Dr. Ezekiel and Dr. Weintraub (cited below) call their studies estimates of "productivity." However, this is merely a difference in terminology. We have preferred to follow John R. Commons in distinguishing efficiency from productivity according to the definition in the footnote on p. 63.

[62] *Reemployment Opportunities and Recent Changes In Industrial Techniques*, National Research Project, WPA.

crease in office work consists of desired services—deliveries, upkeep services, useful information, etc.—it seems probable that a part of this increased manhour input has gone into increased selling and accounting effort, some of which may not benefit the public because of the nature of monopolistic competition described in chapter II.

The above estimates may be low for the following reasons:

1. The durability of many goods has been increased. An increase in the durability of a commodity permits of its longer utilization. Increases in durability are not shown by the indices of physical production. Yet the longer life of a good decreases the rate of replacement, thereby augmenting either the wealth or leisure of society [63] and the efficiency of the productive process as a whole.

2. Manhour input per day has been reduced in all lines of work including farming. This reduction is not taken into account or incorporated in Dr. Ezekiel's estimate, since the indices cited are for "annual production of men employed, regardless of the hours worked." [64]

3. Improved consumer plant (electric refrigerators, sewing machines, tile, concrete, houses, etc.) release manhours for other activities. Such releases increase society's productivity since they increase the working force potentially available though they do not affect the efficiency of production.

For the above reasons, it might be supposed that over-all efficiency had increased somewhat faster than the estimates of Dr. Ezekiel and Dr. Weintraub suggest.

On the other hand, many goods and services are produced and rendered that do not fall under the three headings cited by Dr. Ezekiel. In fact, about half of the gainfully employed are occupied by other activities than farming, mining, and manufacturing. There is reason to believe that efficiency has not advanced in these other branches of activity as fast as in the branches cited. In fact, in certain branches of the services, such as barbering, waiting on table, etc., efficiency may not have advanced at all. In other branches, teaching, nursing, selling, etc., efficiency may or may not have advanced, but a measuring rod is not available. Consequently, we cannot assume that over-all efficiency has increased by more than 3 per cent a year, because the factor last cited may more than neutralize the three factors first cited. It therefore is safe to suppose that efficiency increases annually at an average rate of $1\frac{1}{2}$ to 3 per cent a year. (If interested in comparing this estimate with the growth of national and per capita income in the United States and other countries in recent periods, reference can be made to Table

[63] This increase has been in part neutralized by the fact that the durability of certain goods, in particular consumer goods, has been decreased for reasons of vendibility.

[64] *op. cit.*, p. 6.

V and Appendix B of Evsey D. Domar's article "The Burden of the
Debt and The National Income." *American Economic Review*, December
1944, p. 798.)

APPENDIX 2 TO CHAPTER III.   INCOME VELOCITY.

If, instead of representing demand as the sum of income factors,
demand should be represented as the quantity of money m times its
income velocity, v (i.e., income divided by the quantity of money),
it could be put down thus:

$$E = mv.$$

We can further subdivide this proposition by calling m_1v_1 currency
times its income velocity, and m_2v_2 debit money times its income
velocity.

Then $E = m_1v_1 + m_2v_2$.

Obviously, an increase or decrease in velocity v, could affect the
dimensions of E, just as could an increase or decrease in the quantity
of money, m.

However, an increase or decrease in velocity could also be neutralized
by a decrease or increase in the quantity of money m, and vice versa.
Consequently, an increase in velocity, assuming it could be induced,
would not necessarily increase the effective demand.

The income velocity of money (i.e., income divided by quantity of
money) rose from 2.62 to 3.29 between 1921 and 1929 [65] as business
activity increased, and fell off after 1929, as business activity decreased.
It has tended (1) to drop slightly over the years since more money is
carried in pockets and in bank balances as per capita income increases,
and (2) to increase when income is rising and to fall when income is
falling.

The reason the velocity of currency tends to vary so slightly is easy
to understand.   A workers receives, let us say, $100 a month.   It does
not matter if he spends it in the first week, the last week, or evenly during the month.   In any case, velocity is unchanged unless he holds out
a fraction of it.   And the fraction held out increases slowly but steadily
as is shown by the volume of currency outstanding as given in the
table. [66]

In respect to debit money velocity, v_2, the situation is somewhat different.   At a time of business activity, one would expect, as indeed is
the case, a faster turnover of bank deposits.   But it pays a business man
to hold in his bank deposit account (usually noninterest-bearing) only
that amount of money which he requires in order to do business.   Con-

[65] *The Supply and Control of Money*, Lauchlin Currie, Harvard University Press,
p. 6.

[66] Table V, p. 135.

sequently, variations in activity require variations in the quantity of debit money, m_2, primarily, and variations in velocity, v_2, secondarily.

(If v_2 did not represent income velocity, but represented money velocity, this constancy would be less marked. Money velocity might vary enormously without affecting income velocity or the production of goods and services. A poker game would increase the velocity of money—as would a boiling stock market—without necessarily affecting income velocity or the production of wealth.)

Income velocity bears on our problem for the following reasons: As noted above, an increase in the supply of money might be neutralized in whole or in part by a decrease in income velocity insofar as mathematics are involved. In fact, the increases in the supply of money subsequent to 1934 have in part been neutralized by a decrease in velocity.

However, in practice a decrease in velocity could not wholly neutralize the effect of money injections, if the money were used to employ otherwise unemployed men or to increase unduly low incomes.[67] For the undersupplied can be counted upon to utilize increased income for the purchase of goods and services. Consequently, the possibility of variations in velocity qualifies but does not invalidate the conclusions that will be drawn from Case IV.

In order to simplify our discussion, income velocity will be assumed to be constant in this study. However, should an attempt ever be made to interfere in the equilibrium adjustment by adjusting the supply of money, the variability of income velocity would have to be taken into account.

We would leave the question of velocity without further comment if it were not for the fact that a school of thought advocates measures designed to increase income velocity, measures, it is argued, which will concomitantly increase the national income.

With this in mind, Silvio Gesell (1862–1930) recommended stamped money (currency) which would depreciate with the passage of time. But if currency could not be held without loss, would-be hoarders would turn to debit money and leave their money idle in the form of bank deposits. Contemporary thinkers who suppose income can be increased by increasing the velocity of money have therefore proposed a tax on bank deposits, as well as a tax on currency.

But if both forms of money were taxed, would-be hoarders would turn to call money, foreign money, jewelry, precious metals, land, buildings, even works of art. No matter how widely the list of goods was extended, the holding of which was penalized by taxation, the ingenuity of man

[67] The close relationship between expenditures and the volume of money is described in an article "The Volume of Money and the Price Level" by Clark Warburton, Journal of Political Economy, June 1945.

could be relied upon to discover other goods to hold.   Thus, if money
were taxed, and land and buildings were more heavily taxed, would-be
non-spenders might invest in wheat or copper.   If all durable forms of
wealth were taxed and export of money were forbidden, individuals
would seek out that form of durable wealth subject to the lowest tax.

Essentially, our criticism falls under the following heads:

(a) A valued liberty would be curtailed by taxing money; the liberty
to not spend.   Consequently, measures designed to force spending
would be about as popular as liquor prohibition.   Bootlegging could
be counted upon to nullify, at least in part, any measures designed to
compel spending.

(b) If bank deposits were taxed, owners would reduce them to a
minimum by reducing their loans to a minimum.   Consequently, a
speeding up of v_2 by social decree would probably be neutralized by a
reduction in m_2.

(c) Even if every dollar of income were spent annually at any
feasible rate, our analysis does not indicate that capacity or even full
production would be induced.

We conclude, therefore, that manipulation or management of income
velocity, i.e., the factors v_1 and v_2 in the proposition

$$m_1v_1 + m_2v_2 < (Q + \Delta Q)P$$

even were it feasible, would not induce, alone, an optimum or even
satisfactory production of wealth.

Money and velocity in their relation to the total economy resemble
freight cars and their movements in relation to production and distribution.   A law might be passed taxing idle freight cars.   It is doubtful, however, that commodity shipments would be increased.

CHAPTER IV

The Release of the Wealth Increment

1. THE WEALTH INCREMENT MADE AVAILABLE BY THE ADVANCE IN EFFICIENCY HAS NOT BEEN RELEASED IN RECENT DECADES BY REDUCTIONS IN THE PRICE LEVEL.

IN Chapter II the equilibrium adjustment was scrutinized first in a field of price competition, then in a field of monopolistic competition. It was noted that the adjustment was achieved differently in the two forms of competition. What effect, if any, the different procedures had upon over-all employment and production was not looked into. In fact, no method had been worked out by which the effect upon the over-all adjustment of an event in an industrial field could be gauged. In Chapter III this deficiency was in part remedied.

The four cases reviewed in that chapter represented several possible reactions to an advance in efficiency. The analysis was unrealistic, in that reactions of this kind are seldom if ever confined to one channel (as postulated in the four cases), and was incomplete, since the economy could react in still other ways to an efficiency advance. The cases constitute merely four mathematically possible reactions arbitrarily selected because of their relevance to the argument which follows. Nevertheless, it will further our search to determine to what extent the four mathematically possible reactions release the wealth increments made available by the advance in efficiency in fields of price and of monopolistic competition, and in the economy as a whole.

Let us suppose that an efficiency advance has occurred in an industry engaged in price competition. An efficiency advance may result either in more output per unit of manpower or in fewer manhours per unit of output, or in some combination of the two. In other words, an efficiency advance permits more goods to be produced at the same cost, or the same quantity of goods to be produced at a lower cost.

The logic of Chapter II indicated that a competitor in a field of price competition would find it profitable to operate at his most efficient scale of production. His most efficient scale is determined by the size and nature of his plant. An efficiency advance would not usually alter these factors. Should the competitor continue to operate at his most efficient scale, the introduction of an improved procedure or tool would result therefore in increased production. It would pay him *to produce more at the same total cost*.[1]

Should more goods be produced at the same cost, that is to say, should supply be increased by an increment, while demand, the money paid out in the process of production, remained constant, demand would fall short of the increased supply, and offers would exceed bids for the commodity in question. In price competition, this situation results, it was indicated, in a lower price for the product, the supply of which had been increased. Thus, the equilibrium adjustment would in price competition be effected along the lines of Case I.[2]

Were price competition universal, an efficiency advance would therefore result in an increase in production and in a lower price for the item which was being produced by the improved procedure. Because of the lower price, the demand for this particular item would be stimulated. Per unit profit on this item would be increased for the competitors who had installed the improved procedure since the new price would not reflect fully their lower cost, but would probably reflect the lower average per unit cost of all the industry. New competitors would be tempted to enter the field with improved equipment and perhaps would borrow money in order to do so. The increased demand for labor in the

---

[1] Situations can be imagined for which this would not be true. An improved incubator might not induce the production of more chickens since the brooder pens would still limit production. However, it would usually pay a poultry man in this situation either to expand the balance of his plant or to refrain from purchasing the improved incubator. In most cases an improved procedure increases plant capacity particularly in farming, the one industry which still engages largely in price competition. Thus, the substitution of tractors and gasoline for horses and oats released acres for the production of market crops.

[2] p. 66.

field in which efficiency had advanced would enable the workers to obtain a higher wage since it would pay employers to hire additional men at wages equal to the higher marginal product.

In short, various adjustments would be made all along the line until new prices, new productions, new wage scales, possibly a new money supply were attained which established a new equilibrium. Thus a change in any factor in the hypothetic system of universal price competition was supposed to result in a new equilibrium adjustment which took the new factor into account.

Furthermore, the new equilibrium would be attained without reducing employment, since none of the reactions would result in a net disemployment of men. Because of this feature of the adjustment, theorists have usually supposed as noted in Chapter III [3] that unemployment would be minimized in an economy of perfect price competition and that an optimum production of wealth would be approximated.

In monopolistic competition, on the other hand, it was implied [4] that a deficiency in demand because of an efficiency advance or other cause, would not necessarily result in a compensatory price reduction, but might cause production to be decreased (unless counteracted by some other event) because of the tendency to gear production to demand at the administered price.

These deductions can be checked by referring to the actual events of recent years. Let us therefore refer to the data to determine how the price competition industries and the monopolistic competition industries have in the recent past reacted to unbalances by reviewing their behavior when faced by deficiencies of demand and of supply.

The most conspicuous drop in demand occurred in the 1929 to 1933 period. During the years in question monetary income fell from a total of some 83 billion dollars to some 40 billion dollars,[5] a drop of over 50 per cent. If our deductions are sound, industries engaged in price competition would have reacted to the reduced purchasing power of these years by dropping their prices sharply and their production little if at all. Industries

[3] p. 67.
[4] Chapter II, p. 36 ff.
[5] Table II, end of this chapter.

engaged in monopolistic competition would have lowered production as well as price to meet the reduced demand.

The following table indicates the result of the sharp reduction in demand on the prices and productions of the more important industries. The different behavior of these factors in the several industries is quite conspicuous.

TABLE I

The Relation of Price Drop and Production Drop in Ten Major Industries*
from 1929 to the spring of 1933†

	Per cent Drop In	
	Prices	Production
Agricultural Implements	6	80
Motor Vehicles	16	80
Cement	18	65
Iron and Steel	20	83
Auto Tires	33	70
Textile Products	45	30
Food Products	49	14
Leather	50	20
Petroleum	56	20
Agricultural Commodities	63	6

* The regulated monopolies, railroads, utilities, etc., into which ingress is limited by state control of franchises, and prices are supervised by social authorities, are not included in the above table. However, they fall definitely into the category of the first industries cited above in respect to their price and production policies. During the period in question, their rates (prices) were largely sustained and their operations drastically curtailed.

† *Industrial Prices and Their Relative Inflexibility*, Gardner Means, p. 8.

It appears, then, that prices dropped from 6% to 33%, production from 65% to 83%, in the first five industries. Prices dropped from 45% to 56%, production from 14% to 30% in the next four industries, and prices dropped 63% and production dropped 6% in the remaining industry, that of agriculture.

The American economy, consists in part of monopolistic and price competition, in part of regulated monopolies. Of those engaged in price competition, only agriculture is important. With this in mind, the following generalization in respect to the situation exhibited by the above table would seem to be reasonable.

Industries in which the value of raw materials determined by price competition (farm produce for the most part) was a minor cost factor (such as the first five in the table and the regulated monopolies) translated a drop in monetary demand largely into reduced production.

Industries in which the value of raw materials determined by price competition was an important cost factor, such as the textile, food products, leather and petroleum industries,[5a] lowered both production and price (the latter in large part in order to adjust finished prices to the lower raw material prices when faced by a falling monetary demand).

Industries in which price competition prevailed, such as agriculture, reduced price and largely maintained production when faced by a falling monetary demand.

The figures, therefore support our deduction that price flexibility was effective in maintaining the equality of demand and supply only in industries engaged in price competition. In other industries the drop in price when over-all demand was reduced, was insufficient to maintain the equality of demand and supply. Instead, equality was maintained by production falling until the supply was equal to the demand.

In periods of rising monetary demand such as 1922 to 1929, opposite reactions may be observed. The price of farm products rose when demand increased, and their production increased but slightly. The price of other goods hardly rose at all, as is apparent from the cost of living index,[6] but production increased along with the aggregate monetary income.

In short, the conclusion reached on theoretical grounds, that in price competition an adjustment to a deficiency in demand would be likely to follow the lines of Case I, is conclusively substantiated. Price flexibility in such industries is capable not only of structural adjustments, the ability to reflect changed efficiencies and scarcities, but also of cyclic adjustments, the ability to reflect the relationship of over-all supply and over-all demand. Consequently, in price competition a deficiency of demand does not induce significant changes in production.

The data also indicates that in monopolistic competition a

[5a] The price of crude petroleum was relatively free to reflect demand and supply in the period before the depression of the thirties.

[6] Table II, Column IV, p. 132.

drop in demand results in a drop in production. This event will be considered more fully in later sections.

The reaction of the economy as a whole to the persistent advance in efficiency, is consistent with the above conclusions. If · wealth increments were released by way of lower prices, (Case I), the price index would fall as efficiency increased. But the cost of living index [7] rose from 64 in 1870 to 122 in 1929 and again, after the depression. It is evident that the wealth increment made available by the advance in efficiency was *not* released to the population by means of lower prices in this period.

Although this conclusion is valid for the long trend, since prices have risen since records have been kept, and it applies in particular to recent decades, the data on price and production seems to indicate for the reason which follows that a change in the nature of the equilibrium adjustment occurred at the turn of the century.

Although the price trend was slightly downward in the late 1800's prices did not fall steadily but sharply in moments of crises such as those which occurred in 1873, 1883 and 1893.[8] Production also dropped off sharply during these years of crisis. However, production in this period more than recovered from its downsurges within a few years. Prices, however, did not recover fully. In other words, the price drops of 1873, 1883, and 1893 endured after the crises had passed and production had surpassed its former level.

For the whole period (1870 to 1900) prices fell some $12\frac{1}{2}$ per cent (1). Real income and production increased by some 68 per cent, (2). Evidently part of the increased income and production was released by way of lower prices.

After 1900 this was not the case. Prices held steady or rose except for short periods during which production dropped as much or more than prices. Thus prices fell some 11 per cent (3)

[7] Table II, Column IV, p. 132. The cost of living index is based upon the price of consumer goods. It was preferred to the general price level because the latter includes the price of securities, land and other items of wealth, the prices of which are not included in the available supply, QP, as defined.

[8] See Table, p. 284, "Industrial Price Policy," Brookings Institution for late nineteenth century price and production changes year by year.

between 1920 and 1921. Real income and production dropped some 18 per cent (4). Prices fell some 25 per cent (5) between 1929 and 1933. Real income and production dropped 35 per cent (6) during the same period. It is evident that the wealth increment was not released by lower prices in either of these periods since production dropped more than price, indicating a net reduction in income:

$$(1) \quad \frac{64-56}{64} \times 100 = 12\tfrac{1}{2}\% \qquad (4) \quad \frac{455-374}{455} \times 100 = 18\%$$

$$(2) \quad \frac{316-188}{188} \times 100 = 68\% \qquad (5) \quad \frac{122-92}{122} \times 100 = 25\%$$

$$(3) \quad \frac{143-127}{143} \times 100 = 11\% \qquad (6) \quad \frac{559-365}{559} \times 100 = 35\%$$

Source figures are from Table II.

The record therefore suggests that over-all demand was increased now and again during the late 1800's by price reductions, but that after 1900 it was not increased by this means, except momentarily.[9] Since real income increased during the whole period, it is evident that after 1900 reactions *other than a reduction in price* released the wealth increments made available by the advance in efficiency.

It is plausible to suppose that this change at the turn of the century was due to a shift in the relative importance of price competition to monopolistic competition. Further study, however, would be needed to substantiate this supposition. For our purposes, the important fact is that since 1900, the aggregate income *has not* been *increased* by the reaction of Case I, according to which wealth increments would be released by reductions in the price of the supply.

Another comment is pertinent. Even during the 1800's, when production increased and prices dropped during several periods, the translation of increased efficiency into lower prices and greater buying power was neither smooth nor efficient. Prices

[9] If 1922 be considered by itself, demand was increased for the year by the price reduction, since price dropped and production increased. However, we are not justified in taking this year by itself. If the previous and subsequent years be taken into account, the relationship appears as stated above. (The slight price drops in 1913 and 1928 are too small to be significant.)

dropped off in the main during crises such as those cited in which nonproduction and unemployment curtailed the national income to the accompaniment of want and suffering.   Only afterwards, when production recovered and shortly surpassed its former level while prices failed to come back fully, was general purchasing power increased by way of lower prices.[9a]   It appears, therefore, that the economy failed to fulfill the hopes of the theorists at the time of its heyday when price competition was widespread and under populated areas eased various pressures.   Even during this period (the late 1800's) the American economy was unable to release wealth increments by lower prices except through spasms of nonproduction.   And after 1900 the net annual wealth increments were no longer released by this means.

It is therefore reasonable to conclude that:

a. Wealth increments are released in industries subject to price competition largely by price reductions.   (Case 1)

b. In the economy as a whole, price reductions released part of the wealth increment before 1900.   However, the releases were neither smooth nor painless, but were effected for the most part by crises of nonproduction in the initial stages of which unemployment reduced demand more than lower prices increased it.

c. In the economy as a whole, price reductions have been a minor factor since 1900 in the release of the wealth increment made available by the advance in efficiency even though particular wealth increments made available by particular advances in efficiency continued to be released by price reductions or improved products in certain industries.

2. PART OF THE WEALTH INCREMENT MADE AVAILABLE BY THE ADVANCE IN EFFICIENCY HAS BEEN RELEASED BY WAY OF HIGHER WAGES.   BUT THE WAGE INCREASES HAVE NOT BEEN SYNCHRONIZED WITH THE EFFICIENCY ADVANCES, AND CANNOT BE RELIED UPON TO RELEASE THE WEALTH INCREMENTS.

Case III indicated that a wealth increment could be released by a rise in wages were mathematics alone involved.   Let us

[9a] It seems therefore that before 1900 economic progress (i.e. the release of the wealth increment, etc.) was accomplished by a process not incompatible with that described by Dr. Shumpeter.   (Business Cycles, McGraw Hill.)   After 1900 our thought is that the release has been effected somewhat differently.

therefore examine the available data in order to determine to what extent the rise in real wages has released the wealth increment made available by the advance in efficiency.

The real wage index, constructed by dividing the monetary weekly wage index by the cost of living index is submitted in Column 7.[10] The tabulation indicates that real wages are one of the least variable of the factors affecting the over-all equilibrium adjustment. After wavering within narrow limits between 1870 and 1915, real wages per week started upward in 1916, a movement which continued, though interrupted now and again, until today.

The real wage per week index fails to take into account the number of hours and the number of days worked per week. A separate incomplete table [11] giving the real wage per hours, is therefore submitted. The number of hours worked per week has fallen some 20 per cent during the period, most of the decline having occurred in the ten years before the war.[12] Thus the workers have benefitted during the period not only by way of an increase in buying power per week of work, but also by an increase in leisure per week and per day, increases not indicated by the weekly real wage index. For the period 1909 to 1937, weekly wages per week increased by some 47 per cent,[13] an increase which falls well under the probable increase in efficiency,[14] even if the reduced hours of work be taken into account. Thus, the increase in wages would seem considerably less than that which the increase in efficiency has made possible. However, this deduction is uncertain because of the fewer hours worked per day and per week. Probably the real wage approximates the marginal product of labor in the various industries about as closely in recent peace years as in other periods.

Although weekly wages rose slightly if at all between 1870 and 1915, the buying power of the workers as a whole was augmented (though not shown by the table) because the proportion of the

[10] Table II.

[11] Table III.

[12] The reversal of this trend during the war is probably temporary.

[13] $\frac{107-73}{73} \times 100 = 47\%$. Source figures from Table II p. 132.

[14] 3% for 28 years amounts to 74% uncompounded.

population which worked for wages [15] increased during these years.   However, the increase in the buying power of the working class was probably to some degree counteracted by the reduction in imputed income per capita,[16] since the shift from the farms to industry was reducing the proportion of imputed income to total income during most of this period.

During the war years, 1916 to 1918, monetary wages increased more than real wages because of the simultaneous rise in prices. In 1921 prices fell sharply.   *Monetary* wages per week also fell, but monetary wages per hour fell to a lesser extent, thereby increasing real wages per hour by the largest increase on record.[17]

In 1922 to 1923 per capita income recovered.   Partly as a result of steadier employment, real wages per week reflected the previous advance in real wages per hour and reached a new high which was not exceeded until 1927.

During the period of so-called prosperity—1923 to 1929—both monetary and real wages crept upward, the price level holding relatively steady.

During the downsurge in production, 1929 to 1933, the price level and the per capita *real* income fell sharply, (35%) monetary wages fell slightly less (33%) and real wages per week fell some 15%.   Probably real wages per hour did not fall at all, although we have no data on this event owing to the Labor Department's having discontinued its tabulation.[18]

On the basis of this record, it seems reasonable to conclude that the increase in real wage rates has been an important factor since 1915 in enabling society to purchase the wealth increments made available by the advances in efficiency.   Its importance derives partly from the fact that it has been the only steady factor working in this direction.   Like the advance in efficiency, real wages per hour advanced in both good times and bad times, in time of increasing production and in times of decreasing production.

[15] *Recent Social Trends*, McGraw Hill, New York, 1933, pages 280–1.

[16] Imputed income is discussed on p. 134, and footnote.

[17] Table III.   Real wages per hour rose by some 20% between 1916 and 1921.

[18] The Department of Labor doubtless discontinued the compilations of the wage per hour index because it can so easily be misconstrued.   When the hours worked are omitted, the individual worker may appear to be getting higher pay, when actually the working class is getting much less pay owing to the sporadic nature of employment per week and per year.

During production upsurges, wages may be increased when a specific advance in efficiency or merely increased production increases the marginal product of labor. Sometimes it pays employers in this situation to offer higher pay in order to augment their working force.[19] During production downsurges, real wage rates, in particular per *hour* wage rates, are sometimes increased because of the *inelasticity* of wages. When wage rates fall less than prices, the workers who continue to work receive higher pay. This event which has become commonplace in the 20th Century seems to have been an important means by which the underlying population has been enabled to increase its ability to consume. Like the price drops of the 1800's, this event does not benefit the population until the period after the event. Consequently, the increased real wage per hour in 1921 did not benefit the workers as a whole until employment recovered a year later.

In the same category may be included reductions in the hours worked. As was noted above, the working day has been shortened in the 20th Century. Although a reduction in hours worked may neutralize an efficiency advance in whole or in part by translating the benefit to be received therefrom into an increment of leisure, such reductions are not synchronized with efficiency advances, but are imposed independently. Consequently, they cannot be considered to release the wealth increments, although they may have served in recent decades to diminish the gap between what is produced and what could be produced at full employment, by holding down the latter quantity.

One other kind of reaction is important enough to mention. In recent decades, an increasing proportion of total costs seems to have gone into selling expenses, advertising, executive salaries and bonuses, commercial furbelows, etc. Such expense items serve, as do wage increases,[20] to augment buying power. Like wage increases and other cost increments, they are seldom timed

[19] The result is the same if a labor union by pressure compels a wage advance at such a moment. When a labor union compels an increase in monetary wages at other moments, i.e., when efficiency and the marginal product have not advanced, such an increase is likely to be translated into higher prices and thereby nullified insofar as its over-all effect is concerned.

[20] It is not implied that a bonus to management has the same effect as a wage increase except in respect to the equilibrium adjustment. In respect to income distribution, for example, the first event increases income disparity, and the second reduces it.

to balance an efficiency advance and thereby to release a potential wealth increment.

The situation may be summarized as follows.

A business firm which raised wages by an amount equal to the value of a wealth increment, made available at no increase in cost by an advance in efficiency, would not find, if it produced this increment, that the demand for its product had been increased by the increment of wages for the reason stressed. Such a concern, therefore, would be unable to dispose of the increased production which the advance in efficiency had made possible unless it lowered its price which might, as will be indicated in Section 4 and its appendix, be infeasible. Also, it would not be to the interest of a business firm to install an efficiency advance requiring capital were its advantages to be neutralized by higher wages. Furthermore, to increase wages pari passu with each advance in efficiency would be practically difficult and theoretically unsound, as was stressed in Chapter III, p. 70. Consequently, wage increases have seldom released the wealth increments made available by specific efficiency advances although the wage, as was noted above, has in large part reflected sooner or later such increases in the marginal product of labor as have resulted from the efficiency advance.

In short, though much of the increased wealth made available by the advance in efficiency has been allocated to labor by way of shorter hours and higher pay, these diversions have not been the instrumentality by which the wealth increments have been released either in price or monopolistic competition, but have been an indirect and belated effect of the advance in efficiency. Price reductions also, as was noted in the last section, have not been effective of late in accomplishing this end. Apparently, therefore, the wealth increments have been released, at least to some extent, by other than these means, at any rate in the twentieth century.

3. IN FIELDS OF MONOPOLISTIC COMPETITION, AN ADVANCE IN EFFICIENCY IS LIKELY TO RESULT IN (1) A REDUCTION IN EMPLOYMENT AND DEMAND, AND (2) INCREASED PROFIT EXPECTANCY.

Since the record indicates that all of the wealth increment made available by the advance in efficiency is not released by way of lower prices or directly by higher wages (though the latter reaction, like infantry in the Army, seems to hold territory gained by other means), let us consider what happens to this residue. The data [21] indicates that in some years production increased by more [22] than the wealth increment and in other years it decreased. Since efficiency has probably increased at least to some extent in every year, it is evident that in the years production dropped, the wealth increment made available by the advance in efficiency was not released.

How this event could occur was suggested in the last chapter. A mathematically plausible sequence was presented (Case II) which indicated that if prices were not lowered nor wages or other income source raised the wealth increment made available by an efficiency advance would not be produced but instead a reduction in employment and a downsurge in production would ensue. Our next step therefore is to scrutinize contemporary market procedures in order to indicate to what extent these procedures are responsible for the occurrence of this drastic, uneconomic reaction.

Since in price competition an adjustment to an efficiency advance would be accomplished by a fall in price,[23] our search may be confined to the market procedures described as monopolistic competition. If we suppose that a field of monopolistic competition had attained an equilibrium price and an equilibrium production, as described in Chapter II and represented in Figure II, p. 41, such an equilibrium would be unbalanced by an advance in efficiency which has the effect of reducing unit costs at all levels of production. The question then is, what would a competitor do when faced by this condition or possibility?

[21] The course of production is exhibited most clearly by the figures for per capita real income (Table II, Column 5) since they are corrected to take into account changes in the price level and in the population. An increase in per capita real income would indicate an increase in efficiency were employment (total hours worked) constant.

[22] The potential wealth increment resulting from the efficiency advance (p. 90) was estimated to be between 1½% and 3% per year. This would have amounted to goods and services worth less than $3 billion since the gross national product did not surpass 100 billion until 1941. (Table VII.)

[23] For reasons given in Section 1, of this chapter. Table I, gives the supporting statistics.

It may reasonably be assumed that he would wish to cash in on the opportunity by realizing a profit.   But in order to make a profit, he would not *continue* to operate at his most efficient scale as he would in price competition.   This possibility would not be open to him because he *would not* have been operating at his most efficient scale before the efficiency advance.   As noted in Chapter II, a competitor in monopolistic competition operates at his most efficient scale only under exceptional circumstances.

Furthermore, the competitor would not necessarily produce the increment of wealth made available by the efficiency advance and bring it to market as he would in price competition.   This procedure would be but one of several possible procedures.

The competitor's first concern in this situation would be with price.   In monopolistic competition, as has been indicated, the general practice is for a competitor to set (administer) his price and regulate his production according to the demand evoked at the price established.   Having installed the technical improvement, what price, he would ask, might be expected to maximize profit?   A number of possibilities would be open to him:

1. He might maintain his price and release the men no longer needed to accomplish the production required to meet the unchanged demand for his product.

This policy might reasonably be expected to increase profit since cost would have been reduced by the increase in efficiency, and demand would, he might reasonably believe, be unaffected. Furthermore, he would expect this surplus profit to persist until it attracted newcomers into the field, thereby subdividing the market and reducing the demand for his particular product; that is to say, the situation would appear thus to the enterpriser, although we shall describe in the next section how this policy, were it the net effective policy of all enterprisers in similar situations, and were it not neutralized by some other factor, would upset the applecart by instigating a downsurge in production along the lines of Case II.   But no enterpriser would be likely to take this possibility into consideration even if he had accepted the validity of this study, for the action of each individual enterpriser in the vast field of business is so minute a fraction of the total of actions that it would seldom pay him to apply Kant's categorical imperative.[24]

2. Or the competitor might maintain employment, produce the wealth increment which the efficiency advance had enabled, and reduce his price until demand had risen enough to call for the increased supply. The latter policy might require a price above or below the price at which no profit would be realized.[25]

3. Or he might elect a price lying somewhere between the two extremes cited above.

It is evident that in this situation a competitor would be tempted to choose the first policy since it would seem safe and profitable. The second policy would entail unforseeable risks. The compromise policy might however be chosen if no consideration were involved other than those cited above.

However, another and most important consideration is involved. It was provisionally assumed for the sake of simplicity in our discussion of pricing in a field of monopolistic competition that the competitors of such a vendor would keep their prices constant [26] regardless of his actions. Should they do so, a small price drop on the part of the competitor who had installed the efficiency advance would be likely to draw enough customers from the products of his competitors to enable him appreciably to increase production. Were this the situation, it might well pay the competitor to adopt the compromise policy (3), a policy of lowering price slightly, since such a price might enable him to maintain or even increase his working force and to realize a greater profit than he could expect from standing pat on his original price.

But such an assumption would usually be invalid. In the old days of secret processes, slower transportation, imperfect communications, stricter personal obstinacies, and general conservatism in respect to technical innovations, the assumption that other prices would not be changed even if a producer reduced the price of his particular product, might at times have had a

[24] "Act as if the maxim from which you act were to become through your will a universal law of nature."

[25] See appendix to this section for a graphic representation of this detail.

[26] p. 41.

modicum of validity in the industries subject to monopolistic competition. In our day of published prices and continuous technical change, such an assumption is rarely warranted. The enterpriser must take into consideration the probability, if not the certainty, that his rivals will meet his price and copy his technical procedures. Consequently, the competitor would in most cases [27] assume that any price drop on his part would be shortly followed by an equivalent price drop on the part of his competitors even though they had not yet installed the technical improvement. In other words, he could not expect to obtain an appreciable fraction of his competitor's market. All he could count on would be the increase in demand which would result by reason of his and his rival's products being reduced in price in relation to the price of all other products.

This increase might be appreciable; demand might, as it is said, be elastic, and it often would be elastic in the case of new products, such as automobiles, radios, etc., products whose potential market was enormous in recent decades, since only a few of the possible consumers had been reached. In the case of such products, a price drop might expand the market decisively.

(It is no doubt because of this condition and owing to the further fact that new products are usually more subject than others to technological improvements, that the products whose price has dropped in the twentieth century counter to the general trend, have largely belonged to this class.)

Or the increase might be inconsiderable. For example, the demand for such products as machine tools, flour mills, etc. would probably be unaffected by a slight drop in price because the cost of equipment usually is but a minor factor in the cost of production, with the result that a drop in price would not tempt enterprisers to increase their supply of these products appreciably. This condition of inelasticity which applies to perhaps the largest class of producers' goods, also applies to the cheaper classes of consumer goods and to many basic materials.

---

[27] In some cases the technical improvement would be covered by patent. However, even in this situation the competitors would be likely to drop their prices while they were seeking to develop an equivalent or better technical improvement, should the innovator lower his price.

For example, a drop in the price of steel products [28] increases consumption, but not by much. The demand for steel depends upon other factors, chiefly the demand for buildings, automobiles, cans, cannon, ships, etc., factors largely independent of the price of steel. A drop in the price of bread or overalls increases demand but not by much. Those using bread and overalls for the most part consume all they need in any case. When their income is incapable of satisfying their needs, as it is for the majority of citizens during peacetime even in the United States, meat and coats are sacrificed rather than bread and overalls.

Consequently, the demand for most products is inelastic when the price of the product is changed in concert and the possibility of any one enterpriser encroaching on his competitor's market is excluded.

In this situation, an enterpriser would be hardy indeed to risk lowering his price. As usual, a lower price would increase demand. But the step-up in demand would be so small that the increased returns from the increased turnover would not balance the reduced returns from the lower price.[29] Consequently a voluntary price reduction sufficient to release the wealth increment and maintain employment cannot be expected.

The statistical record supports the above interpretation. As noted in the foregoing sections, the price index has tended to hold steady or to rise slightly during periods of sustained production.[30] Its course, therefore indicates that the lower per unit costs due to the increased efficiency of production have not resulted in lower over-all prices.[31]

[28] The demand for intermediate products is further discussed in Chapter VI, page 206.

[29] For a mathematical justification of this deduction, see discussion of Figure IV (p. 113).

[30] Table II. Theoretically a lower price, a price which eliminated surplus profit, would, as was noted in Chapter II, eventually be compelled, as newcomers tempted by the surplus profit enter the field, dividing the market. Apparently this event is effected in practice largely by the periodic down surges in overall demand which are considered in Chapter V.

[31] Other reasons for maintaining prices, even when a technical improvement has lowered costs, are sometimes given. For example, the enterprisers, aware that any price cut will be followed by their competitors, may prefer not to cut prices and thereby initiate a price war. The product may be of such a character that price-cutting would make the customers suspect quality had suffered, thereby reducing demand. Prices are sometimes set by custom and tradition. A price cut may at

But if price was not lowered, demand would not increase and the wealth increment would not be produced and sold. Instead men *would be released* and the same volume of goods produced, though at a lower cost.

It seems reasonable to conclude, therefore, that an advance in efficiency in an industry engaged in monopolistic competition, would usually result in:

1. A price being maintained substantially above the level needed to evoke a demand sufficient to remove the potential wealth increment from the market.

2. A reduction in employment, in money paid out as costs and in over-all demand since fewer men would be needed to satisfy the demand for the product after the efficiency advance than previously.

3. Increased profit expectancy owing to the spread between cost and selling price at the new cost schedule—an expectancy which would not be fulfilled, at least in its entirety, should a downsurge of production be touched off by the reduction in over-all demand due to result 2.

APPENDIX TO SECTION 3. THE SITUATION OF A COMPETITOR IN A FIELD OF MONOPOLISTIC COMPETITION WHO HAS INSTALLED A TECHNICAL IMPROVEMENT, IS REPRESENTED GRAPHICALLY.

Let us suppose that price has come to rest at the equilibrium price, QB, and production at the equilibrium production OB, as described in Chapter II and as represented by Figure II,[31a] and that a competitor introduces a technical improvement which increases the efficiency of his productive process. The result would be lower costs per unit produced. This event may be represented by introducing in our diagram (Figure III) a new cost curve, such as the curve CC_2. This curve is drawn to represent the lower per unit costs of the competitor at every scale of production except the smallest [32] at which operating costs are insignificant. The question is: What would the competitor do under the circumstances?

first decrease sales, since in certain lines customers are likely to hold off buying in the expectation of further price cuts. A sentiment has gradually evolved in many industries that it is unethical to cut prices to get business. The above and other similar conditions as well as the reason cited in the text, serve to deter price-cutting.

[31a] p. 41.

[32] Overhead costs as noted elsewhere have an irreducible minimum.

The competitor would seek to realize a profit. The diagram indicates that price, *PE*, would now maximize profit, were the curves as drawn, for the reasons given in Chapter II.

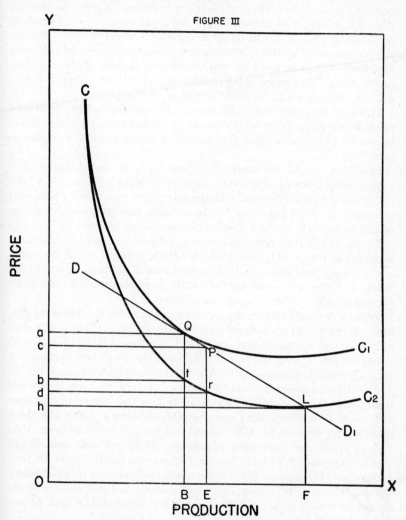

FIGURE III

Y

PRICE

C

D

Q

a
c

P

C₁

t

b
d
h

r

L

C₂

D₁

O

B E

F

X

PRODUCTION

(Profit is represented by the areas bounded by per unit profit—price less cost—multiplied by quantity. Thus, an area such as *Qtba* represents profit at price *QB*. the area *Prdc* represents profit at price *PE*. Such an area would be largest at price *PE* were costs established by curve *CC₂* and demand by curve *DD₁*, because of the shapes of the curves.)

The enterpriser, however, would not know what price would maximize profit. A number of possibilities would be open to him as was noted in Section 3. He could maintain his price at QB in the hope of realizing profit $Qtba$. He could seek, by lowering his price, to discover price PE, which, *if his competitors kept their prices constant*, would result in maximizing profit. Or he could maintain his working force, produce the increment of wealth made available by the advance in efficiency and lower his price until he was enabled to dispose of the resulting production. This latter policy might require a price above or below LF, the price at which no profit would be realized.

Probably the competitor in his attempt to maximize profit would set a price above LF, a price which would be higher than his costs (determined by CC_2) and a price therefore that would promise to realize a profit.

However, should the enterpriser drop his price to a point on DD approaching price LF, the wealth increment might be released and the reduction in over-all demand which results when costs (money paid out) are reduced, might not occur.[33] In practice, however, such an action would be unlikely as the following discussion will indicate.

Figure IV [33a] is therefore submitted, a figure representing the same situation as Figure III, one in which LF, the price at which the value of the supply produced equalled the new cost of production, would fall below MN, the price at which the wealth increment made available by the advance in efficiency would be released.

Price MN would release the wealth increment for the following reason. Were the curves as drawn, area $cNOg$—the cost of ON goods after efficiency had advanced and costs had fallen from CC_1 to CC_2—would equal the area $QBOa$, the cost of producing OB goods before efficiency had advanced. Consequently BN would represent the quantity of additional wealth which could be produced at the former cost of production. And these additional goods as well as the former production, OB, could (if our statement was complete) be sold at price MN since demand, represented by DD_1, would call for ON goods at price MN.

As a result, an enterpriser apparently might not only release the wealth increment BN and still make a substantial profit,—area $MCge$— by dropping his price to MN, but he might even increase his production beyond this point by hiring additional workers and still make a profit should he choose to set a price somewhere between MN and LF on demand curve DD_1.

Should he do so, he would pay out more money in the process of production after the technical improvement than before he had installed it, and thereby increase over-all demand.

[33] $LFOh$ might be greater than $QBOa$.
[33a] The new demand curve, EE_1, will be explained shortly.

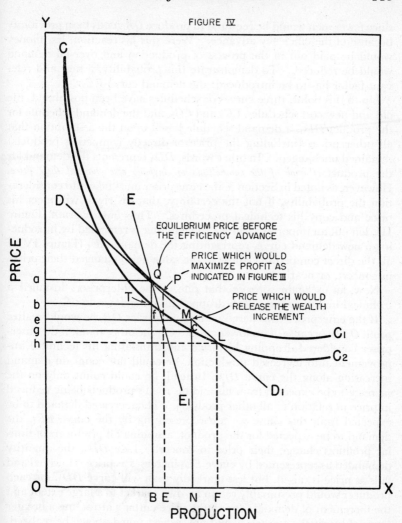

FIGURE IV

EQUILIBRIUM PRICE BEFORE THE EFFICIENCY ADVANCE

PRICE WHICH WOULD MAXIMIZE PROFIT AS INDICATED IN FIGURE III

PRICE WHICH WOULD RELEASE THE WEALTH INCREMENT

PRICE

PRODUCTION

However, in most cases, the enterpriser would set a price at or close to his former price QB,[34] with the result that *employment would be curtailed*,

[34] The prospective profit, area $QTba$ at price QB, is less than the potential wealth increment, area $MNBf$, because the enterpriser who increased production from OB to ON under the circumstances would realize not only lower costs due to his improved efficiency—the vertical distances between CC_1 and CC_2—but also lower costs due to his increased production as represented by the downward slope of both cost curves.

Consequently, the cost saving would be greater at production ON than it would be at production OB, the production he would have to maintain should he retain price QB and use the efficiency advance merely to lower costs.

since fewer men would be required to produce *OB* goods than previously because of the efficiency advance. Were this his reaction, less money would be paid out in the process of production and over-all demand would be reduced. To demonstrate this probability, a new and relevant factor has to be introduced: the demand curve *EE*₁.

Up to this point, three curves or schedules have been postulated, the old and new cost schedules, *CC*₁ and *CC*₂, and the demand schedule for the product *DD*₁, a demand schedule based upon the assumption that all other prices (including the price of directly competing products) remained unchanged. In other words, *DD*₁ represents the demand for the product *if none of the competitors or anybody else changed their price*. However, as noted in Section 3, the enterpriser must take into consideration the probability, if not the certainty, that his rivals will meet his price and copy his technical procedures. Thus our diagram, Figure III, left out an important factor. The matter is remedied by introducing a new demand curve, representing the demand *EE*₁ (Figure IV) if all the direct competitors (those in the same field) changed their prices in concert, or nearly so.

Now, let us again suppose that one of the enterprisers installed a technical improvement which dropped his costs down to *CC*₂.

If the enterpriser considered maintaining price *QB*, he would realize profit *QTba* because of his lower costs. On the other hand, if the enterpriser considered dropping his price and translating his technical improvement into increased production, he could not count on demand increasing along the curve *DD*₁. Instead, he could count only on the increase to be expected from his and his rival's products being reduced in price in relation to all other products. The increased demand to be expected from this cause we are representing by the curve *EE*₁, the demand to be expected for the product, assuming all producers of similar products change their price in concert. Like *DD*₁, the quantity demanded as represented by curve *EE*₁ increases as price is lowered and falls as price is raised, but less markedly than will curve *DD*₁, for each producer would presumably retain his own market to a large extent and the increment of demand, due to the price cutter's attracting a greater share of his rival's market, would not, as was noted above, be realized.

The slope of *EE*₁ might approach the horizontal, *DD*₁ lying still nearer to the horizontal. But this event, it was stressed in Section 3, would be unusual. An elastic demand cannot be expected for *most* products when all the competitors change their price in concert. The slope of *EE*₁ would be more likely to approach the vertical. In fact, in the case of most intermediate products—products coming between raw materials and finished goods—*EE*₁ would be likely to lie close to the vertical, even though *DD*₁ might still be elastic (i.e. approach the horizontal) were the item produced by many manufacturers.

Should demand approach the vertical, the situation represented by EE_1 in Figure IV, an attempt on the part of the enterpriser who had installed the technical improvement to maintain his former working force would prove disastrous. The reduction in costs due to the efficiency advance would enable some ON goods to be produced at the same cost as OB goods formerly cost (if area $cNOg$ = area $QBOa$, as postulated). But if all competitors lowered their price in concert then, in order to evoke a demand that would call for ON goods (the potential production of the original working force) price would have to be dropped *not* to MN but to some price on EE_1 far below the cost of production. In this situation an enterpriser would be unlikely to risk lowering the price of his product even when an increase in efficiency lowered his cost of production.

(The diagram suggests that ON goods could not be given away if EE_1 were still nearer to the vertical and if the other competitors lowered their price and increased production to their respective ON's. This result conflicts with the well-known dictum that a demand exists for every product if the price is dropped low enough. Owing to the possibility of substituting one product for another, it is probably true that the curve EE_1 somewhat falsifies the situation, for certain products. Thus, if the price of steel fell below the price of wood, brick, etc., the demand for steel would start to rise sharply. Likewise, if the price of wheat fell below the price of corn and oats, farmers would begin using wheat in preference to the present cheaper grains to feed their stock and the demand for it would rise sharply. But though we must qualify our representation (Figure IV) by admitting that a curve like EE_1 would be true in most cases only for a short distance, our argument is not invalidated. Even though curve EE_1 holds good only for a short distance, a low price policy would be rendered difficult if not impossible under the circumstances. A steel manufacturer who has instituted a technical improvement could not afford to operate full speed and drop his price low enough to sell his product. We can be quite definite on this point, for just such a reaction occurred several times in the prewar years (1938 and 1939). Price cutting started in steel sheets. Demand expanded only slightly. Profits, which were already slender at the existing rate of operations due to the heavily divided market, became negative. Production did not rise to capacity or anywhere near it. With general bankruptcy inevitable should the policy be continued, the competitors quickly came to terms with each other. Soon the published, administered price was the only price openly obtainable. A move toward price cutting had been stifled.

Examples of this kind can be found in most fields of monopolistic competition.)

4. A REDUCTION IN MONEY PAID OUT AS COSTS IN A FIELD OF
MONOPOLISTIC COMPETITION WOULD TOUCH OFF A DOWNSURGE OF
PRODUCTION, UNLESS ITS EFFECT ON OVER-ALL DEMAND WAS
COUNTERACTED BY SOME OTHER EVENT.

It was concluded in the last section that a management which
had introduced a technical improvement in a field of monopolistic
competition would usually maintain the price of its product and
release the men no longer needed to provide the demanded quota
of goods.   Since money paid out as costs would be reduced by
the release of the men made unnecessary by the efficiency advance, and the value of the output would not be reduced by an
equal amount, demand would be diminished in respect to supply.

The resulting deficiency, however, would *not* pertain particularly to the competitor who had installed the technical improvement and who would continue to gear his production to the demand evoked by his price.   In fact, should he lower his price,
even a little, the demand for his particular product would increase.   The deficiency would pertain, therefore, not to any
particular competitor or any particular field of effort, but to the
over-all demand-supply adjustment since the total of money paid
out as costs would be reduced more than the value of the total
supply being produced.

Furthermore, if no other event intervened the deficiency in
demand would not be made up by an increase in profit because of
the peculiarity of profit, noted in the last chapter, which prevents
it from being realized until the supply is sold.   And all the supply
could not be sold were demand deficient.[35]

It is true, if the management or managements paid out the
prospective profit before it was realized, that is to say, before the
goods were sold, the producers would continue to pay out as
costs plus profit the same total that they took in through sales.
But this procedure would be unusual.   In all probability the
producers would produce the goods, paying out whatever money
was necessary to cover costs and put the product up for sale before
increasing profit payments.   The result would be, momentarily,[36]

[35] p. 75.
[36] According to the theory of monopolistic competition, as described in Chapter
II, the realization or even the promise of surplus profits would attract newcomers to
a field who would set out to produce additional goods, spending money in the

at any rate, that less money would be paid out in the over-all process of production than the value of the supply at the prices asked.

In price competition such an over-all deficiency would result in price being lowered on the market.   In monopolistic competition price tends to be sticky as our logic and the available data [37] both indicate.   As a result, a deficiency of demand in respect to supply would not induce a price drop sufficient to maintain production at its former level.[38]   In fact, when it is recalled that competitors in monopolistic competition are acutely aware of each other's actions, and that in many industries a price reduction on the part of anyone may lead to a greater price reduction on the part of another, the fact that price reductions are sometimes introduced appears more surprising than their comparative rarity.

But if the deficiency in demand were *not* met by a compensatory drop in price, it would induce a reduction in production, because the vendors of differentiated products and other monopolistic competitors gear production closely to demand at the administered price, as was brought out in an earlier chapter. Consequently, an over-all deficiency in demand induced by the efficiency advance would result, if our statement was complete, in a curtailment of over-all production.

But this is the reaction given as Case II.   Its effect on the over-all equilibrium adjustment was there described.   Were a deficiency of demand in respect to supply met by reducing production, demand would be further reduced in respect to supply. Were this second deficiency met by a further reduction in production . . . etc.   In sum, a downsurge in production would be touched off.

Thus, in monopolistic competition the efficiency advance might, result in a cumulative downsurge in production.[39]

process.   Thus the deficiency in demand might shortly be eliminated as the new producers started to spend money.   This possibility is the subject of the next section.

[37] Table I, p. 98.

[38] See Appendix to this section for a graphic representation of this probability.

[39] Since price would probably fall as well as production (because certain groups of enterprisers might choose to lower price as well as production) though not enough to inhibit a decline in production, the event would not be a pure example of Case II, but rather a combination of Case II and Case I with Case II dominant, since Case II is cumulative and Case I is not.

The conclusion reached above by logical deductions is supported by the statistical record. The data covering the 1929–1933 depression was summarized in Table I. The record shows that industries such as the automotive, cement, steel, rubber, etc., in which the cost of agricultural produce is minor, reacted to the falling demand of the period by dropping production from 65% to 85% while price drops were held between 6% and 20%, except for tires, the price of which dropped some 33% (while their production fell 70%) owing no doubt to the fall in crude rubber prices.

More convincing even than this general picture is the relation or production and price on a month to month basis. The record in nearly every non-agricultural industry brings out clearly that production in good times as well as bad wavers erratically reflecting even the little ups and downs of demand, while price clings stubbornly to each successive position, following the basic up or down trends in a lingering, hesitant and most reluctant manner.

But have we not proved too much by the above argument? If an advance in efficiency in a field of monopolistic competition would result in a reduction in costs and thereby in over-all demand, and if such a reduction would touch off a downsurge in production, why is it that production increased in some twenty of the last thirty-three years? To answer this question, let us refer again to the conclusion reached in Section 3.

APPENDIX TO SECTION 4. THE SITUATION OF A PRODUCER IN A FIELD OF MONOPOLISTIC COMPETITION FACED BY A REDUCTION IN DEMAND IS REPRESENTED GRAPHICALLY.

Let us assume that price had come to rest at the equilibrium price *QP*, and production at the equilibrium production *OB*, as described in Chapter II. Now let us suppose that owing to the installation of a technical improvement on the part of one or more going concerns, men were disemployed and the money issued in the productive process dropped below the value of the supply being produced at asked prices, as described in the preceding section. As a result, the demand curves of individual producers such as *DD* and *EE* [40] would drop, that is to

[40] Figure V. *EE* was defined on p. 116.

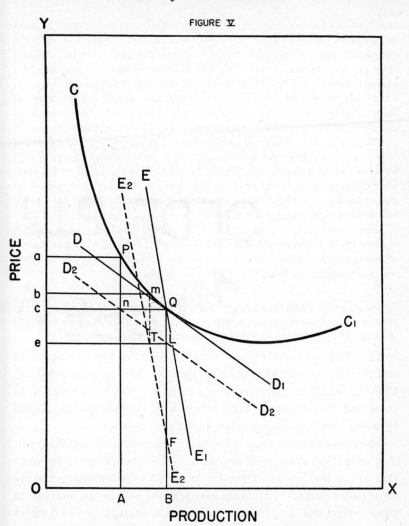

FIGURE V

say, would move to the left, to DD_2 and EE_2 for example. What would the enterpriser do under the circumstances?

He might maintain price QB, reduce his production to OA on demand schedule DD_2 and accept loss $Pnca$; or he might drop his price to LB, the price which would evoke a demand sufficiently great to enable him to continue producing OB goods, the quantity formerly produced, and accept loss $QLec$ should demand curve DD_2 govern. In fact, if the competitor *could count* on his rivals maintaining the existing price, this latter procedure would be probable since loss $QLec$ might be greater or

less than loss *Pnca* depending on the slope of the cost curve and the drop
in demand.   However, it was indicated in the last section that the
competitor must expect his rivals to follow his price moves.   Should
they do so, demand curve EE_2 would govern and the quantity demanded would not be *OB* at price *LB* but would fall to quantity *eT*,
where his loss would be *mTeb*.   However, the significant factor is not
the probably increased loss but the fact that *OB* goods, his former production, could not be sold at any reasonable price and therefore would
not be produced.   Price *LB* would evoke a demand for some *eT* goods
only.   In order to evoke a demand for *OB* goods, the producer would
have to cut his price to *FB*, which would be less than half of his costs
were demand as inelastic as in the illustration.   It, therefore, would be
disastrous for a producer to meet a drop in demand entirely by a price
adjustment were the curves as drawn.

Since curve EE_2 would be likely to approach the vertical for the
reasons given in Section 3, it would be unusual for a producer in a field
of monopolistic competition to meet a deficiency of demand by lowering
his price enough to maintain his former production.

5. INCREASED PROFIT EXPECTANCY IN A FIELD OF MONOPOLISTIC
COMPETITION MIGHT INDUCE THE CREATION AND SPENDING OF NEW
MONEY SUFFICIENT TO TOUCH OFF A PRODUCTION UPSURGE.

The effect of an efficiency advance on a field of monopolistic
competition was analyzed in Section 3.   It was concluded (p.
112) that such an advance would usually result in a reduction in
costs and in increased profit expectancy because of the spread
between cost and selling price at the new cost schedule.

The reduction in costs, it has just been indicated, would result
in a reduction in over-all demand, and a downsurge of production along the lines of Case II, "unless it was counteracted by
some other event."   Such an event might well be an increase in
money paid out and in over-all demand from the second effect
of the efficiency advance, the increase in profit expectancy.

Let us suppose for example that at some equilibrium level an
inventor introduced a technical improvement and that one or
more competitors prepared to install it.   The news spread
quickly.   Other competitors on one basis or another also prepared to install it.   Credit would usually be available.[41]   A
sudden requirement for money and men on the part of certain
enterprisers, sold on the profit potentialities of a new invention

[41] p. 4.

might well result in promotions in some time period in excess of the money being set aside for investment in that period. The banks to meet the drain would create additional money as described in Chapter I. Demand as a result would be increased as the new money was spent.[42] Possibly the increase in demand from this event would more than equate the decrease in demand from the cost reduction described in the previous section. As a result, over-all or net demand would be increased.

In a field of monopolistic competition an increase in demand, when production is short of full, is more likely to induce increased production than higher prices.[43] The reason is that excess capacity, a normal characteristic of such fields of effort, permits surplus profit to be realized at higher productions without risk and without raising prices. And a rise in price, owing to its depressing effect on demand, usually contains an element of risk. Other reasons, such as the sentiment against raising prices, the fear or awareness that competitors would not follow suit, etc. are also present. But the point need not be labored since the price record of nearly all non-agricultural industries fully supports our deduction. In any case, that is to say, whether production only is increased or whether price is raised as well as production, surplus profits would be realized.[44]

Surplus profits tempt new concerns into a field of effort. Newcomers require men and money in order to start production. Should the banks provide the money by creating new money, and should the men be drawn from the ranks of the unemployed, over-all demand would again be increased. Should production be increased once more to meet the increased demand, etc., a cumulative upsurge in production would be initiated along the lines of Case IV.

The difficulty involved in increasing an individual's profit unless some other individual's profit were decreased (noted in Chapter III) [45] would not be encountered owing to the increase

[42] Case IV.

[43] If a total system of price competition were in effect, a demand for money and men in excess of the supply being used, would raise prices, wages, interest rates, etc. The increased monetary demand would be neutralized by the increased value of the supply and the scale of production might not be affected.

[44] The relation is represented graphically in the Appendix to Section 5.

[45] p. 75.

in net over-all profit resulting from the influx of new money along the lines indicated. Thus an individual concern's profit increment would come out of the increment [46] of over-all net profit made available by the spending of new money.

It is reasonable to conclude, therefore, that an efficiency advance, should it lead to plant expansion and the creation of new money, might result in a cumulative upsurge in production [47] which would eventually level off at a new equilibrium level as full production was approached, or sooner, as per unit costs started to rise.[47a]

It appears therefore that the introduction of an efficiency advance in a field of monopolistic competition not only might touch off a downsurge in production, but also, in other circumstances, might touch off an upsurge in production, were production less than full at the time. Let us see if the statistical data will permit such an interpretation.

The fact that production tends to vary erratically from year to year and seldom gets close to full production in times of peace, cannot be put forward as proof of the analysis since other causes might account for this event. Should, however, the records indicate that profit and the supply of money increased during upsurges and declined during downsurges, our deduction that cyclic movements are accounted for in large part by reactions along the lines of Case II and Case IV would be strongly supported for the following reason.

Case IV showed how a wealth increment made available by an advance in efficiency would be released were enough new money thrown into the spending stream to increase demand by an amount equal to the value of the wealth increment. Case II showed that if production were reduced when demand proved insufficient to command the potential increase in supply made available by the advance in efficiency, a production downsurge

---

[46] Case IV, p. 87. This conclusion is qualified in Chapter V by indicating a situation in which the release of the wealth increment by new money spending would not increase profit.

[47] The fact that some prices would probably rise (even in the early stages of the movement owing in part to certain raw materials being subject to price competition) though not enough to inhibit a series of increases in demand and production, does not render the above conclusion invalid. It merely complicates the relationships.

[47a] This probability is considered in Chapter V.

would be induced. The first event, it was indicated, would increase profit disproportionally. The second event would reduce profit disproportionately and, in a modern economy, the supply of money, although this latter effect is not brought out by the formula. It may, however, be accounted for quite simply.

In modern economies, the great part of the money supply consists of debit money [48] which is withdrawn when not required. Borrowers, as a matter of course, regulate their supply of borrowed money by their need for money.[49] Thus, when plants are in process of expansion and the demand for money exceeds the supply, new money is created as described. Furthermore, when little or no plant expansion is taking place, as in periods of falling production, the supply of money is likely to exceed the demand for money. At such times loans are repaid and the supply of money is contracted.

The three quantities therefore would rise and fall together profit increasing and decreasing disproportionately were the reactions described as Cases II and IV indicative of the actual event. Let us check our deductions by referring to the relevant data.

Table IV starts with the year 1921 and lists the national monetary income, the supply of money and corporation profits.[50]

A fourth column has been appended giving the index of employment. It parallels closely the national income, Column I. It is a convenient check on Column I since it is unaffected by changes in the price level.

Chart I shows the relationship of the first three quantities between 1921 and 1938. Arbitrarily starting them off together, as of the year 1921, the chart shows how they rose and fell together

[48] p. 3 and Table V, p. 135.

[49] Borrowers reduce their debt when they do not need all the money on hand and increase it when they need additional money, if their credit is good.

[50] Total profits could be estimated. However, by limiting profits to corporation profits, the profit of monopolistic competition is roughly segregated. This follows because few corporations engage in price competition, a field largely preempted by farmers, and some 90 per cent of monopolistic competition is carried on by corporations. It does not seem necessary to correct the quantities for the increase in population or the changes in the price level. Although the changes in the price level reduced somewhat the amplitude of the cyclic swings, its effect may be disregarded because price has risen on upsurges and fallen on downsurges.

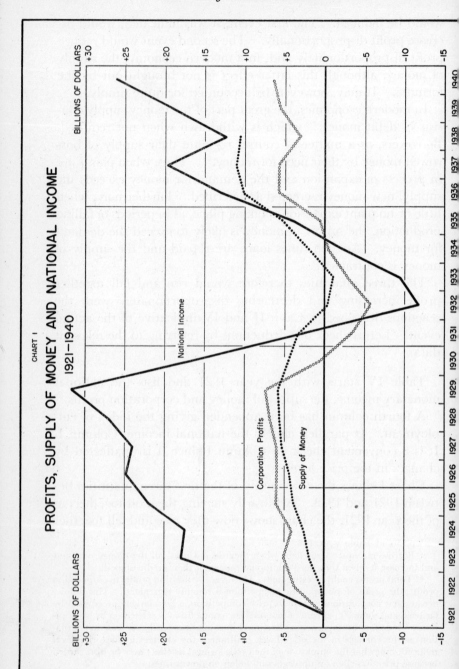

CHART I

PROFITS, SUPPLY OF MONEY AND NATIONAL INCOME
1921–1940

during the subsequent years. Increases in money were accompanied by increases in profit and production,[51] and vice versa. Profit followed money closely, dropping more than money in the depression but rising by about the same amount during the 1922–29 upsurge and by lesser amounts during the recovery period.[52]

As would be expected from the relationship described as Case IV, net over-all profit increased and decreased as the supply of money increased and decreased. The increment of corporation profit corresponded roughly to the dimension of the increment of new money.[53] Production usually increased and decreased by more than the supply of money and profit in absolute amounts because money increments in excess of that quantity needed to release the wealth increment have a cumulative effect as noted in Chapter III.[54] Profit however increased and decreased by greater percentages than did production as is evident from the fact that profit became negative at about the 55 billion production level in recent decades.

Thus the data support the foregoing analysis which indicated that in recent decades that fraction of the wealth increment made available by the advance in efficiency which was not released either by lower prices (Case I) or higher wages (Case III), has been released, when it has been released, largely by injections of new money which served to increase net over-all profit and usually resulted in a production upsurge as described in Case IV.[55] At other times, a fraction of the wealth increment has not been released, which event results in a production downsurge along the lines of Case II.

[51] In 1924 money increased slightly and profits and production fell slightly. The divergence however is slight. Probably the money increment was insufficient to release the wealth increment. Chart I data on p. 134.

[52] Between 1929 and 1932 net over-all profit dropped by considerably more than did the supply of money. This event is probably accounted for by the measures the government took during this period to sustain the debt structures and thereby indirectly the money (i.e., debit money) supply. After 1932, money increments were sometimes greater than the increments of corporation profit. The lower velocity of money in the post depression period in part accounts for this fact.

[53] Were entrepreneurial and other non-corporative profits and capital gains included, profit increments would be greater than money increments as is to be expected because of the velocity of money. Profit increments become less sensitive to money increments as the upsurge matures for reasons presented in Chapter V.

[54] p. 88.

[55] Further aspects of this relationship are considered in Chapter V.

Thus the contemporary economy incapable because of the procedures of monopolistic competition of reacting to the advance in efficiency by appropriate price changes, has adjusted itself to the advance in efficiency [56] by a series of back and forth movements usually known as the business cycle.

Since any deviation from full production constitutes nonproduction, full production cannot be realized when the equality of demand and supply is maintained by varying production.   Consequently, the *equilibrium adjustment imposed by monopolistic competition accounts for nonproduction.*

The above analysis leaves changes in the volume of production subject to incidental events.   If the above account comprehended all relevant factors an efficiency advance might result either in a downsurge or upsurge in production depending on whether the interested competitors increased the money they paid out on capital formation, etc. by considerably more than the enterprisers who had installed the technical improvement reduced their costs. If the aggregate demand increment (ΔE) was insufficient to release the wealth increment and other factors balanced each other, a downsurge would be touched off.   If the aggregate demand increment was sufficient or more than sufficient to release the wealth increment and other factors balanced each other, an upsurge would be touched off.   Since efficiency is advancing in many fields simultaneously, and since the reactions to it are various, the analysis, were it complete, would leave us with what might be called a principle of indeterminism.

Such a conclusion would be unsatisfactory.   It would not, for example, account for the observed tendency of production to increase and decrease in cycles of a certain rough regularity in respect to duration.   Furthermore, were the choice of upsurge or downsurge subject to chance, "pump-priming" would be in order whenever the forward march of production lost its momentum. But "pump-priming" alone cannot be counted upon to sustain production.[57]   It seems, therefore, as if more is involved in the

[56] It is not maintained that efficiency is the only factor which disturbs the over-all equilibrium, but merely that it is the most persistent and probably the most important factor.

[57] Reasons for this judgment are submitted in Chapter V, pp. 167 ff.

equilibrium adjustment than the chance alternation of the reactions described above as Cases II and IV.

Despite the limitation suggested above, the analysis has served to narrow the scope of our inquiry since it has shown how the inability of price in industries engaged in monopolistic competition to effect cyclic adjustments induces nonproduction. There remains to discover the factors which determine the choice of one or other of the two reactions described above when the advance in efficiency or other event increases the potential supply without increasing the effective demand.

Summary. Part of the wealth increment made available by the continuing advance in efficiency has been released by way of lower prices (Case I). Since this reaction occurs for the most part in that fraction of the economy which is subject to price competition, and in industries promoting new products, its relative proportions have been small in recent decades.

Part of the increment has been released by way of higher wage rates, shorter hours of work, increased payments to salesmen, advertising agents and executives, improved products, etc. (Case III.) However, these developments, are secondary effects of the advance in efficiency serving to hold part of the ground gained when the wealth increment has been released by other means.

The release of the residue of the wealth increment, has apparently been accomplished largely by the creation and spending of new money along the lines of Case IV. Whenever enough new money was created and spent as in 1922 to 1929, 1934 to 1937, and 1939 to 1944, production increased and the wealth increment was produced and purchased. Whenever enough new money was not created and spent, as in 1929, 1930, 1931, 1932, and 1938, production turned downward and the potential increment of wealth was not produced and consumed. The factors which bear upon the selection of one of these opposite reactions will be considered in Chapter V.

In short, our analysis and the data suggest that all of the potential wealth increment made available by the annual advance in efficiency has not of late been released by reductions in the price level (Case 1), nor directly by way of wage increases (Case III).

Instead, the residue of the wealth increment has at times been released by the spending of increments of new money (Case IV) and at other times the efficiency advance has in effect been nullified by nonproduction (Case II).   As a result, the economy, instead of forging ahead steadily by producing each year the increment of additional wealth made available by the advance in efficiency, has been subject, at any rate, in times of peace, to wide cyclic swings and has realized, in consequence, a production well short of full production.

APPENDIX TO SECTION 5.   THE SITUATION OF A PRODUCER IN A FIELD OF MONOPOLISTIC COMPETITION FACED BY AN INCREASE IN DEMAND IS REPRESENTED GRAPHICALLY.

It is being supposed that new money has, in its spending, increased over-all demand as described in Case IV.   An increase in over-all demand increases the demand for particular goods and services.   We can represent this result in a field of monopolistic competition by supposing that the demand curve EE_1 of Figure V has been moved to the right instead of to the left. E_3E_3 of Figure VI (page 131) therefore represents an increase in demand, an increase which is likely to be equally great at every price as shown on the diagram, and which will apply to all competitors since it is the result of an increase in over-all demand.   The question is, what would a competitor do under the circumstances?

Evidently he might maintain price QB, step up production to OV to meet the increased demand, and content himself with profit *mneb*. (Such has been the usual reaction, judging from the relative stability of the price level during recent peace time upsurges in production). Or he might apparently maximize profit by increasing his price to RS, drop *production* to OS and realize profit $RKca$, *could he count on every competitor doing likewise.*[58]   Other prices might be tried out depending on the competitive situation, since profit would be increased even were price dropped slightly below QB or raised above RS.

However, a rise in price would be unlikely because of the probability or rather certainty [59] were competition effective, and were production

[58] To represent the increase (or decrease) in demand which would result if the competitors did not raise their prices would serve no end, since such a price increase would a priori defeat its purpose.

[59] A price rise would be less likely after an efficiency advance than previously since it would be less needed.   Usually its possibility would have *been explored* in the period *before* the influx of new money when the competitor supposedly was breaking even.   Were the competition fictive, that is to say, were monopoly in effect, the several units might of course raise their price in concert.

appreciably short of full, that the competitors would not follow suit. If they failed to do so and maintained their prices, the enterpriser who raised his price would find the demand for his product so reduced that his prospective profit would not be realized. Consequently in this situation an enterpriser possessing the usual excess capacity of monopolistic competition would be likely to play safe and content himself with the profit to be obtained by increasing production, thereby spreading his overhead costs over more units.

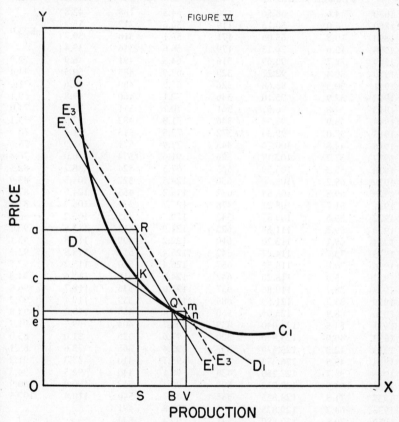

FIGURE VI

The realization of an increase of profit from zero at price QB production OB to an appreciable quantity at price QB production OV would be made possible without risk by the expansion of the money supply and demand as described in Case IV.

APPENDIX TO CHAPTER IV.   STATISTICAL TABLES.

Table II lists income, price, and wage data, between 1870 and the advent of war.   By dividing the total monetary income (Column I) by

TABLE II

	(1)	(2)	(3)	(4)	(5)	(6)	(7)
Year	Monetary Income	Population	Monetary Income Per Capita	Cost of Living Index	Per Capita Real Income Deflated	Monetary Wage Index	Real Wage Index
	$ Billions	Millions	1÷2	1935–39=100	3÷4	Weekly	6÷4
1870	4.6	38.56	120	64.3	188	42.8⎤	
1880	6.0	50.15	119	56.6	212	35.7 ⎬ ±73.0	
1890	10.8	63.06	171	55.1	310	39.7 ⎬	
1900	13.6	76.13	179	56.6	316	39.4⎦	
1909	28.7	90.69	316	64.3	491	46.9	72.9
1910	30.4	92.27	329	67.9	485	50.5	74.4
1911	30.5	93.68	326	67.9	480	48.6	71.6
1912	32.9	95.10	346	72.1	480	49.8	69.1
1913	34.8	96.51	361	70.7	511	52.3	74.0
1914	33.9	97.93	346	71.8	482	52.5	73.1
1915	37.0	99.34	372	72.5	513	51.4	70.9
1916	44.8	100.76	445	77.9	571	58.9	75.6
1917	53.7	102.17	526	91.6	574	70.0	76.4
1918	58.3	103.59	563	107.5	524	88.7	82.5
1919	68.2	105.00	650	124.5	522	104.5	83.9
1920	69.5	106.54	652	143.2	455	124.6	87.0
1921	51.7	108.21	478	127.7	374	106.9	83.7
1922	59.5	109.87	542	119.7	453	103.2	86.2
1923	69.5	111.54	623	121.9	511	113.5	93.1
1924	69.1	113.20	610	122.2	499	113.8	93.1
1925	73.7	114.87	642	125.4	512	115.8	92.3
1926	76.6	116.53	657	126.4	520	117.2	92.7
1927	75.9	118.20	642	124.0	518	117.6	94.8
1928	78.7	119.86	657	122.6	536	118.7	96.8
1929	83.3	121.53	685	122.5	559	119.1	97.2
1930	68.9	123.09	560	119.4	469	110.8	92.8
1931	54.5	124,040	439	108.7	404	99.7	91.7
1932	40.0	124,840	320	97.6	328	81.0	83.0
1933	42.3	125,579	337	92.4	365	78.6	85.1
1934	49.5	126,373	392	95.7	410	87.3	91.2
1935	55.7	127,250	438	98.1	446	92.5	94.3
1936	64.9	128,053	507	99.1	512	100.0	100.9
1937	71.5	128,825	555	102.7	540	110.4	107.5
1938	64.2	129,825	495	100.8	491		
1939	70.8	130,880	541	99.4	544		
1940	77.8	131,954	590	100.2	589		
1941	96.9	133,060	728	105.2	692		

Sources:

Col. 1—1870–1900 Robert Doane. 1909–1928, unpublished and unofficial estimates of the Dept. of Commerce, obtained by extending the Commerce 1929 estimate by means of National Bureau of Economic Research data. 1929–1941, unpublished estimates of the Dept. of Commerce.

TABLE III

INDEX NUMBERS OF WAGES PER HOUR, COST OF LIVING, AND REAL WAGES

	Wages Per Hour	Cost of Living		Real Wages Based On	
		1913 = 100	1935–39 = 100	C.L. 1913 = 100	C.L. 1935– 39 = 100
	(1)	(2)	(3)	(4)	(5)
1913	100	100.0	70.7	100.0	141.4
1914	102	101.6	71.8	100.4	142.1
1915	103	102.5	72.5	100.5	142.1
1916	111	110.2	77.9	100.7	142.5
1917	128	129.6	91.6	98.8	139.7
1918	162	152.1	107.5	106.5	150.7
1919	184	176.1	124.5	104.5	147.8
1920	234	202.5	143.2	115.6	163.4
1921	218	180.6	127.7	120.7	170.7
1922	208	169.3	119.7	122.9	173.8
1923	217	172.4	121.9	125.9	178.0
1924	223	172.8	122.2	129.1	182.5
1925	226	177.4	125.4	127.4	180.2
1926	229	178.8	126.4	128.1	181.2
1927	231	175.4	124.0	131.7	186.3
1928	232	173.4	122.6	133.8	189.2
1929	233	173.3	122.5	134.4	190.2

Source: Bureau of Labor Statistics, Dept. of Labor.

the population (Column 2) and by dividing the resulting per capita monetary income (Column 3) by the cose of living index (Column 4), the income per capita in dollars of constant purchasing power is obtained.   Column 5 therefore may be called the per capita real income, since it represents the production and consumption of wealth per person.

Per capita real income (Column 5), like the national monetary income (Column 1) increased erratically over the years, occasionally dropping back, and seldom approaching the income of full production.

TABLE II—*Continued*

Col. 2—1870–1930, Statistical Abstract of the United States, 1939, p. 10.
   1931, 1933, 1935–41, Statistical Abstract of the United States, 1943, p. 6.
   1932, 1934, Statistical Abstract of the United States, 1941, p. 10.
Col. 3—Col. 1 ÷ Col. 2.
Col. 4—1870–1912, Index of estimated costs of living in U. S., Federal Reserve Bank of New York, linked to cost of living index, Bureau of Labor Statistics.
   1913–1941, Statistical Abstract, 1943, p. 404–405.
Col. 5—Col. 3 ÷ Col. 4.
Col. 6—Bureau of Labor Statistics.
Col. 7—Col. 6 ÷ Col. 4.

TABLE IV

	(1) National Monetary Income	(2) Supply of Money	(3) Corporation Profits	(4) Index of Employment
	Billion $	Billion $	Million $	
1921	51.7	21.33	−244	83.7
1922	59.5	21.70	3986	99.1
1923	69.5	23.25	5371	105.7
1924	69.1	23.85	4481	101.9
1925	73.7	25.34	6451	102.6
1926	76.6	25.78	6275	104.0
1927	75.9	26.66	6379	101.2
1928	78.7	26.90	7042	103.5
1929	83.3	27.14	7546	110.3
1930	68.9	26.11	840	98.3
1931	54.5	24.65	−3687	81.2
1932	40.0	20.97	−5929	71.2
1933	42.3	20.30	−2970	85.0
1934	49.5	23.29	−502	89.0
1935	55.7	26.58	961	95.2
1936	64.9	31.53	6135	104.4
1937	71.5	32.48	6121	109.1
1938	64.2	31.92	3271	93.3
1939	70.8	33.4*	5946	
1940	77.8	38.7*	6770	
1941	96.9	45.5*	9166	

Sources:

Column 1, As in Table II.
Column 2, As in Table V.
Column 3, As in Table VI.
* Federal Reserve Board, Banking and Money Statistics, Washington 1944, pp 34 and 35. Dr. Currie's figures end with 1939. Hence the additional figures are not strictly comparable with the proceding ones but range slightly higher.

Despite its erratic course, real income has risen from $188 per capita in 1870 to $559 per capita in 1929, an increase of some 300 per cent, or some 5 per cent a year on the average. This increase would suggest that our estimate of the advance in efficiency was too low were it not for the fact that imputed income is not included in the estimate.[60] Since imputed income constituted about one-half of the total income in 1870 and some one-sixteenth only in 1929, the total per capita income

[60] Imputed income consists largely of the imputed rent of owned houses, farms, etc. and the value of home production, foodstuffs, etc. It was not included in the table because our concern is with that fraction of the national income produced for sale.

TABLE V

TOTAL SUPPLY OF MONEY IN THE UNITED STATES, 1919–1938

In Millions of Dollars

June 30	Adjusted Demand Deposits	U. S. Government	Foreign Bank Deposits In American Banks	Total	Currency Outside Banks	Total Supply of Money
1921	17,030	463	138	17,631	3,700	21,331
1922	17,990	203	150	18,343	3,360	21,703
1923	18,860	364	274	19,498	3,760	23,258
1924	19,570	233	390	20,193	3,660	23,853
1925	21,150	205	400	21,755	3,590	25,345
1926	21,610	241	310	22,161	3,620	25,781
1927	22,250	261	575	23,086	3,580	26,666
1928	22,340	294	622	23,256	3,650	26,906
1929	22,620	416	450	23,486	3,660	27,146
1930	21,870	347	514	22,731	3,380	26,111
1931	19,910	491	580	20,981	3,670	24,651
1932	15,670	471	190	16,331	4,640	20,971
1933	14,450	885	177	15,512	4,790	20,302
1934	16,650	1,804	165	18,619	4,680	23,299
1935	20,540	922	317	21,779	4,810	26,589
1936	23,860	1,840	573	26,273	5,260	31,533
1937	25,260	763	929	26,952	5,530	32,482
1938	24,390	1,470	598	26,458	5,470	31,928

Source: Lauchlin Currie, formerly of Federal Reserve Bank.

TABLE VI

NET INCOME OF ALL CORPORATIONS AFTER PAYMENT OF ALL TAXES
BUT BEFORE PAYMENT OF DIVIDENDS

(In Millions of Dollars)

1916	$ 7937	1929	$ 7546
1917	7958	1930	840
1918	4513	1931	−3687
1919	6241	1932	−5929
1920	4248	1933	−2970
1921	−244	1934	−502
1922	3986	1935	961
1923	5371	1936	6135
1924	4481	1937	6121
1925	6451	1938	3271
1926	6275	1939	5946
1927	5379	1940	6770
1928	7042	1941	9166

Source: U. S. Bur. of Internal Revenue.

TABLE VII

GROSS NATIONAL PRODUCT, CAPITAL FORMATION AND CONSUMERS' OUTLAY
1919–1940

In Billions of Dollars

Year	Gross National Product	Gross Capital Formation	Consumers' Outlay
1919	68.8	19.3	49.5
1920	82.8	22.1	60.7
1921	66.1	11.5	54.6
1922	67.2	13.3	53.9
1923	78.2	18.2	60.0
1924	79.8	15.2	63.6
1925	83.4	19.2	64.2
1926	88.8	19.0	69.8
1927	86.8	18.2	68.6
1928	90.1	17.8	72.3
1929	93.6	20.3	73.3
1930	82.7	13.7	69.0
1931	64.8	8.5	56.3
1932	47.1	3.1	44.0
1933	46.0	3.7	42.3
1934	55.2	5.5	49.7
1935	61.6	9.4	52.2
1936	72.7	13.8	58.9
1937	80.8	17.5	62.5
1938	70.3	12.7	57.3
1939	77.0	15.6	61.4
1940	82.0	18.5	63.5

Sources: Monograph No. 37, "Savings, Investment and National Income," U. S. Govt. Print. Office, Wash. D. C. 1941.

"Hearings before the Temporary National Economic Committee," Part 9, page 4007. Data there presented were taken from "National Bur. of Econom. Research," 1937, and "Commodity Flow and Capital Formation in the Recent Recovery and Decline, 1932–38; Bulletin 74, N. Y. Natl. Bur. of Econ. Res., 1939.

has increased [61] no faster than the technological advance permitted, as we know, a priori, in any case.

Column 7, the real wage index, has also advanced over the period, though not as much as per capita real income. However, as noted in the text, the real wage index does not include the shortening of work hours which occurred in the latter decades and therefore understates the improvement in the wage earners situation. The contrast between the

[61] If imputed income per capita amounted to $188 in 1870 and to $37 in 1929, as suggested above, total income would have been $376 per capita in 1870 and $596 in 1929, an increase of $220 or some 58 per cent during the 60 years. If the above rough estimate approximated the actual event total income advanced in the period by considerably less than our lowest estimate of the advance in efficiency would have permitted for $1\frac{1}{4}\% \times 60 = 90\%$ uncompounded. However, the imputed income estimate is little more than a guess and probably overstates the 1870 quantity.

TABLE VII(a)

In Billions of Dollars

Year	Gross National Product	Producers' Durable Equipment (Private)	Business Construction (Private)	2 + 3	Consumers' Purchases
	(1)	(2)	(3)	(4)	(5)
1919	74.8	6.2	2.2	8.4	49.9
1920	83.1	6.2	3.0	9.2	58.1
1921	67.0	3.4	2.2	5.6	51.3
1922	68.6	3.4	2.4	5.8	52.2
1923	79.8	5.3	3.1	8.4	58.3
1924	80.4	4.8	3.2	8.0	59.2
1925	85.0	5.3	3.5	8.8	63.3
1926	91.6	5.8	4.1	9.9	66.8
1927	90.3	5.6	4.2	9.8	66.3
1928	93.2	6.0	4.1	10.1	68.1
1929	99.4	7.4	4.7	12.1	70.8
1930	88.2	6.0	3.9	9.9	64.9
1931	72.1	4.2	2.4	6.6	54.2
1932	55.4	2.4	1.2	3.5	43.0
1933	54.8	2.1	0.9	3.0	42.8
1934	63.8	3.1	1.1	4.2	47.7
1935	70.8	4.0	1.2	5.2	52.5
1936	81.7	5.2	1.6	6.8	59.1
1937	87.7	6.3	2.3	8.6	62.5
1938	80.6	4.5	1.6	6.1	58.5
1939	88.6	5.5	1.7	7.2	61.7
1940	97.1	6.9	2.1	9.0	65.7
1941	120.5	8.9	2.7	11.5	74.6
1942	151.5	5.1	1.8	6.9*	81.9
1943	187.8	3.1	1.1	4.2*	90.9
1944	198.7	4.0			97.6

* Private capital formation was supplemented in 1942, '43, etc. by vast public formations, thereby permitting consumers' purchases to continue increasing in these years.

Sources:

Col. 1—1929–1944, *Survey of Current Business*, May 1942, April 1944, February, 1945.

1923–1928, based on Hagen, E. E. and Nora Boddy Kirkpatrick, *The National Output At Full Employment in 1950*, *American Economic Review*, Sept. 1944, Table 1, p. 476, by adding income originating in the Armed Forces.

1919–1922, estimates of Marvin Hoffenberg linked to Hagen's estimate for 1923.

Col. 2—1919–1928, estimated by Marvin Hoffenberg.

1929–1944, same source as Column 1.

Col. 3—Excludes farm and nonfarm residential construction. *The Construction Industry in the United States*, Bureau of Labor Statistics, Bulletin No. 786, 1944.

Col. 4—Col. 2 + Col. 3.

Col. 5—1919–1928, estimates prepared by Marvin Hoffenberg.

1929–1944, *Survey of Current Business*, May 1942, April 1944, February, 1945.

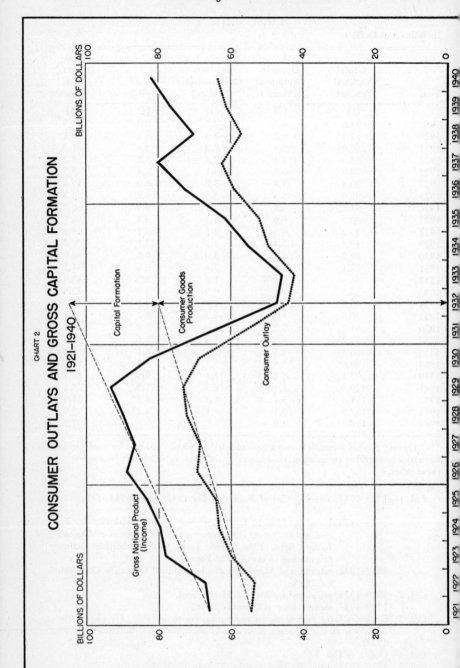

CHART 2

CONSUMER OUTLAYS AND GROSS CAPITAL FORMATION
1921-1940

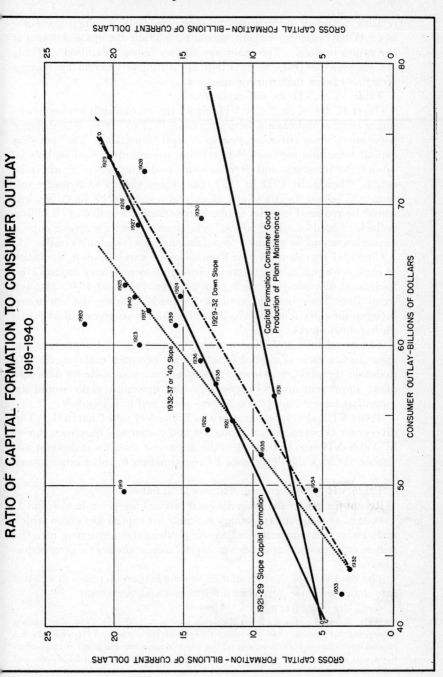

RATIO OF CAPITAL FORMATION TO CONSUMER OUTLAY

1919-1940

relative steadiness of the wage and the volatility of income is also notable. Wage rates, it is evident, do not reflect fully the ups and downs of
per capita income. The real wage *per hour* index, submitted in Table
III, suggests that real wages per hour rise during production downsurges
sometimes faster than during upsurges.

Table IV to VII are self-explanatory.

Chart II, based on Table VII, shows the relationship between consumer outlays and capital formation from 1921 to 1940. The distance
between the two curves represents capital formation. The fact that
capital formation increases [62] in relation to consumer good outlays on
production upsurges, and decreases on the downsurges is clearly indicated. Should the 1921 to 1929 relationship govern some future upsurge, 25 billion dollars worth of capital formation or its equivalent
would be required in order to obtain a consumer's outlay of 80 billion
dollars. Should the 1933 to 1937 relationship govern, a greater capital
formation would be required to obtain an equal consumer's outlay.

Chart III represents, by the location of the various points, the ratios
of capital formation (the vertical distances) to consumer outlays (the
horizontal distances) for each year between 1913 and 1940. Rough
trend lines have been superimposed which indicate the variations
between the rates of increase in the ratios during upsurges and decreases
during downsurges.

The trend line, *OH*, drawn through the year 1931 represents the
approximate ratio of capital formation to consumer outlay needed to
maintain the plant.[63] However, *no* allowance was made for desirable
plant improvements. Consequently the optimum ratio would be
somewhat higher than *OH* indicates, as stressed in Chapter V.

Table VII (a) is supplementary to Table VII and Chart III. The
divergence between capital formation and consumers' purchases shown
by Table VII is so important to the argument that it was thought advisable to check the divergence by re-estimating it, using other source
data.

Table VII (a) differs from Tabel VII as follows.

Recent figures for the gross national product are given in Column 1.

Instead of using the customary estimate for capital formation which
includes increased inventories, private residential construction, etc., the
two most important categories of capital formation were segregated as
shown.

The data verifies the fact that capital formation increases at a faster
rate than consumer purchases on upsurges and vice versa.

[62] Chapter V, pp. 144 ff.

[63] Dr. Kuznets estimates a net disinvestment of .3 billion in 1931, the smallest
divergence on record. On the assumption that the ratio of 1931—namely 8.5
capital formation to 56.3 consumer outlay—would maintain the plant at all productions within the probable range, the ratio 8.5 : 56.3 was extended forward and
backward.

The Business Cycle

1. THE DEMAND-SUPPLY RELATION IS RE-STATED IN ORDER TO CONCENTRATE UPON THE CRITICAL PHASE OF THE EQUILIBRIUM ADJUSTMENT WHICH PERTAINS TO NONPRODUCTION.

IN each field of effort as well as in the economy as a whole, various factors are continually in process of adjustment, so that a rough balance between demand and supply is always being approximated, as described in Chapter II.

The sources of change are many. Two general classes of events: (1) changes in consumer taste and (2) changes in technics, were stressed because of their inevitability and ubiquity in a free, healthy economy. An event of either kind might be reflected by an alteration in the demand, production and price of the affected goods and services.

However, changes in consumer taste are likely to be met by appropriate inter-product (i.e., structural) adjustments. Should consumers, for example, increasingly prefer wool to cotton, certain mills would be forced out of business and other mills be expanded with secondary adjustments that might reach into many communities. The adjustments could be made without affecting over-all demand or the value of the supply produced, since the increased production of woolens would probably be roughly balanced by a decreased production of cotton textiles. Consequently such events might not affect the size of the total supply, the price level, or the money issued in the process of production, nor change these over-all quantities appreciably. Since our concern is with events which affect the dimension of over-all production, changes in consumer taste require no further consideration.

Changes in the technics of production on the other hand, must be reflected by a compensatory change in one or more of the three quantities, as the formula indicates (p. 65). Consequently, the persistent advance in efficiency will continue to be the focal point of this inquiry, although it is convenient at this point to revise our statement of the over-all equilibrium adjustment so that we can continue to use the mathematical straitjacket, which is our formula. Let us, therefore, modify slightly the Chapter III version, which was concerned with the total wealth increment, ΔQ, made available by the advance in efficiency. Instead, let us segregate that fraction of the wealth increment made available each year by the advance in efficiency which is left over after adjustments such as price drops (Case I), wage increases (Case III), improvements in quality, etc. all of which release some of the wealth increment, have been accomplished. Thus, our attention can be focused on the reactions or adjustments described as Cases II and IV, which, it was indicated in the last chapter, account in large part for the so-called business cycle, and nonproduction.

This segregation which can be represented symbolically by replacing the total wealth increment made available by the advance in efficiency, by what may be called "the residual wealth increment," is not meant to reflect on the importance of the other reactions. On the contrary, it is the writer's impression that the facility with which the economy of the United States has released part of the wealth increment by raising wage rates, albeit by delayed action, postponed the nonproduction crisis of the 1930's, the first nonproduction crisis in the United States which did not bring its own correction. Had wage rates and other compensations risen less, this unprecedented crisis would, if our logic is sound, have come sooner.

Furthermore, the greater difficulties of the German and Japanese economies in disposing of their production on the home market may have been due to their lesser facility in releasing the wealth increment by this means. As a result, they may have had to devise drastic ways of voiding wealth at an earlier date than did the United States.[1] Such suppositions, however, are speculative, and the data by which they could be checked are not available.

At any moment, many adjustments are occurring simultaneously. One enterpriser, for example, who installs an improved

---

[1] The "voiding wealth" solution of the Fascist states is described on page 229.

machine maintains his price and discharges part of his working force, thereby reducing demand in respect to supply. Another enterpriser who had improved the efficiency of his operations borrows new money to hire additional men to enlarge his capacity, thereby increasing demand in respect to supply. Such opposite events to some extent cancel each other out in respect to the over-all adjustment. If we consider the various pluses and minuses, such as the above, cancelled out, an unbalance remains, which may be represented in the terms of our formula. It is this net residual unbalance which results in an upsurge or downsurge in production as described in Chapter III.

Since the adjustments such as price drops, wage increases, etc. release some of the wealth increment made available by the advance in efficiency, as described in Chapter IV, it might be asked, is there necessarily a residual wealth increment? The answer would be:

1. The discussion indicated that an efficiency advance in a field of monopolistic competition would result in making available a potential wealth increment—a potential which would not in the ordinary course of events be entirely released by a drop in price or by a rise in wages, but which would either be released by an increase in demand due to the injection of new money or would not be released at all.

2. The data (Chart I and Table IV) indicates that production has increased and the wealth increment been released *only* in years in which the money supply has appreciably increased; and has not increased, *when the money supply has not increased.* [2]

These two considerations taken in conjunction are explicable on the assumption that a residual wealth increment as defined above is to be expected in the contemporary economy, an increment which may or may not be released.

The situation may, therefore, be re-stated as follows:

The advance in efficiency makes available a wealth increment which could be produced at no increase in costs. This wealth

[2] In 1922 prices dropped augmenting the increase in demand resulting from the small money increment. In 1924 the small money increment may have been insufficient to release the residual wealth increment. In 1933 extraordinary factors were involved. The other seventeen years need no qualifications.

increment may be in part released by lower prices, in part by higher wages, reduced hours of work, increased selling costs, higher salaries, better quality, etc. As a result, only part of the wealth increment made available by the advance in efficiency would need to be released by some other means. This fraction will be called the residual wealth increment and designated by the symbol $\Delta_r Q$. The replacement of ΔQ, the total wealth increment made available annually by the advance in efficiency, by $\Delta_r Q$, the residual part of it, enables us to concentrate on the two reactions (Case II and Case IV), which, the foregoing analysis has indicated, account for nonproduction and the so-called business cycle.

2. WERE THE RESIDUAL WEALTH INCREMENTS RELEASED BY THE SPENDING OF NEW MONEY BY PRIVATE AGENCIES, CAPITAL FORMATION WOULD INCREASE IN RESPECT TO CONSUMER GOODS PRODUCTION.

In order to make our discussion easier to follow, let us briefly run through the successive steps of this final disquisition, not pausing to support or qualify several of the assumptions encountered on the way. In the appendix to this chapter, these omissions will be taken up separately.

The residual wealth increment as defined in the last section either is released by the increment of demand created by the spending of new money, Case IV, or it is not produced, in which case men are disemployed and a downsurge of production is touched off along the lines of Case II. Our initial question then is: What circumstances would induce the creation and spending of new money by private [3] agencies sufficient to release the residual increment?

It was brought out in Chapter III that private enterprisers borrow funds in addition to ordinary receipts for many reasons. However, the "*private* borrowings" which concern us because they are likely to persist for a long period or indefinitely, thereby altering [4] the dimensions of the money supply, are devoted usually

[3] Spending by public agencies which would have much the same effect is discussed in Section 5, pp. 175 ff.

[4] Borrowings, even of new money, which are made and repaid shortly, would not alter the over-all annual quantities appreciably, as was noted in Chapter III. Footnote p. 72.

to capital formation or to capital purchase. Capital formation and capital purchase are functions of profit expectancy.[5] By that is meant merely that enterprisers and inventors put more money into capital when business is or is expected to be profitable than when it is unprofitable.[6] Furthermore, the loans or "borrowings" used to promote private capital formation require the creation of new money only when the demand for money is so great that funds in addition to the money withheld from consumption are required to make up the requisite amount. Consequently, our question may be answered as follows:

Equilibrium would be maintained, the residual wealth increment released and industrial expansion enabled along the lines of Case IV, were profit expectancy such that capital formation was induced, requiring not only money withheld from consumption, but in addition *new money* [7] in quantities at least sufficient to step up demand in its spending by an increment equal to the residual wealth increment.

Since the increased demand resulting from the new money spending would pertain to all products and not only to the products of those industries in which efficiency had increased, it would not be the specific wealth increments made available by the specific efficiency advances which would be released, but *their over-all equivalent.* Thus the demand for the products of the producers who had improved the efficiency of their operations

[5] Fig. 6, p. 5, *Survey of Current Business*, Department of Commerce, March 1941, illustrates the close relationship between profit and capital expenditures. The relationship is closer than that between capital expenditures and any other factor. (Text same page.)

[6] The volume of investment may be varied regardless of the investment money on hand (i.e. withholdings) because of the elasticity of the money supply. Section 4, Chapter III.

[7] Using the spending-saving breakdown of Chapter III, pp. 78 ff., this theorem can be restated in symbols as follows: If $GE + SE = GPQ + SQP$ an unbalance such as $GE + SE < G(Q + \Delta_r Q)P + S(Q + \Delta_r Q)P$ would be corrected if profit expectancy were such that a capital formation was induced sufficient to necessitate the spending of $(SE + m)$ money, m, the *new* money being in sufficient volume to create in its spending an increment of demand $\Delta E(= \Delta_r QP)$ so that $E + \Delta E = (Q + \Delta_r Q)P$ before income was redivided between saving and spending in the subsequent period. The introduction of this income increment, ΔE would, it is evident, enable demand to command supply, thereby releasing the residual wealth increment, $\Delta_r QP$. The introduction of an increment of demand greater than the wealth increment would also release the wealth increment as will be described in Section III.

would not be increased enough to permit the retention of their former working force. However, the men released by these producers would assumably be rehired by the producers who had *not* improved the efficiency of their operations, but who would nevertheless increase production in response to the increased over-all demand.[8]

The spending of *m* new money, as was noted in Chapter III (p. 86) would enable society to build *m* dollars worth of capital. This capital formation would be in addition to the capital formation paid for in the ordinary course of events by money withheld from consumption and would require for its formation manpower in addition to the manpower currently employed.[9]

It might be asked why the additional capital would not be made available by the efficiency advance, since efficiency increases in the processes involving capital formation as well as in those involving the production of consumer goods. The answer is that the efficiency advances which occurred in the field of capital formation would have been largely released by price reductions since the price of capital (in particular construction, custom made equipment, etc.) is established for the most part by bargaining. Thus the price of capital tends to reflect such advances in efficiency as occur in the field of capital formation. The price of capital, therefore, would probably be dropped enough to permit the increment made available by the efficiency advance, or most of it, to be purchased by money withheld from consumption. As a result, capital, in addition to what might be called the available supply[10] of capital, would have to be

[8] pp. 122 ff.

[9] If $GE + SE = GQP + SQP$, the increased capital formation initiated by spending additional money would call for increased manpower if efficiency had not increased in the field of capital formation, or if the increment made available by increased efficiency were released by lower price as explained in the next paragraph.

[10] The expression 'available supply' is quite meaningless in respect to capital, as was brought out in Chapter III. At any time, additional capital can be formed, of sand and stones if other materials are lacking. Consequently, that part of the expression represented by $S(Q + \Delta_r Q)P$ is an indefinite quantity, and therefore nothing is gained by representing the reduction in price and the increase in quantity which would occur within this expression under the conditions cited.

However, were it desired to represent the total capital formation in the situation under discussion, it might be put down as $S(Q + \Delta_r Q + \Delta_{r2} Q)P_{-1}$, in which the reduction in price is assumed to neutralize $\Delta_r Q$, the wealth increment *made available by the advance in efficiency*, so that $\Delta_{r2} Q$ would be left to be produced by additional manhours and to be paid for by *m* money.

formed in order that money in addition to money withheld from consumption would be spent on its formation. Such an addition to capital [11] would *require additional manhours.*

As the promoters, technicians, vendors of materials, and workers got paid for forming the capital increment, they would receive as described in Chapter III the increment of new money and in their and their successors' spending of it create, as they spent it, an increment of demand equal, it is postulated, to the residual wealth increment. It is this secondary effect of the introduction of new money which releases the residual wealth increment.

The release of the *residual* wealth increment which pertains largely to consumer goods production for the reason given above would continue into the future,[12] because the additional spending power which accrued in the first place to the wage workers, vendors of material, promoters, etc., who received the additional wages, salaries, etc., paid out in creating the additional capital (paid for by m dollars), would accrue subsequently, as was indicated in our discussion of Case IV, to the vendors of goods and services who would be enabled to sell the supply increment [13] (produced without additional cost) without lowering prices.

Consequently, were demand increased by an increment equal to the value of the residual wealth increment, net employment in the consumer goods industries would be little [14] changed, the equivalent of the residual wealth increment would be produced and sold, and the expectations of increased profit, induced by the efficiency advances as described in Chapter IV, might be realized.[15]

Moreover, this reaction has a further feature which needs to be

[11] This addition to the capital plant need not be incorporated in our symbolic statement because the investments and capital formation "of any year is a kind of residuum cast off by the economic activities of the year and is not included in the demand-supply adjustment of the subsequent period." p. 81.

[12] That part of the wealth increment pertaining to capital formation which is released by lower prices, also continues to be released indefinitely as was indicated in our discussion of Case I. It is not included in the "residual wealth increment" by definition.

[13] Or its equivalent, as noted on p. 145.

[14] Theoretically, employment in the consumer goods industries would not be changed at all, as noted on p. 146. However, in practice, the increase in profit would usually stimulate some increase in selling, promotional and research activities and therefore some augmentation of the working force.

[15] The effect of this event on profit is reviewed in Section 3.

brought out because it bears on our central problem.   As given above, the new money would largely accrue on its first spending to the workers, promoters, material suppliers, etc., occupied with the capital formation, who would lose their jobs or sales after the work was completed unless similar operations were promoted in the subsequent period.   On its second and subsequent spending the new money would largely accrue to the vendors of goods and services and would serve to enhance enterpriser and property income (profit, interest and rent).

It appears, therefore, that the release of a wealth increment by way of new money spending on capital formation would largely increase the total of wages in its first spending and would increase the total of profit, interest and rent payments on its second and subsequent spendings.   The increase in the wage total would occur but once, that is to say, in the first spending. The increase in the profit, interest and rent totals, on the other hand, would continue until some other event intervened.

(Wages might, and to some extent, do rise, sooner or later, as has been indicated, to meet a higher marginal product resulting from an increase in efficiency.   Our analysis suggests, however, that surplus profits in monopolistic competition would tempt new going concerns bringing new capital into the field, thereby subdividing the market and holding down the marginal product.   This latter event, as will be indicated, might increase interest payments and reduce profit payment to such an extent that the marginal product and wages would be left after the efficiency advance little higher than they had been.   This reaction is further developed in Section 4.)

Since money is spent several times a year on the average,[16] enterpriser and property income would rise therefore in relation to wages, should the wealth increment be released by the spending of new money on capital formation.

This deduction is compatible with the statistical record since profit has increased in relation to production on upsurges.   Thus corporation profit which dropped below zero in recent decades each time the national income fell below 55 billion dollars, rose on each upsurge, as Table IV indicates, proportionately more than

[16] p. 92.

production. The relationship is brought out clearly by a diagram recently published in *Current Business*.[17] The figures indicate that manufacturers' net profits before sales were zero when sales dropped below 40 billion, were some 4 billion dollars or about 1/15 of sales when sales approximated 60 billion, were 8 billion or 1/10 of sales when sales were slightly above 80 billion, and rose to 14 billion dollars or nearly 1/8 of sales when sales approximated 120 billion dollars in 1942. It is evident therefore that the proportion of income which is paid out as profit, *increases* as *sales* and *income increases*.

Property income which consists largely of interest and rent also rises with production as the capital plant is expanded and additional resources are utilized. It would rise disproportionately should interest and rent rates increase with production, as occurred during the 'twenties.

Since enterpriser and property income become a larger fraction of the total income as income increases, it is evident that wages become a smaller proportion of the total, for the national income (money paid out) consists of the above three categories. Consequently, our deduction that enterprises and property income would rise in relation to wages should the wealth increment be released by the spending of new money on capital formation is substantiated by the record of those recent years in which the residual wealth increment was released by this means.

Other factors[18] are probably involved as well as the one stressed above. Also the "pure" situation which was postulated, is exceptional. In recent upsurges, total wages increased as well as profit because in practice more new money was introduced, than was needed to release the wealth increment. Consequently production and employment were increased as well as profit and interest. However, in every case, as the record indicates, enterprises and property income rose disproportionately.[18a]

[17] "How Can Business Analyze Its Markets," Louis J. Paradiso, *Survey of Current Business*, March 1945, p. 6.

[18] An increasing proportion of the net increment would probably be diverted from profits to interest as the upsurge developed. This tendency will be considered in the next section.

[18a] For further evidence of this relationship the reader might refer to an article by R. S. Tucker, "The Distribution of Income among Taxpayers in the United States." *Quarterly Journal of Economics*, Aug. 1938. p. 586.

An increase in net over-all profit (which would accrue largely to corporations and their propertied owners) and property income, when total wages are increasing at a slower rate, augments income disparity. An increase in income disparity increases the proportion of income, which is withheld from consumption. (Assumptions [19] II and III to be reviewed and qualified in the appendix to this chapter). Increased withholding requires increased capital formation to maintain equilibrium along the lines postulated.[20]

In short, were equilibrium maintained by injections of new money, withholdings would increase in respect to consumer goods spending. Consequently, capital formation would have to increase in respect to consumer goods production, for the withheld money to be invested and the balance maintained.

This conclusion, which by the way is generally accepted, is fully supported by the data. Tables VII and VIIa, indicate that *capital formation rose in respect to consumer goods production* during recent production upsurges.

It appears, therefore, that maintaining equilibrium by injecting new money *necessitates increased capital formation in respect to consumer goods production*, from year to year. Such a trend would result in an increase in the capital plant in relation to the consumer goods produced by that plant.

No difficulty would be encountered in effecting an increasing capital formation. As described in Chapter II, an increase in profit tempts newcomers to enter a field of effort and existing competitors to expand their facilities. As a result, the incentive to form capital would increase when profit increased. But the new capital would not only increase over-all efficiency [21] but

---

[19] pp. 186 ff.

[20] If $GE + SE + \Delta E = G(Q + \Delta_r Q)P + S(Q + \Delta_r Q)P$ and the equal quantities $\Delta E = \Delta_r QP$ and $GE = GQP$ are subtracted, we have $SE = SQP$. Thus, if SE increases, SQP must also if $\Delta E = \Delta_r QP$. (The probable reduction of P to P_{-1} in the expression $S(Q + \Delta_r Q)P$ would augment the requisite increase.)

[21] As will be brought out in Chapter VI the new capital is likely to be more efficient than the capital in place. Since it does not replace existing capital on an upsurge but augments it, the net increase in efficiency would probably be in line with the long trend. The expansion of the plant when excess profits are realized is facilitated by the corporation practice of withholding and investing part and sometimes all of net returns instead of distributing it as dividends. The practice is discussed by S. P. Dobrovsky in the *American Economic Review*, Sept. 1945.

would also *expand existing facilities* as was brought out in our description of monopolistic competition.[22]

Before following up this important lead in Section 4, let us pause a moment to consider more carefully what happens to profit during the upsurge.

3. DURING A PRODUCTION UPSURGE JUST SUSTAINED BY THE SPENDING OF NEW MONEY, PROFIT WOULD BE LIKELY TO INCREASE AT A DIMINISHING RATE, AND EVENTUALLY TO DECREASE.

At any moment in time, profit expectancy induces a capital formation requiring new money sufficient, more than sufficient, or insufficient to create an increment of monetary demand equal to the residual wealth increment.

The last possibility has already been considered. It would result in a deficiency of demand in respect to supply, a deficiency which would probably be translated into nonproduction.[23]

Certain aspects of the first possibility were noted in the last section. It was indicated that capital formation would have to increase in relation to consumer goods production were the wealth increment to be released year after year by increments of new money spent on private capital formation. Since private capital formation depends upon profit expectancy, an increase in its proportions would not normally occur unless profit expectancy also increased. Other factors have little bearing on its dimensions. For example, the volume of money withheld from purchasing consumer goods does not control the dimensions of capital formation.[24] Whenever withheld money exceeds the demand for money, the excess is applied to reducing the total of debt outstanding. Likewise, when withheld money falls short of the money required for capital formation, money in addition to the withheld money is created and expended. Thus withheld money does not govern capital formation despite the fact indicated in the last section that to maintain equilibrium, capital formation would have to increase as withholding increased.

It is necessary, therefore, to consider if profit expectancy may be expected to increase from year to year, were the residual

[22] p. 37.
[23] Case II, pp. 68, Chapter IV, pp. 118–122.
[24] pp. 78 and 145.

wealth increment released by increments of new money allocated to capital formation.   Such an increase would seem probable on the basis of the reaction described as Case IV [25] and recalled in the last section, which indicated that at such times as efficiency increased, the vendors of goods and services would be able to dispose of the resulting wealth increment or its equivalent without lowering their prices were new money, sufficient to increase demand by the amount of the wealth increment, created and spent on capital formation.   Profit, it was indicated, would be increased by the increment of demand resulting from the spending of the new money, less the interest on it.   Since an increase in profit would increase profit expectancy [26] which would stimulate capital formation, which would require additional money, it seemed reasonable to suppose that the operation would touch off an upsurge in production that might continue until full employment was approached.

However, Case IV, was oversimplified, in that it did not take into account certain relevant ramifications.   In order to correct this omission, it is necessary to include in our formularization money withheld from consumption, since its increase would increase overhead and diminish the increase in profit for the reason which follows.

Should the residual wealth increment made available by the efficiency advance be *just* released by new money spending, a most exceptional situation but useful as an illustration, the new money increment would vary inconsequentially from year to year because the rate of advance in over-all efficiency does not accelerate appreciably in a short time span. [27]   As a result, the demand increment which we are supposing just equals it cannot be assumed to increase from one year to another. [28]   That part of the increment which was paid out as interest, on the other hand, would increase from year to year even were the interest rate constant, because interest is paid normally on all borrowed money and new capital is formed not only on borrowed new money, but also on borrowed withheld money.   But withheld money, it was

[25] p. 88.
[26] Assumption IV, qualified in appendix to this chapter.
[27] p. 190 and footnote page 150.
[28] Assumption VI.

indicated in Section 2 [29] would increase from year to year should the residual wealth increment be released by the spending of new money. Consequently, profit would be increased from year to year by a positive quantity which would vary inconsequently, less a negative increasing quantity. In other words, profit would increase at a diminishing rate. The event would *not* reduce the demand increment,[30] but would increase the fraction issued as interest (a cost item) and decrease the fraction assigned to profit.

Consequently, at some point in time the diminishing annual increase in profit would reduce profit expectancy below the point where it was sufficient to induce the increase in capital formation needed to induce the creation of money sufficient to release the wealth increment. As a result, new money creation would thereafter be insufficient to release the residual wealth increment, men would be disemployed and demand would drop off. Presumably stock market values, which also depend in large part on profit expectancy, would have slipped into a nose dive sometime previously.

As given above, the event may seem on the metaphysical side. Actually its symptoms are as tangible to the business man as labor unrest. Salesmen first apprehend increased buyers' resistance owing to the falling off in over-all demand. Sales managers report this condition to management when enough straws indicate a changed wind. Managements direct plant superintendents to reduce inventories, thereby augmenting the reduction in demand, and call the new trend to the attention of Boards of Directors', etc. Some of the directors attempt to strengthen their position by selling stock to the public who always decide at this moment, or so it is reported, to get rich with the country. Stocks, it is said, change from strong to weak hands. At any rate, a not necessarily extraordinary event results soon after in a stock market break. The unduly drastic reduction in the price of stocks is a signal for outside investors to unload. Torrential selling follows.

[29] pp. 144 ff.

[30] See appendix to this section for a mathematical statement of this deduction. An increase in interest or other cost item augments demand just as does an increase in profit.

Loans are based on collateral. As the collateral falls in value, the loans are called in. This event reduces the supply of money which too reduces the demand for goods and investments directly and indirectly, etc.

It is not maintained that the next downsurge will follow the above pattern, based on our memory of 1929, in every detail. Many procedures have changed in the intervening years. It is however deemed probable that a reduction in profit, because the market for goods and services has been overly divided by many prosperous concerns expanding their capacity to produce and overhead per unit has been increased thereby,[30a] will again, as it has in the past, lead to an arrest of such expansion, a stock market break, a contraction of loans, a reduction in demand and a production downsurge unless steps are taken to eliminate the basic cause.

Even without stock market liquidation (which substitutes capital losses for capital gains, debt repayment for debt incurrence, money cancellation for money creation, etc.), the falling off in demand would change the reaction from industrial expansion (Case IV) to industrial contraction (Case II). Industrial contraction along the lines of Case II, as indicated in Chapter III, also includes factors which arrest and reverse its direction in time.

Furthermore, the time necessary for the diminishing increment of profit to reduce profit expectancy below the point where it induced the requisite capital formation would not, under the somewhat special circumstances cited above, be long because profit expectancy was assumed to be *just* sufficient to induce a capital formation requiring enough new money to increase demand by the residual wealth increment. (If it had been more than *just* sufficient, a greater capital formation and new money creation would have been induced.) Such a profit expectancy might be called "critical."

[30a] It might be asked why the capital formation expanded the plant instead of increasing its efficiency. Actually it would accomplish both purposes. The increased efficiency results in making available the wealth increment ΔQ. The expansion is the result of the monopolistic procedures described in Chapter II. The first process goes on all the time. The second mainly during upsurges. Compare our description with that of Gottfried Haberler, *Prosperity and Depression*, League of Nations, Geneva. Pp. 367–370 and p. 487.

However, this aspect is not directly significant because the condition represented above in which the increment of demand was assumed to be equal to the residual wealth increment would be unusual. In the ordinary course of events, the increment of demand would probably be greater than, or less than, the residual wealth increment, since nothing in the situation causes them to be equal.

There remains to consider the second possibility, the effect of a profit expectancy so great that capital formation is induced requiring the creation and spending of sufficient new money to increase demand by an increment greater than the residual wealth increment. This situation was touched upon in Chapter III, p. 89. It was decided that the resulting excess of demand over supply would probably set off a production upsurge were employment less than full.[31] Should over-all production be increased to meet the excess demand, equality would not be restored because the additional production would cause additional money to be paid out for labor and material thereby again increasing demand by a further increment. The resulting excess of demand over supply might again induce production to be increased, etc.

This possibility could be explored [32] by means of the formula. However, it would be premature to express the reaction accurately in symbolic form, because the formula does not include a further factor which influences the situation. Though there is no physical limit to the creation and spending of money which pays for the capital, and though there may be no financial limit to it, as was suggested in Chapter II, the amount of *excess capital* which

---

[31] Were $E < (Q + \Delta_r Q)P$ and were $m_1 + m_2$ money created and spent on capital formation so that the spending of m_1 resulting in demand being enhanced by the quantity $\Delta E(= \Delta_r QP)$, and the spending of m_2 resulted in demand being enhanced by the quantity ΔE_2, equality would not be restored. Instead $E + \Delta E + \Delta E_2 > (Q + \Delta_r Q)P$. Presumably production and employment would increase in response to the excess of demand over supply, which in turn would increase demand and so on. The series is cumulative as described in the text. It is important to note that the increment ΔE would result in increased enterpriser and property income and the increment ΔE_2 would result in *increased employment* (on consumer goods production as well as on capital formation). Increased employment might also enable greater profit to be realized, but only under certain conditions which will be considered in the next section.

[32] As in footnote p. 161.

the economy will in practice support *is limited.* In order to gauge the importance of this latter limitation, it will be necessary to take into account the position of production in respect to zero and full production.

By including this further factor, it will be possible to indicate why upsurges often do not continue until full production is closely approached and why the alternation of upsurges and downsurges which constitute the business cycle is not haphazard nor wholly indeterminate.

APPENDIX TO SECTION 3. THE DEDUCTIONS OF SECTION 3 IN RE-SPECT TO PROFIT DURING AN UPSURGE INDUCED BY THE SPENDING OF NEW MONEY ARE REPRESENTED IN SYMBOLIC TERMS.

Should $E = QP$ and $GE + SE = GQP + SQP$ in any year, and should the efficiency advance make available a residual wealth increment, $\Delta_r Q$, and should profit expectancy be such that sufficient new money, m, was allocated to capital formation in addition to withheld money, SE,[33] to increase demand by an increment ΔE[34] $= (\Delta_r QP)$, equality between demand and supply would be maintained, and the residual wealth increment would be released because the incorporation of both events results in the equality $E + \Delta E = (Q + \Delta_r Q)P$ for the year after the year in which both events occurred.

Splitting E into two components, C, total costs, and D, over-all net profit,[35] $C + D + \Delta E = (Q + \Delta_r Q)P$ in the year after the two events occurred. As a result, the increased supply $(Q + \Delta_r Q)P$ could be sold and profit D would be increased by the quantity ΔE, less an increase in interest. It was therefore supposed in Case IV which left interest on withheld money out of account, that:

Supply − costs (plus interest on m) = profit + ΔE (less interest on m) [36]

If interest be represented by $1/d$, since interest usually comes to a percentage or fraction of a quantity, the equation given above could be stated as:

$$\underset{\text{Supply}}{(Q + \Delta Q)P} \; - \; \underset{\text{Costs}}{\left(C + \frac{m}{d} \right)} \; = \; \underset{\text{Profits}}{D + \Delta E - \frac{m}{d}}$$

[33] Savings may be represented by $SE \pm m$ as noted. In the subsequent year, that part of income created by the spending of m which is withheld from consumption is included in the new SE. Thus SE represents money withheld from consumption before increments of money are added or subtracted as described in Chapter III.

[34] ΔE consists of the new money, m, times its velocity as described in Chapter III.

[35] As defined in Chapter III, p. 76.

[36] Footnote, p. 87.

Were the above expression the whole story $(\Delta E - m/d)$ would represent the increment of profit which would result in the above situation from the spending of m new money on capital formation.

But the situation is complicated by "withholding" a complication omitted in our provisional presentation. It is evident that withheld money will draw interest in the future just as does the new money.[37] As a result, a fuller statement would incorporate interest on withheld money, namely SE/d. Thus, the increment of interest, that is to say, the increment of overhead costs could be represented by $(SE + m)/d$,[38] and the demand-supply adjustment by:

$$
\underset{Supply}{(Q + \Delta_r Q)P} - \underset{\substack{Former \\ Cost}}{C} + \underset{\substack{Cost \\ Increment}}{\frac{SE + m}{d}} = \underset{\substack{Former \\ Profit}}{D} + \underset{\substack{Profit \\ Increment}}{\Delta E - \frac{SE + m}{d}}
$$

Evidently the release of a wealth increment along the lines of Case IV would increase:

Capital by	$SE + m$
Demand and supply by the quantity	$\Delta E = \Delta_r QP$
Profit by the quantity	$\Delta E - \dfrac{SE + m}{d}$
Overhead and costs by the quantity	$\dfrac{SE + m}{d}$

Since capital formation, which depends on profit expectancy, would have to continue to increase in relation to consumer goods production for equilibrium to be maintained [39] and since profit expectancy depends on the trend of net over-all profit,[40] it is evident that industrial expansion along these lines could be maintained only if profit was increasing. But it is also evident that the quantity, $\Delta E - (SE + m)/d$, which represents the *increase* in profit, would be a diminishing quantity. For if the first term, ΔE, which determines the dimensions of the requisite money injection, m, equalled $\Delta_r QP$ as postulated, and if $\Delta_r QP$, m, and d varied inconsequently [41] and SE increased, as maintained in the last section, the total expression would diminish. In other words, the overhead increment, $(SE + m)/d$, would increase in relation to ΔE, and the

[37] From the ethical viewpoint, interest on SE—which represents a refrainment—is justified to a greater extent than intrest on m, a creation.

[38] Such reductions in the cost of carrying capital as are effected by paying off of debt and paying up on equipment (amortization) are included in the formula as it stands. Assumption V, p. 190.

[39] Section 2, p. 150.

[40] Assumption IV, p. 188.

[41] Assumption VI, to be qualified in the appendix to this chapter, p. 190.

profit *increment* would decrease from year to year were no other factor involved. As a result, net over-all profit $D + \Delta E - (SE + m)/d$ might eventually cease to increase and start to diminish during an upsurge. (Profit would be drastically reduced on the downsurge.)

Were $\Delta E > \Delta_r QP$, this result might be postponed as noted in the text.

4. IN THE CONTEMPORARY ECONOMY, PRODUCTIONS ABOVE AND BELOW A CERTAIN PRODUCTION WOULD BE UNSTABLE. THE LIVING STANDARD DEPENDS LARGELY UPON THE LOCATION OF THIS EQUILIBRIUM PRODUCTION.

During a production upsurge, the proportion of effort allocated to capital formation increases.[42] During a downsurge, the proportion of effort allocated to capital formation decreases. In fact, when the demand for consumers goods is low and much capital equipment, as a result, is redundant, so little new capital is formed that the diminishment of the plant by way of depreciation and scrapping of equipment sometimes exceeds new capital formation. When this occurs, the over-all plant suffers a net reduction, as in the early 'thirties.[43] Thus capital formation varies under present procedures from an insignificant fraction to a high proportion of the total effort.

Early in this study,[44] it was maintained that the capital plant could be greater than the plant needed to meet the demands being made upon it. A capital formation which increased such an unbalance would therefore be excessive.

Although this deduction is indubitable, it might be maintained that such an event would be unlikely because the "roundaboutness "[45] of production can always be increased thereby increasing efficiency. Should this occur, the capital formation might contribute to the wealth or leisure of society.

[42] Section 2, p. 144, and Chart II, p. 138.
[43] Chart III.
[44] p. 15.
[45] "Roundaboutness" is used by certain economists to express an increased division of labor achieved by adding to the capital plant. A machine which accepted a steer at one end and delivered shoes, packaged meat, etc., at the other, would be an extreme example of "roundaboutness," though to an engineer it might seem like a straightforward operation. In any case, machines of this kind can be multiplied indefinitely. Thus, capital which would reduce the manhours required for operations could in theory always be formed.

In practice, as was stressed in Chapter II, excess capital is formed during production upsurges, capital which does not significantly reduce manhour input or costs.

It is not necessary to refute this contention. Although efficiency *might* always be increased by additional capital, the analysis of monopolistic competition in Chapter II indicated that additional capital often in practice does not advance over-all efficiency significantly, nor lead to the discarding of less efficient equipment. Instead, the new capital is added to the existing plant with the result that "excess capacity has become a permanent and normal characteristic of producing units engaged in monopolistic competition." [46]

Such excess capital would be formed, it was indicated, because of the tendency of newcomers to enter a field of monopolistic competition and of existing concerns to expand their facilities whenever surplus profit was being realized even though the facilities in place were quite sufficient to satisfy the effective demand. And this superfluous capital formation would not be balanced by an equivalent reduction in the capital in place because of the reluctance of competitors to leave a field of effort so long as profit was realized or even longer.

Thus a certain "actual" capital plant may be considered "optimum" for every actual scale of production although every "actual" plant, like other human constructs, can in theory be improved. Less capital than this optimum would be insufficient to permit the most efficient production of the demanded consumer goods, more capital (of the kind actually built) would not be used with effectiveness. And the carrying charge of the redundant capital would increase per unit costs.

For every consumer goods production, the capital formation (actual) just sufficient to maintain this optimum plant at peak efficiency would be economic. Let us call such a ratio of capital formation to consumer goods production the *optimum ratio*.[47] This optimum ratio would vary little from one level of production to another when production was above some low point below

[46] p. 39.

[47] "The optimum ratio" would be definite only for that form of capital called the "means of production," since the optimum quantity of public works—monuments, bridges, roads, skeleton armament plants, etc.—depends in part on other than economic considerations. For the sake of simplicity, this source of uncertainty will be disregarded for the time being. In later sections, "borrowings" in order to construct "public works" will be taken into account.

which mass production and the efficient use of certain kinds of capital equipment would be infeasible.

At full production, the capital formation of the optimum ratio as defined above would maintain the plant at peak efficiency, which we are defining to include not only replacing worn out equipment but also obsolescent equipment, that is to say, such equipment as had been rendered obsolete by a technical advance or invention. Such a capital formation would be desirable at any production level since a lesser capital formation would preclude society from realizing its economic potentialities, and a greater capital formation at full employment would curtail the production and consumption of consumer goods unnecessarily—a curtailment which might never be made up.[48]

It is evident that somewhere on the up and down surges, actual capital formation would *coincide* [49] with the optimum capital formation as defined, since actual capital formation varies from zero or less as in 1932 (when the existing plant was not maintained because obsolescence depreciation and scrapping was greater than capital formation) to the high ratios of 1929, and 1937 [50] when capital formation was excessive for the reason recalled above.[51]

Below the point of coincidence every capital formation would by definition be insufficient to maintain a capital plant capable of producing efficiently the consumer goods demanded at full production. Above this point, every "actual" capital formation would create more capital than needed to maintain the plant capable of producing efficiently the consumer goods being demanded.

In an economy such as that of the United States consisting largely of monopolistic competition and marked by *excess plant capacity*, (1) decreasing costs would be realized on production increases when the volume of capital formation was such that the capital plant would be increased by *less* than that necessary to maintain it; (2) increasing costs would be realized when the

[48] If our guess, p. 186, is accurate, the optimum capital per unit product would gradually decrease as efficiency increased.
[49] See Figure VII, p. 170 for a graphic representation of the relationship.
[50] Chart II, p. 138.
[51] p. 159.

capital plant was increased by more than was needed to maintain it at peak efficiency. The point of coincidence demarcates these two conditions because any capital formation less than the optimum would by definition fulfill condition (1), and any capital formation above the optimum would fulfill condition (2). Thus, at productions below the point of coincidence, the increase of profit as the reduction of excess capital lowered per unit costs, would favor capital formation and a production upsurge. At productions above the point of coincidence the decrease in profit as the capital plant became more and more excessive would lead, sooner or later, to a reduction in profit and profit expectancy and a downsurge in production, unless some other event intervened.[51a] Production at the point of coincidence has therefore the nature of an equilibrium, because productions above and below it are not likely to stand.

Let us, therefore, call the production at the point of coincidence which results in an optimum capital formation, the equilibrium production.[52]

[51a] John H. Hobson on *The Economics of Unemployment*, 1922, considers this event is the cause of production downsurges. However he supposed excess capital formation was the result of oversaving. (Over-withholding in our terminology.) Our analysis indicates that withholdings do not govern capital formation. Instead excess capital formation is shown to be the result of the increase in profit expectancy during upsurges in fields of monopolistic competition, when the wealth increment is released along the lines of case IV.

[52] The effect of changes in the ratio of capital formation to consumer goods production during production upsurges and downsurges could be presented in terms of the formula. Thus, the profit increment resulting from the spending of m money, namely (1) $\Delta E - (SE + m)/d$, would be positive, SE being small, when production was below the equilibrium level. (Should SE, money withheld from consumer goods spending, exceed capital formation, the excess would be applied to reducing outstanding debt and m would be a minus quantity.) However, as production rose, the increase in $(SE + m)/d$ in relation to ΔE (which equals the residual wealth increment $\Delta_r QP$ by definition), would reduce the increase in profit as noted in the last section. Thus net profit would sooner or later cease to increase and start to decrease from this cause.

However, more money, m_2, would probably be created than needed to release the wealth increment. Should this happen, demand would be increased by more than $\Delta E = \Delta_r QP$. The further increment, let us call it $\Delta_2 E$, which results from spending m_2 money, would induce a production increase $\Delta_2 QP$ when production was short of full. Money would be issued in the process of producing $\Delta_2 QP$. ($\Delta_2 QP$ unlike $\Delta_r QP$ is not made available by the advance in efficiency). This money would be divided between costs and profit. Thus, in the subsequent period, the effect of the spending of m_2 could be represented by (2) $\Delta E_2 = \Delta C + \Delta D = \Delta_2 QP$.

This expression also is affected by *the location of production*. When production is below the equilibrium production, profit would be increased disproportionately by

The equilibrium production, then, is *that actual production at which capital formation is just sufficient to maintain the optimum (actual) plant at a high efficiency level.*[53]

As was brought out in earlier chapters, production tends to move in more or less sustained up and down surges owing to the cumulative nature of both movements. These movements range above and below the equilibrium production as defined above. Downsurges, despite their cumulative tendency are likely to be arrested not far below the equilibrium production, partly because enterprisers, even during depressions, have in recent periods been quick to promote capital formations which promised profit, partly because society actively intervenes, at any rate in recent periods, to neutralize deflationary forces, especially when they become

the spending of m_2 because an increase in production (when less capital was being formed than was needed to maintain the plant) would enable the existing plant to be used more efficiently. When production was above the equilibrium production, costs would be increased disproportionately because an increase in production (when more capital was being formed than needed to maintain the plant) would augment the proportion of excess capital and would result in the total plant being used less efficiently.

The net effect of the creation and spending of $m_1 + m_2$ money would therefore be the combination or addition of the two effects (1) and (2) represented above.

An upsurge would not be likely to reverse its direction at the equilibrium production level because production might not turn downward until net profit started to decrease. Although the *increase* in profit would start to diminish at about the equilibrium production unless m_2 were increased from year to year, because of the combined effect of the two events noted above, net profit as noted in the last section might increase, although at a diminishing rate, for some time longer. In fact, if new money creation and spending $(m + m_2)$ were increased by unusual circumstances as during the war years, production and profit might continue to rise until full employment was attained.

At other times, new money creation would probably not be sufficient to create a demand increment greater than or equal to the residual wealth increment for long after the equilibrium production was passed because the rise in overhead costs as the market was increasingly subdivided would be likely fairly soon to dampen speculative enthusiasm.

Fundamentally, the production at which the movement reversed itself and the equilibrium production *do not coincide* because the two productions *are subject* to different and to some extent *independent factors*. The first is established by financial relationships expressed in terms of money. The second by a ratio between two physical quantities. The physical quantities, though basic, could and often are submerged for a time by financial events. Thus, should money be created for war purposes, speculation, public works, new industries, etc., the underlying physical unbalance might as suggested above be concealed for a time. The more important of these possibilities are taken up in Section 5.

[53] This definition includes as was noted such formations as are needed to incorporate technical advances. Its actual calculation would have to take into account wage rates and other relevant cost factors.

dangerously acute, by artificially sustaining wages, spending money on public works, relief, and other measures. Upsurges, on the other hand, are likely to rise far above the equilibrium production, partly because enterprisers during the optimism and easy credit of an upsurge can often finance capital formations which are not justified on the basis of cold calculations, partly because the authorities sometimes foster such movements.[54]

Since a movement in either direction would meet increased resistance, the farther it traveled from the point or location of the equilibrium production (the opposing forces just described increasing with the distance),[55] neither movement is likely to continue indefinitely. In fact, recent peacetime upsurges, such as those ending in 1929 and 1937, have been arrested before full production was attained. This event is due to the probability that the gap between the equilibrium production and full production has become so wide that the cumulative force of the upsurge is negated by the deflationary effect of increasing costs [56] before the physical limit set by the supply of manpower is reached. Thus, if Dr. Kuznets' estimate is valid, that a capital formation of 8.8 billion dollars was sufficient in 1931 to maintain the plant, the equilibrium production of that year would have approximated 65 (or perhaps 75 billion dollars more or less if allowance is made for desirable capital improvements).[57] Such a production was some 60 or 70 per cent only, of full production. An upsurge, therefore, would in that period have had to surpass

[54] The economy could not stabilize itself at the equilibrium production unless the wealth increment was released by price reductions (case I) because other releases, for example by way of money injections (case IV), would as we have seen increase the proportion of capital formation and the volume of production. Since an economy dominated by monopolistic competition cannot release the wealth increment by way of price decreases or wage increases for the reasons brought out in Chapters II and IV, these possibilities are only of theoretical interest. However production could linger in the area between the level at which capital sufficient to sustain the existing low consumer good production was formed, and the higher lever at which capital sufficient to support the existing plant was formed, as will be indicated in the appendix, p. 172. The history of the recent depression seems to support these deductions.

[55] Should the upward movement approach full employment, profits would be curtailed by the lesser efficiency of the *last quota* of *manpower*, by certain industries, in particular the extractive industries, surpassing their optimum operating level, etc., which events would supplement the factors stressed in the text.

[56] Footnote p. 161.

[57] Table VII, p. 136, and Chart 3, p. 139, line *OH*.

the equilibrium production by nearly 60 per cent in order to approach the level of full production.

Furthermore, the equilibrium production is likely to become a still smaller fraction of full production as time goes on, although the equilibrium production, like full production, increases in time. The gap between full production and the equilibrium production tends to increase, for the following reason.

As efficiency advances, the production of full production is increased. The advance in efficiency would, however, not alter appreciably the optimum capital formation [58] nor the ratios which prevail between actual capital formation and actual consumer goods production at each level of production, since these ratios are determined by factors not directly affected by the degree of efficiency. The release of a wealth increment made available by the efficiency advance, would, therefore, *not affect* the location of the equilibrium production in relation to zero, though it would widen the gap between the equilibrium production and full production because the latter quantity *would have increased* with the increase in efficiency.[59]

However, the above statement evidently is not complete. If it were, the equilibrium production would be permanently established for all time. Since the standard of living is a function of the equilibrium production, as will be shown shortly, and since the standard of living has risen steadily in the United States,[60] such a conclusion would not be in accord with the facts.

Changes in the location of the equilibrium production may be accounted for as follows. The actual ratio of capital formation to consumer goods production is determined, if our analysis is accurate, largely by the way the economy reacts to an advance in efficiency.[61] It might be plotted, as in Chart III, for any pro-

[58] Assumption I, p. 185.

[59] Full production would increase by ΔQP as illustrated by Figure VII, p. 170.

[60] Table II, p. 132.

[61] Should the economy react along the lines of Case 1, the ratio would not change as production increased; should the wealth increment be released along the lines of Case III, income disparity would be reduced and the ratio would fall; should, however, the wealth increment be released largely by increments of new money spent on capital formation, as occurs in monopolistic competition when wages and prices are stable, the ratio of capital formation to consumer goods production would rise rapidly. As noted in our discussion of the residual wealth increment in Section 1, the proportions of the wealth increment released along the several lines vary.

duction upsurge. But the ratios of the upsurge would not be followed on the subsequent downsurge. On the contrary, capital formation would be curtailed on the downsurge, our data suggests,[62] more drastically than it had been increased on the upsurge. Consequently, the location of the equilibrium production would end up higher (farther from zero production) after an upsurge and a downsurge than the position from which it had started.[63] Thus, the movement known as the business cycle would raise the equilibrium production in respect to zero. Whenever the equilibrium production advanced at a slower rate than full production, the gap would widen. The widening of this gap accounts for the increasing extent of nonproduction and unemployment.

Production, consumption, and the living standard depend on the location of the equilibrium production, even though the equilibrium production is but touched in passing on the upward and downward surges. Thus, were the equilibrium production close to the level of full production, there would be little amplitude for the cyclic swings and the resulting nonproduction of wealth, since the downsurges do not surpass the equilibrium production by very much. The wider the gap between the equilibrium production and full production, the wider would be the cyclic swings and the greater would be the nonproduction of wealth. (And so accustomed have people in general become to this seesaw motion, which deprives them for no physical reason of goods and services required for living and sometimes for life, that the irrationality of nonproduction, when additional goods and services are sorely needed and human and natural resources are available, is for the most part overlooked.) The dependence of the living standard upon the location of the equilibrium production is also indicated by the behavior of the marginal product during a production cycle. As noted in Chapter I, in a competitive economy, the wage rate tends to

[62] Table VII, illustrated by Charts 2 and 3, pp. 138 and 139.

[63] Figure VII, p. 170, indicates that a decrease in the proportion of capital formation on a downsurge (which could be shown by a line more horizontal than *EH* starting from any point on *EH* somewhat short of full production) would cut the line of plant maintenance higher up on the scale of production, and thereby raise the point of coincidence and increase the equilibrium production.

equal the marginal product of labor and surplus profits tend to disappear.[64] The marginal product of labor, like the average product of labor, is reduced by a rise in overhead cost per unit product and vice versa. As indicated above, overhead costs decrease at productions below the equilibrium production because the plant decreases in relation to production, and overhead costs increase at productions above the equilibrium production because the plant increases in relation to production. Consequently, the tendency of the marginal product of labor and the wage rate to rise with the increase in efficiency is augmented at productions below the equilibrium production by the fall in overhead costs and counteracted at productions above the equilibrium production by the increase in overhead costs.

Thus at some production level [65] on an upsurge, the increase in overhead costs per unit due to excess capital, described in Section 3, would equate the decrease in operating costs per unit due to the efficiency advance, with the result that the marginal product would thereafter diminish. Thus, the paradox of labor asking for more pay because an industry has become more efficient, and the employers refusing more pay because their operations were being conducted at less profit, is resolved by the above analysis which indicates how efficiency might increase without the increase resulting in greater profits or permitting higher wages.

The interrelationships described above fill in our explanation of nonproduction, since they indicate that:

1. The increased amplitude of the business cycle measured in terms of physical production is the result of the widening of the gap between the equilibrium production and full production.

2. Chronic nonproduction is the result of the gap between the

---

[64] p. 9. Surplus profit was defined as profit above that minimum return necessary to keep the enterpriser in business. This minimum would be the return the enterpriser would earn as a wage or salary worker if he gave up his business. Thus, the minimum profit would tend to approach the maximum (the marginal product) which the wage would tend to approach. This relationship, however, is mainly of theoretical interest. In practice, many profiteers, in particular shareholders of industrial concerns, have to content themselves with much less than this minimum. In fact, many if not most stocks pay no dividends at all. And many farmers, shopkeepers, etc., earn for long periods less than their hired hands. Also, the wage earners hired by going concerns operating in the red, earn more than the marginal product of their labor. Thus, the presumptive limits are often exceeded.

[65] This level would probably be above the equilibrium production.

equilibrium production and full production becoming so wide that upsurges in production, unless augmented by events to be reviewed in the next section, fail in peacetimes to attain the limit of production set by the physical factors. Consequently, a residue of nonproduction and unemployment persists, even at the peaks of the peacetime cycle, as in 1929 and 1937.

3. Living standards vary in economies of comparable skills and resources, in part because the equilibrium production is higher or lower on the scale of production in certain economies than in others. Thus, the relatively high location of the equilibrium production in the United States has permitted a greater wealth production per individual than that of other comparable economies in which the equilibrium production falls lower down the scale of production.

4. The presumptive "indeterminism" noted on p. 128 has been qualified. The direction of the business cycle, our discussion has indicated, is subject to at least two sets of forces. In the first place, a movement in either direction tends to be cumulative. If no opposing forces intervened, the movements might continue until the high limit set by full production or the low limit set by society's endurance were approached. However, after the upsurge or downsurge has passed the equilibrium production level, the factors described above intervene and eventually reverse the direction of the movement. Because of this situation, pump priming (deficit spending) is likely to be an effective way to initiate an upsurge when production is below the equilibrium production level, as in 1933; and its opposite, money cancellation by the calling in of loans or other event, is likely to be an effective way to initiate a downsurge when production is above the equilibrium production level as in 1929. Furthermore, when production is above this level, as in 1937, an arrest or diminution of pump priming or even a reduction in bank reserves is likely to lead to a reversal of the trend as was exemplified by the events of that year.

5. Most important of all, the relations represented by the formula have been given a footing in the physical world. Our statement of the equilibrium adjustment was presented by necessity in monetary terms since dollar value constitutes the common

denominator for all forms of wealth and effort. Thus, the disequilibria were also given in terms of monetary value although some of the quantities represented physical facts. But monetary relations are subject to arbitrary manipulation since values [66] do not exist in the physical world. As a result, the unbalances which were revealed, could be corrected insofar as logic and mathematics are involved, by purely monetary or financial measures. For example, should the demand increment during an upsurge be exceeded by the overhead cost increment, and the profit increment as a result become negative, the condition could be changed by an additional injection of new money,[67] thereby inhibiting the diminishment of profit and its disastrous after effects. However, a purely financial corrective, such as the above, though feasible under certain conditions, as will be described in the next section, *would be undesirable* because the indefinite creation and spending of money would result in unneeded capital or unwanted public works or other products, and in the loss to society of the desired forms of wealth that could be provided by the diverted labor and capital. Furthermore, such financial measures would be effective only so long as confidence in the buying power of money was maintained. Thus, the formula as presented omitted an essential factor, which left our statement incomplete, thereby obscuring important features of the problem which would need to be taken into account in order to effect a satisfactory resolution.

By introducing the relationship between physical capital and physical production, a relationship which underlies and affects the financial phenomena represented by the formula, though indirectly and with some leeway in time, the omission has been largely remedied. Proposed corrective adjustments, even though certain of them probably should be of a financial character for the sake of convenience, could be checked by reference to the capital production relationship. Should they leave untouched the tendency of capital to increase proportionately more than production, the measures would sooner or later prove unavailing,

[66] As defined, p. ix.

[67] Should $\Delta E - (SE + m)/d$ be negative, the spending of enough additional new money would increase ΔE and m and make the expression positive.

perhaps disastrously so. Should, however, the proposed adjustments inhibit the basic physical unbalance described in this section, they would, were other aspects in order, promise relief.

6. Finally, we have related monopolistic competition to the over-all equilibrium, the two economic procedures scrutinized in this study. It is true the discussion in Chapters III and IV brought out the fact that neither price reductions nor wage increases would be likely to release all the wealth increment in an economy of monopolistic competition, thereby indicating one way in which the procedures of monopolistic competition affected the over-all adjustment. However, this effect would not preclude full production since new money sufficient to release the residual wealth increment might be created and spent.[68] The further fact that capital in monopolistic competition tends to increase in relation to production regardless of the need for additional capital, were the wealth increment released by new money spending, and that this tendency results in an *unbalanced* situation, not only accounts for the business cycle and nonproduction as described above, but also *puts responsibility* for *nonproduction directly* upon that *aspect* of *monopolistic competition* which *induces excess capital formation.*

It therefore seems permissible to conclude (a) that measures which did not inhibit excess capital formation would fail to achieve "capacity production" even though such measures might, as in prewar Germany, induce,[69] at least for a while, a balanced demand-supply adjustment at full employment; (b) that measures which equated demand and supply at a desirable level of employment and also *inhibited excess capital formation* would achieve capacity production and solve the problem with which this study has been concerned.

APPENDIX TO SECTION 4.   THE RELATIONSHIP DESCRIBED IN SECTION 4 IS REPRESENTED GRAPHICALLY.

A simple diagram will illustrate the relationship between the scale of production and the cyclic movement under scrutiny. Let us suppose that the vertical distances between the line OS and the x-axis on Figure

[68] p. 175.
[69] pp. 172 and 177.

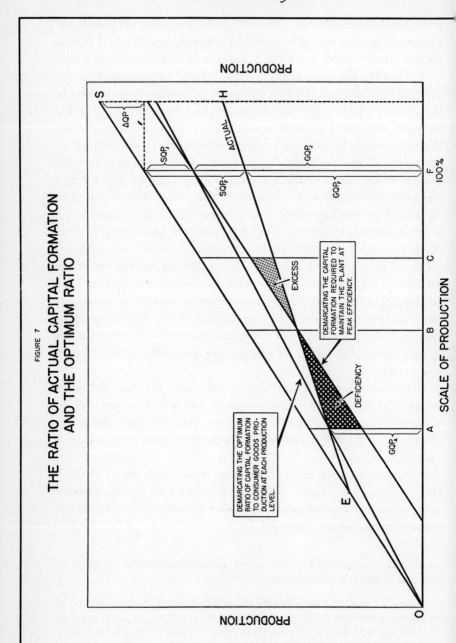

FIGURE 7

THE RATIO OF ACTUAL CAPITAL FORMATION
AND THE OPTIMUM RATIO

DEMARCATING THE OPTIMUM RATIO OF CAPITAL FORMATION TO CONSUMER GOODS PRODUCTION AT EACH PRODUCTION LEVEL.

DEMARCATING THE CAPITAL FORMATION REQUIRED TO MAINTAIN THE PLANT AT PEAK EFFICIENCY.

EXCESS

DEFICIENCY

SCALE OF PRODUCTION

PRODUCTION

PRODUCTION

VII [70] represent production. Then every vertical distance between zero and full production would represent a particular production, and its location on the scale of production would be shown by the point at which it cut the *x*-axis.

Productions, such as *A*, *B*, *C* and *F* (which latter represents full production) may be divided between capital formation *SQP*, and consumer goods production *GQP*. Let us draw the line *EH* to represent the actual division between capital formation and consumer goods production which occurs during a production upsurge. As deduced logically and proved statistically (Chart 2, page 138), capital formation increases in relation to consumer goods production, when production increases. Since *SQP/GQP* increases as production increases from *E* [71] to full, line *EH* satisfies this condition.

(Because the ratio of *SQP* to *GQP* differs in each actual upsurge and downsurge, as shown on Chart 3, [72] nothing would be gained by plotting *EH* from the data of a particular up or down surge.)

Let us draw another line to represent the optimum division between capital formation and consumer goods production. For reasons noted in Section 4, the ratio of these quantities would be constant, that is to say, would vary little when production was above some low point below which mass production would be infeasible. The line therefore must start from zero (although its lowest segment has no validity) since only a straight line starting from zero divides a triangle so that the segments of the divided side maintain a constant ratio.

Finally, let us draw a line parallel to the line *OS* limiting production, and passing through the intersection of the line of the optimum ratio and the vertical full production line. The distance (a constant quantity) between this line and the line *OS* limiting production, represents then the capital formation which would maintain the optimum plant (the plant best suited for full production) at peak efficiency. This line intersects *EH* at production *B*. *Actual* capital formation therefore would be optimum only at production *B*.

At any production below *B* the capital plant would run down since capital formation would be insufficient to maintain the plant. As the plant diminished, the units which remained would acquire larger shares of whatever market existed. This condition permits more efficient utilization. As a result, losses would be reduced and profits increased. Sooner or later new promotions, plants expansions, etc. would be initiated.

It is relevant to note that production *A*, at which *EH* intersects the line demarcating the optimum ratio, lies below production *B*. At pro-

[70] p. 170.
[71] Net capital formation becomes negative at some low production because of plant depreciation exceeding capital formation.
[72] p. 139.

duction A, capital formation would be insufficient to maintain a plant capable of producing efficiently the small quantity of goods and services being demanded. Although this point may be surpassed in downsurges as in 1932, production is unlikely to stay long below A. Production, however, might linger between A and B for a period since the capital formation in this area would maintain the plant required for the existing demand.[73] However, as time went on, an invention, election or other event would be increasingly likely to touch off an upsurge since the capital plant would be gradually whittled away by scrapping and decay should production linger in this area.

It is probable therefore that a downsurge unaffected by incidental events would proceed until A was surpassed. Below A the stage would gradually be set for an upsurge as noted above. The upsurge when it came would be likely sooner or latter to surpass B since depreciation would not be offset by new construction until the point was passed.

At productions above B, excess capacity would increase, thereby setting the stage for the next downsurge.

The diagram also illustrates the discrepancy between full production and capacity production noted in Chapter I. It is evident that *any* combination of consumer goods production and capital formation running through F would constitute full production in the sense that no more could be produced without an increase in efficiency since every available man would be employed.

Capacity production, on the other hand, would by definition be $SQP_J + GQP_J$, neither more nor less. Only this particular production would maximize satisfactions in a free economy over a period of time.[74] Thus, full production might be attained by producing anything. Capacity production, however, predicates, as defined, a maximum production of consumer desired wealth. Munitions, pyramids, etc. presumably would not fall under this category, at any rate in the United States of this century.

[73] No definite probabilities can be hazarded for movements between A and B owing to the relative importance of incidental factors in this area. However, below A and above B the physical relations under discussion would quickly make themselves felt unless neutralized by deliberate compensatory money creation and spending, or other events along the lines discussed in the next section.

At production above B, capital formation would be in excess of that formation needed to maintain the plant at peak efficiency. As a result, the market would be divided and overhead costs increase. Sooner or later profit expectancy would fail to induce the spending of the requisite quantity of new money and the movement would be reversed. Consequently production B constitutes the equilibrium production were the lines as drawn.

[74] A greater consumer goods production would increase satisfactions momentarily to be paid for later when the neglected plant would fail to maintain the standard of living.

Furthermore, the diagram illustrates the fact suggested by the statistical analysis of the *NSPPC* that the living standard of the population would be unnecessarily low even at full production should the equilibrium production fall below full or 100 per cent production. Thus, should the equilibrium production fall at B, consumer goods production would presumably range from below GQP_a to about, or just below GQP_f (disregarding the extension which represents ΔQP). Should, however, the equilibrium production fall at F, consumer goods production would approximate GQP_j, a quantity greater than even the maximum consumer goods production GQP_f, were the equilibrium production at B. In other words, should the equilibrium production fall at full production, *full production and capacity production would coincide*.

From this condition, it follows that in order to maximize satisfactions, it would not be enough to approximate full production, even were this possible without resorting to the various devices utilized for voiding wealth. To maximize satisfactions, it would be necessary to *approximate capacity production*.

SECTION 5. THE EFFECT OF SPENDING CREATED MONEY ON NEW INDUSTRIES, PUBLIC WORKS, EXISTING EQUITIES OR CHARITY, IS CONSIDERED AS WELL AS THE POSSIBILITY OF A RISE IN THE PRICE LEVEL.

Before closing our analysis and drawing such conclusions as seem warranted, it is necessary to consider the effect on the demand-supply adjustment of certain possibilities which were slighted in passing but need to be included in order to fill out the statement. Also, a number of obscurities remain, which have not as yet been integrated with the central discussion. This section, therefore, will be devoted to tying up loose strands.

Withheld money and new money, as was noted in Chapter III [75] are spent in other ways than those considered in the foregoing pages. For example, new money is sometimes allocated to the promotion of new industries, to the formation of noncompeting forms of capital, to the purchase of existing assets and to public charity (relief, etc.), as well as to the improvement and expansion of the existing plant, the allocation on which our discussion has centered. Let us consider the effect of these possibilities.

[75] pp. 78 ff.

The promotion of new industries might serve to postpone the reversing of a production upsurge.

When new industries are promoted with part of the investment funds, the capital plant available for the production of the goods and services formerly demanded is not increased. Nevertheless, the market for the products of the existing plant is encroached upon. Instead of the new producers competing directly for the market with goods similar to that of other concerns, they compete indirectly by means of dissimilar goods, but just as effectively and often more effectively. However, the promotion of new industries, like other promotions, increases demand by causing money to be paid out in the process of construction, promotion, production, etc. Thus the promotion of new industries does not necessarily effect the demand-supply adjustment, since both demand and supply are increased thereby.

Nevertheless, the promotion of new industries differs from other promotions in certain respects. The development of new industries is likely to take more time and more man-hour input before the industries became active producers of goods for sale than does the expansion of existing industries. And new industries are not able to satisfy the additional demand they create until they are ready to put goods on the market. Thus the market of the existing going concerns is likely to be increased by an increase of demand without a concomitant increase of supply for a longer period of time than is the case when the capacity of existing industries is expanded.

Even more important than this delay is the fact that the capital formed to equip a new industry would not be excess capital of the kind discussed in Chapter II, which increases the capital plant in respect to existing consumer goods production. A new industry creates new wants as well as the capacity to satisfy them. Thus, capital formed to equip a new industry does not contribute to the widening of the gap between the equilibrium production and full production. For these reasons, the promotion of new industries might delay the onset of that critical stage in profit expectancy which results from disproportionate capital formation and the dividing up of the market into smaller and smaller segments. As a result, the onset of diminishing returns and the arrest of an upward surge in production tends to be later, when many or large new industries are promoted during an upsurge, than when the new promotions involve only such industries as are already in the field.

The formation of capital for public purposes does not imperil profits or incur the other dangers inherent in excess private capital formation.

Money is allocated to non-competing forms of capital, such as roads, bridges, libraries, monuments, armaments, and to relief and other charities. Money for such purposes is obtained in large part by taxation and borrowing.

Taxation is a method of transferring purchasing power. It does not in itself create purchasing power. Consequently, it has no direct effect on the over-all equilibrium adjustment, though it may affect the distribution of income and thereby the propensity to consume. When the receipts from taxation are insufficient to cover the projected works, the additional sum needed is usually borrowed from the banks or directly from the public by means of bond issues. In so doing, the available funds, that is to say, withheld money is drawn upon and spent before the creation of new money is resorted to. Since spending withheld money does not alter effective demand, public works and charities accomplished with withheld money, as well as with tax receipts, have no direct effect on the over-all equilibrium adjustment, that is to say, on the balance of supply and demand. Like the private investment of withheld money the public investment of withheld money on monument, armaments, relief, etc., merely transfers buying power from the original recipients to the men hired to construct the public works and to the vendors (and to their working force) of the supplies which are utilized in the public works; or to the receivers of relief, if the money is handed out directly. Consequently, our concern is only with public works, relief, etc., undertaken with funds *in excess* of the funds withdrawn from current income by way of *taxation* or *borrowings* from income.

The spending of new money on public works, relief, etc., increases demand just as the spending of new money on private works increases demand. Insofar as the mathematical relations are involved, the two procedures are identical. Nevertheless, spending new money on public works needs to be distinguished from the spending of new money on private capital formation for at least three reasons:

(a) Private capital formation is a function of profit expectancy. Consequently, private capital formation is arrested, as has been described, when the rise in costs due to the increase in the carrying charges of the increasing capital plant, or other reason, reduces profit and profit expectancy below the point at which the requisite capital formation is induced. Public spending is not a function of profit expectancy. Consequently, the release of the residual wealth increment by means of new money injections spent on public works, etc., need not be halted by a fall in profit expectancy.

(b) Spending money on armaments, monuments, public works, relief, etc. does not increase plant capacity. Consequently, the ratio between the production of consumer goods and services and the capital plant used to produce them, is not disturbed by the allocation of money and effort to these purposes. Any proportion of effort therefore can be allocated to public works of this character without subdividing the market of those engaged in production for sale. (Obviously, if public funds were used to increase the productive plant, as for example when public funds are used to construct hydro-electric stations, this observation does not hold good).

(c) Spending money on armaments, monuments, public works, relief, etc. increases overhead costs, just as spending money on excess private capital increases overhead costs. In the former case, the increased costs which consist of interest on the money borrowed, are collected by taxation; in the latter case, these additional costs are collected by selling goods for more than the cost plus profit of the most efficient scale of production.[76]

In both cases, the public, as it is said, foots the bill.

However, when public works, etc., are constructed by borrowing new money and spending it, (1) the carrying cost of the debt is likely to be less than in the case of private works, since the security is greater.[77] As a result, the carrying cost of public works, etc., would usually be less per dollar spent than the carrying cost

[76] p. 46.
[77] Taxation is usually a more secure source of returns than commerce.

of an equivalent private capital formation; (2) the social authorities can collect the carrying cost from the larger income recipients by means of graduated income and inheritance taxes, thereby inhibiting the increase in income disparity which usually results when excess capital is formed under private auspices; (3) the social authorities, by manipulating the money supply, could decrease the interest rate on its debt as the total of its debt increased,[78] thereby reducing the increase or even inhibiting an increase in overhead cost; (4) the social authorities could utilize new money for meeting its debt (since its borrowing capacity is not a function of profit expectancy) thereby enabling society to spend money on public works, etc., indefinitely, or rather up to the limit set by the ability of society to produce goods and services to meet the increased demand. (So long as goods are produced to meet the effective demand, inflation does not result.)[79]

It appears, therefore, that public spending of newly created money differs from private spending in that no factors inherent in the procedure necessarily arrest the upward movement initiated by the spending short of full production.

This supposition, though at variance with general opinion, would seem supported by the prewar experience of the German, Japanese and possibly Italian economies. Although all three spent more money on public works, war, etc., than it was possible to collect from themselves by taxation and voluntary withholding, neither inflation nor bankruptcy resulted.[80]

It seems therefore that the wealth increments made available by the advance in efficiency might be released and unemployment eliminated or reduced by the social authorities allocating new money to public works and charity without incurring the disequilibria or being halted by the limitations [81] inherent in private capital formation on borrowed money.

[78] Such a decrease may be noted in the United States in the early 1930's.

[79] Inflation is considered on p. 180.

[80] The foreign trade difficulties of these economies would seem to have been due to their inability to produce as much value for sale abroad as the value they desired to import. This difficulty has little to do with the practice of internal deficit spending under discussion.

[81] Deficit spending in the 1930's did not eliminate unemployment in the United States, presumably because the deficit spending of the government was on too small a scale. The deficit spending of the 1940's was on a larger scale and eliminated unemployment with something to spare—the so-called inflationary gap.

On the other hand, releasing the wealth increments and maintaining employment by using new money for armaments, monuments, relief, or even public works of a wealth-creating character (such as reforestation, etc.) would hardly seem likely to maximize satisfactions, in the United States [82] and consequently cannot be considered a desirable solution of the problem. It seems however to be a feasible solution and will be referred to in a later chapter as Solution II.

The allocation of new money to the purchase of capital assets would increase profit and profit expectancy.

Withheld money is allocated to the purchase of capital assets as well as to capital formation. Since the spending of withheld money is balanced by an equal refrainment from spending, the utilization of withheld money for the purchase of capital assets has no effect on the demand-supply adjustment. The utilization of new money however is not balanced by an equal refrainment. As stressed previously, were enough new money devoted to capital formation, private or public, non-production would be decreased, and unemployment reduced. Were the new money used to purchase capital assets, the effect would be to raise the price of these assets since the supply of existing assets is fixed by definition.[82a]

An increase in the price of the existing capital plant enhances its value and thereby the wealth of the owners, at least on paper. Such increments of wealth are commonly called capital gains and constitute a variety of profit. The dimensions of this profit would be established by the increment of increased value less its cost of production.

But the production cost would be little since the broker's fee and transaction taxes would be the only operating costs involved. Consequently, profit in the form of capital gains would be augmented by nearly the total of the new money. Such a utilization of new money would also enhance profit expectancy, since an

[82] A philosophy of faith was devised and inculcated by the Fascists, Nazis, Japanese and others, which put the values of national aggrandizement above those of individual development. Since values are subjective, true devotees of this faith doubtless obtain greater satisfaction from national conquest than from the freedom deriving from a higher standard of living, thereby compelling us to submit this qualification.

[82a] p. 79.

increase in the value of capital assets augments profit expectancy nearly as effectively as the realization of increased profits from the production and sale of goods or services.

On the other hand, such a transaction would not contribute directly to consumer demand by way of increased wages, since the only cost of production would be brokers' fees, transaction taxes, etc., as noted above, and the interest on the new money. [83] It appears, therefore, that in certain circumstances, this type of transaction, which is signified by a rising stock market, might postpone the arrest and reversal of an upsurge by delaying the reduction in profit expectancy that otherwise would ensue for the reasons cited in Section III.

It does not seem necessary to delve further into these somewhat elusive relations, since our purpose in touching upon them at all was merely to indicate that the profit increment resulting from a new money injection equal to or in excess of that needed to release the residual wealth increment might be smaller or larger, or even of a different sign than it would be if the various more or less arbitrary factors, such as the promotion of new industries, social policy, speculation, manipulation, publicity, government favor, ill favor, etc., did not interfere at times with the more fundamental economic factors.

Thus the fact that withheld and new money may be apportioned variously among numerous possible outlets, increases the uncertainty in respect to the duration of a production upsurge. All that can safely be concluded is that the creation and spending of new money in excess of the quantity needed to release the residual wealth increment results in an excess of demand over supply. Should this excess be translated in whole or in part into increased production, an upsurge in production would result.

[83] The speculator who increases his holdings at the broker's by borrowing money has to pay interest on this money, which counts in the total economy's balance sheet as a cost item. Thus, interest on a marginal account is part of total interest and must, like taxes, be included in an estimate of the overhead costs of production. In our representation, it is incorporated in $(SE + m)/d$, since this expression represents the interest on such new capital formations and purchases of the year as are effected by withheld and created money.

The possibility of a price rise at some point in a production upsurge also increases the uncertainty in respect to the duration of an upsurge.

A further source of uncertainty needs to be touched upon. Reasons were submitted which indicated [85] that the increment of excess demand resulting from the spending of new money in excess of the residual wealth increment would be translated "largely" into increased production when employment was less than full. But a fraction of the excess demand might be deflected into a rise in commodity prices. It is necessary, therefore, to consider what bearing this possibility has upon the relationship under scrutiny.

Let us suppose, as in the theoretical cases reviewed in Chapter III, that the sole reaction to an excess of demand was higher prices. It is evident that if prices were raised so that the value of the supply was increased by the full amount of the excess of demand, equality would be reestablished. Furthermore, the price rise would permit the realization of an increment of profit equal to the demand increment less a small increase in interest since costs would be increased only by the interest on the new money. [85]

Apparently a new equation would be established at the higher price level. But in this case the profit increment, unlike the profit increment dealt with previously would *not* be balanced by a wealth increment made available by increased efficiency, or by increased production. The profit increment would have been made available by raising the price and thereby reducing the quantity of wealth which recipients of fixed money incomes could buy.

[84] The situation of a field of monopolistic competition in which demand exceeded supply was considered on pp. 122 ff.

[85] If $E < (Q + \Delta_r Q)P$ and new money $m_1 + m_2$ is spent in amount greater than that needed to release the residual wealth increment so that $E + \Delta E + \Delta E_2 > (Q + \Delta_r Q)P$ and we subtract the equal quantities $\Delta E = \Delta_r QP$, we obtain $E + \Delta E_2 > QP$.

If E be divided into costs, C, and profits, D, and price P is raised enough to restore equality so that $C + D + \Delta E_2 = QP_2$, then

Supply less costs = Former profit plus additional profit

$$QP_2 - C = D + \Delta E_2$$

except for the increase in interest omitted from the symbolic representation.

The event is known as inflation. It is cumulative if unchecked, for the reason which follows:

Inflation not only increases income disparity, by increasing the share of the enterpriser at the expense of the wage workers, but also (unlike the injection of new money allocated to wealth production) lowers the buying power of the wage worker and of those property owners whose receipts are fixed by contract for periods of time. With the rich getting richer and the poor poorer, the demand for low priced consumer goods would fall. As a result, withheld and new money, instead of being allocated largely to capital formation, would be used for the most part to acquire assets, raw materials, land, etc. thereby forcing up their price. As a result, prices would spiral upward even as employment fell, society becoming rapidly poorer.

However, the translation of a money increment into higher prices would, as we have seen, be most unlikely if not impossible were employment less than full and were the new money injected at a rate at which it could be absorbed [86] by increased production. Our analysis of the individual field [87] indicated that the pressure to raise price in fields of monopolistic competition would be reduced by the spending of new money since the alternative, a higher rate of production would increase returns per se. Thus, were prices stabilized at the "break even" level, [88] there is no reason to suppose that they would rise should an increase in demand enable a more profitable production level. Consequently an upsurge initiated or accompanied by the creation and spending of new money would not under usual conditions result in a significant increase in price, a deduction substantiated by the history of recent peacetime upsurges, in which prices and wages kept in step with each other, some rising, some falling, but the net changes being inconsiderable.

Furthermore a dash of inflation, by which is meant the neutralization by higher prices of a small fraction of an increment of

[86] In 1941 and 1942 new money was spent somewhat faster than it could be put to work thereby raising prices. In 1943, 1944 and 1945 more new money was injected than could be put to work. Consequently price controls were needed during these years to prevent prices from getting out of hand.

[87] pp. 122 ff.

[88] Figure VI, p. 131.

excess demand, may have an opposite effect on the real wage from that to be expected from larger scale inflation. The reason is that a slight price rise, when it accompanies, marks or instigates a reversal of a downward cycle, is likely to raise the income of two of the lowest income groups and thereby decrease income disparity and increase the demand for consumer goods.

When production is low, an increment of demand resulting in an excess of demand over supply is likely to be translated (1) in part into increased production of processed goods, (2) in part into higher prices for raw materials. The first result is due, it was indicated, to the condition of increasing returns among the processors because of their idle equipment. Self-interest, in this situation, usually is served better by stepping up production than by raising prices.

The second result is due to the prevalence of price competition among the farmers. An excess of demand over supply in a field practicing price competition, such as agriculture, automatically raises prices, thereby permitting marginal producers to enter production and increasing the profits of those already in the field. Both results increase disproportionately the demand for consumer goods, since both results raise the incomes of the receivers of the lowest incomes—the unemployed and the farmers. Neither result reduces anyone's income, since a slight rise in raw material prices can usually be absorbed without loss by a processor who is concomitantly increasing production.

Thus when production is low a dash of inflation, one which is restricted largely to an advance in the price of farm produce in relation to the average wage, is likely to increase the income of the farmers and to reemploy workers without reducing the income of anyone. If raw material prices continued to advance to a point where it impelled the processors to raise their prices as well as their operating rates, the procedure would begin to cut into the purchasing power of those whose incomes were fixed or rising at a slower pace. It is this secondary stage which has the serious consequences suggested above.

One further comment seems relevant. The foregoing analysis obviously did not go into every economic distortion. Certain going concerns tend to hold their prices above the price which maximizes profit. Other enterprisers, by legal and illegal agreements, patent rights, or the mere nature of the industry, successfully combine to render the ingress of new concerns difficult. As a result, price in such industries is likely to be maintained at a higher level than it would be were ingress free and monopolistic competition effective.

On the other hand, other enterprisers accept prices, for one reason or another, below the price which returns a profit. And in certain fields of effort, ingress is so easy that the industry chronically operates at a loss. Thus it is fortunate that the analysis does not depend upon the existence of the much publicized imperfections (monopolistic controls, price rigging, closed markets, secret agreements, etc.) since actual prices, sometimes lie below as well as above the prices of perfect or pure monopolistic competition.[89]

SUMMARY

The foregoing analysis may be summarized as follows:

1. In the American economy, the advance in efficiency makes available an increment of wealth at no increase in cost.

2. Because of the nature of *monopolistic competition*, the *full* amount of the annual increment is seldom if ever released by way of lower prices, higher wages, increased selling expenses, etc.

3. The residual wealth increment which is not released by the above routes, either results in the discharge of workers thereby touching off a downsurge in production or it is released by the creation and spending of new money.

4. Such a creation and spending is induced if profit expectancy is at a certain level, or if society intervenes to create and spend new money for military or other purposes. (a) During upsurges effected by the spending of new money capital formation increases in relation to consumer goods production. During downsurges, the reverse occurs. (b) Because of the nature of *monopolistic competition*, the capital formed after the equilibrium production is passed consists largely of excess capital which increases overhead costs thereby subdividing the market and diminishing

[89] As described in Chapter II, Section 3.

the profit of the participating firms. (c) Capital formation is a function of profit. As a result, capital formation and new money spending fall off, eventually from result (b) thereby reducing over-all production.

In short, the economy because of the nature of monopolistic competition is unable to translate increased efficiency into lower prices. Instead, the equality of demand and supply is maintained in part by varying production. Thus, the equating of demand and supply at levels short of full production *is inherent* in current economic procedures thereby accounting for "nonproduction."

Our study might be closed at this point, since the irrational procedure we have been calling nonproduction has been explained in terms of current working procedures. It is true the logic needs to be reviewed by other minds not involved in its formulation. And the various probable adjustments indicated by the logic should be checked in greater detail against economic history and the available data. However, to do such a job thoroughly requires a study beyond the scope of this paper.

A further problem remains to be explored. Supposing the relationship set forth in the foregoing pages accurately describes economic procedures, what is implied in respect to the future? What measures might be taken to delimit the so-called business cycle so that the demand-supply adjustment would be accomplished at a high production level, thereby holding nonproduction and unemployment to a minimum.

These questions cannot be attacked in the same way as the questions that have occupied us up until now. The matter is speculative, and speculation, always hazardous, is peculiarly so in the social sciences where the check of controlled experimentation is rarely feasible. Yet it seems to the writer that he would be omitting matter of interest if he did not summarize certain thoughts bearing on this aspect of the problem. The following chapters are therefore submitted in the hope that their content, though controversial and certainly subject to qualifications, will increase our understanding of the problem.

APPENDIX TO CHAPTER V. CERTAIN ASSUMPTIONS ARE EXAMINED.

In the foregoing exposition, a number of relations, some of them important, were left in the form of assumptions and passed over without scrutiny to avoid interrupting the line of the argument. These assumptions which are listed below had better be examined and verified or qualified, although several of them are more or less self-evident. It was assumed:

1. That the capital required per unit product would not be increased by an advance in efficiency.

2. That disproportionate increase of enterpriser and property income increases income disparity.

3. That an increase in income disparity increases the proportion of income which is withheld from the purchase of consumer goods.

4. That profit expectancy varies directly with net over-all profit.

5. That such reductions in the carrying charge of capital as occur either through debt repayment or the amortization of equipment are included in the formula as it stands.

6. That the dimensions of the residual wealth increment, the demand increment, and the interest rate, would *not* vary in such a way as to invalidate the relations deduced in the text.

Assumption I. It was assumed that the amount of capital needed per unit product would not be increased by an advance in efficiency.

An efficiency advance can increase or decrease the amount of capital needed to produce most effectively a certain quantity of goods. The introduction of the steam shovel, for example, probably increased the proportion of capital needed for most efficient digging operations. The development of the 200-egg-a-year hen decreased the quantity of capital required to produce a dozen eggs. Similarly, improvements in management, collective skill, working conditions, etc., increase the output per man-hour without increasing the need for capital. It is difficult to ascertain which trend has been dominant during a period. The writer's guess would be that the amount of capital needed to produce an item most efficiently increased during the opening decades of the steam power age, since the revolutionary innovations consisted in the main of inventions which substituted natural energy and machinery, for human energy and tools. In recent decades, the revolutionary innovations have for the most part replaced less efficient machines with more efficient machines. Such innovations reduce the amount of capital needed per unit product. (A modern motor produces more energy per man-hour expended on its construction, installation, operation and maintenance, than an older motor). It therefore seems reasonable to suppose, as is done in the text, that these opposite trends would largely cancel each other out and recent changes in the ratio would be too small to affect appreciably the relations being scrutinized.

In any case, the argument is not rendered invalid. Even should more capital per unit product be required as efficiency advanced, a result which the writer believes to be unlikely, the necessary increase in overhead has evidently been less than the actual increase in overhead. This is indicated by the increase of excess capacity, the dimensions of which are suggested by the statistical surveys cited in Chapter I, and by the war record.[90]

Should less capital [91] per unit product be required as efficiency advanced, a result which the writer believes probable, at any rate in recent decades, then the unbalance described in the text between capital and production would be augmented. Since this probability was not needed for the argument, it was disregarded by assuming that the ratio of capital to production required for most efficient operations has been constant in recent times.

Assumption II. The assumption that an enhancement of enterpriser and property income increases income disparity is generally accepted. Yet it may be worthwhile to consider the basis of this assumption.

When profit and property income are increased by new money spending, the increment of profit consists largely of corporation profit and to a relatively minor extent of individual profits (listed by the Department of Commerce under entrepreneurial withdrawals). The reason is that processing, as well as such services as utilize natural energy (railroads, utilities, etc.), fields in which monopolistic competition and regulated monopoly largely prevail, are performed for the most part by corporations. Price competition, on the other hand, is still largely engaged in by individual enterprisers, since the six million unincorporated farmers constitute the only large price competition [92] group.

But price administration and production control, the procedures which enable surplus profits to be realized when new money injections release, or more than release, the wealth increments made available by efficiency advances, are feasible only in fields of monopolistic competition.

This conclusion, reached in the first place by logical deductions, is supported by the statistical data. In the 1921 to 1936 period, entrepreneurial withdrawals increased and decreased proportionately with production and the national income. Corporation profit, on the other hand, was subject to wider variations.[93]

[90] The industrial plant (excepting ordinance, aeroplane and other war goods plants) had to be increased but slightly, some 10 or 12 per cent in steel and less in most other commodities, to enable production to be about doubled between 1939 and 1943. Manpower shortages rather than plant capacity eventually halted the production increase.

[91] The supposition that less capital is required as efficiency advances, is supported in Brooking's study of *Productivity, Wages, and National Income*, pages 46 and 175.

[92] Chapter II, Section 1.

[93] Table IV, p. 134.

The statistical evidence, therefore, supports the above inference that the increment of profit resulting from the creation and spending of new money, accrues largely to corporations.

Of the part which goes into corporation profit, the larger fraction is issued in the form of dividends, bonuses, salary raises, new executive jobs, etc. Another part is reinvested by the corporation in capital formation and in the securities of other corporations, both diversions usually affecting individual incomes by enabling capital gains. (The ploughing back of profit when unneutralized by other events, increases the value of the corporation).

Also, a small part, that is to say, relative to the other segments, is likely to go into increased wages and into services (athletic fields, company houses, etc.) designed to make the workers more content.

The bulk of income from dividends, high salaries, capital gains, etc., and the bulk of income deriving from property, in particular from corporation debt (bonds, etc.) goes largely to a half million families more or less, and the income from wages and entrepreneurial withdrawals is divided among 33 million families, more or less.

It is evident, therefore, that a disproportionate increase in corporation profits and property income from any cause will increase income disparity. Thus, under present operating procedures, the release of the residual wealth increment made available by advances in efficiency by way of new money injections, *increases income disparity*, as was assumed in the text.

Assumption III. The assumption that an increase in income disparity increases the proportion of income which is withheld from the purchase of consumer goods, like the previous assumption, is seldom disputed. It may be of interest nevertheless to suggest why it is so.

Each civilization evolves a more or less defined minimum norm of respectable consumption. Individuals unable to enjoy this norm feel more or less deprived, even though they may not suffer physically. Consequently, individuals living at or below this norm tend to withhold little or none of their income. Individuals living above this norm tend to withhold and invest an increasing proportion of their income, as the gap between their income and the norm widens. The wider the inequality of incomes, the farther, that is to say, the higher incomes stretch above the minimum norm, the greater the proportion of the total income which is withheld. Consequently, withholding is a function of the disparity of incomes; the greater the disparity, the more withholding; the nearer the equality (the less disparity) the less withholding.

This fact not only can be logically deduced and individually observed, but also is indicated by the available statistics. If every American family had enjoyed an income of $3,000 in 1929 (90 billion dollars divided by 30 million families) only some 13 per cent would have been withheld instead of the 20 per cent actually withheld,[94] according to the tabulation of Brookings Institution. We may conclude, therefore, that the proportion of income which is withheld depends in part upon the disparity of incomes.

There would therefore seem to be no reason to doubt that the fraction of the total income which is withheld increases as income disparity increases. Consequently, an increase in corporation profits and property income increases the proportion of income which is withheld.

Furthermore, *much money is invested directly* by corporations when surplus profits are realized, as noted above. For this reason, too, the proportion of income which is invested increases when corporation profits are increased.

It may be concluded, therefore, that maintaining equilibrium as efficiency advances by the creation and spending of money, increases corporation profits, property income, income disparity and the *proportion of the total income which is withheld from the purchase of consumer goods*, as was assumed in the text.

Assumption IV. The assumption that profit expectancy is dependent upon the trend of net over-all profit is occasionally questioned. Certain commentators substitute the word "confidence," presumably confidence in further profits, for profit expectancy and point to its psychological and therefore unreliable nature. It is, of course, true that profit expectancy is a state of mind, and that it is difficult, if not impossible, to measure directly a state of mind, although one of its products, namely, capital formation and purchase, can be measured. But if the factors upon which profit expectancy depend can be measured, then profit expectancy itself is subject to measurement.

The state of mind known as profit expectancy depends on both objective and subjective factors. Most of the subjective factors, such as the individual's health and the pleasantness of the weather, probably even out in time. They may therefore be eliminated from consideration, although certain of them, for example, the entrepreneurial community's confidence in or fear of society's administrative authorities, may affect the state of mind for a considerable period. However, it is unlikely that subjective influences such as the one cited are strong enough to more than intensify or diminish the mental state induced by the objective factors. By this we mean merely that in 1936, for example, the distrust of the executive on the part of the entrepreneurial community in the United States may have reduced somewhat the onrush of capital formation stimulated by the favorable objective factors in that year. But it would seem unlikely that sentiments such as these could neutralize the objective factors for a sustained period.[95]

[94] Table, p. 96, *America's Capacity To Consume.* Brookings Institution.
[95] Our division of factors into objective and subjective is arbitrary and none too exact. For example, "distrust of the executive authorities" would have an objective

The situation is much simpler in respect to the objective factors, for these center upon the "trend of profit," a trend represented by changes in the dimensions of profit, as described in the text.

It seems reasonable to conclude, therefore, that profit expectancy depends in general upon the trend of profit, even though the psychological (subjective) factors can and do influence the intensity of the expectation and may obstruct a change in its direction, momentarily.

Perhaps one qualification of this general rule is sufficiently important to note. Withheld money is applied in part to capital formation, in part to the purchase of assets, as noted in the text. The profit expectancy which induces capital formation depends by and large upon the trend of profit, since self-interest would rarely be served by the formation of capital unless it appeared that the new capital could be utilized profitably.

The profit expectancy which induces the purchase of assets, however, often depends on other factors than the profitability of the going concern whose stock is considered for purchase. It often depends upon the prospective demand for this stock which may be more or less independent of the profits of the concern. For example, if potential investors believe, for any of a number of reasons, that the stock of a corporation, or a section of land, is going to be demanded by other potential investors, they are likely to seek to purchase it, regardless of its so-called intrinsic value, and regardless of the general trend of business, that is to say, of profit prospects. This practice of buying assets because it is believed others are going to be buying the assets soon, a practice which attained large dimensions in the 1920's, is associated for the most part with stock exchanges and real estate developments,[96] although it occurs to some extent in all markets.

No further elucidation of this well recognized phenomenon needs to be submitted, since John Maynard Keynes,[97] in a brilliant chapter, has analyzed the more important factors involved. It may however be relevant to recall [98] that whenever stock manipulation, publicity, or a popular stampede diverts money into the purchase of capital assets in quantities which the trend in over-all net profit would not justify, the creation and investment of new money, in addition to money saved, may be stimulated. As a result, an upsurge in production might apparently be sustained beyond the duration indicated by the objective factors, should speculative fervor possess what might be called a certain "momentum."

basis if the distrust were well founded. However, the distinction, though slight and uncertain, will serve, it is hoped, to clarify somewhat the shadowy influences involved.

[96] Such as the Florida land boom.
[97] *op. cit.*
[98] p. 178.

Assumption V. It was assumed that such reductions in the cost of carrying capital as are effected by the paying off of debt or the paying up on equipment (amortization) are already included in the formula as it stands.

The cost of carrying capital, a part of overhead costs, is reduced every time a debt is refunded, since the carrying cost of the debt is thereby eliminated. And refunding operations are going on all the time. However, these reductions are incorporated in the formula as it stands. For the quantity, m, is a net quantity, consisting of the net increase in new money—i.e., the increment of new money after such reduction in the money supply, as occurred, have been subtracted. Consequently, overhead costs would be increased by the full amount of m/d. No deduction, therefore, need be made for the cancellation of money.

It is also necessary to consider if the using up of capital (equipment) reduces the carrying charge of capital. Many concerns withhold a fraction of their income and invest it (put it in the bank, buy bonds, etc.) in order to have it available at a later date when their capital is worn out and needs to be replaced. The first transaction increases the quantity SE, since it constitutes a withholding of funds, and therefore is already incorporated in our formula. The second transaction, the selling of the investment and the utilization of the proceeds for capital formation, may or may not increase SE, depending on what the vendors of the investment do with their receipts. If they choose to reinvest it, or any part of it, and do not spend all of it on consumer goods, then SE again would be augmented. But the only point we need to make is that these operations (refunding and amortization) are already included in the formula as it is constituted, since SE represents net withholding (money withheld less money withdrawn from investment and used to purchase consumer goods) with the result that no deduction need be made to represent the paying off of a debt or the amortization of capital.

Assumption VI. It was assumed that the dimensions of the residual wealth increment $\Delta_r QP$, of the demand increment ΔE and of the interest rate $1/d$, would not vary in such a way as to invalidate the relations deduced in the text.

Let us consider each in turn.

The residual wealth increment $\Delta_r QP$, is a fraction of the wealth increment ΔQP, made available by the advance in efficiency. It was indicated in Section 1, Chapter III, and elsewhere, that this latter increment established by the advance in technology, would be largely independent of financial events and business conditions. Although efficiency advances by leaps and lapses in the individual branches of industry, the over-all advance in efficiency, which consists of all the various advances added together, would seem from the available data to be a somewhat steady quantity. Thus the data suggests that over-all efficiency has been advancing by $1\frac{1}{2}$ to 3 per cent a year.[99]   Should this estimate be low, a larger increment of demand would be needed to release the residual wealth increment and vice versa.   The relations, however, would be unchanged.   In sum, our argument does not depend on the statistical estimate which is subject to error.

$\Delta_r QP$, is a fraction of ΔQP.   This fraction is probably quite variable. In certain years, prices dropped abruptly, monetary wages holding steady, or dropping by less.   These and similar events alter the size of $\Delta_r QP$, which consists by definition of the wealth made available by the advance in efficiency not released or neutralized by lower prices, higher wages, etc.

However, in such years as the wealth increment was being released by the injection of new money allocated to capital formation under the stimulus of profit expectancy, the residual wealth increment, $\Delta_r QP$, has apparently held quite steady.   For in these years, the period 1923 to 1929, for example, prices and monetary wages have varied relatively little.[100]

In respect to our analysis, changes in the dimensions of $\Delta_r QP$, would not invalidate the relationships deduced unless $\Delta_r QP$ should diminish as production increased.   Nothing in the nature of an upsurge in production along the lines cited would seem to effect such a result.   On the contrary, prices and wages tend to rise together during upsurges in production.   It therefore seems reasonable to assume, as was done in the text, that changes in the dimensions of $\Delta_r QP$ would not invalidate the deduced relations.

On the downsurges in production $\Delta_r QP$ has been radically reduced by events of various kinds.   Such reductions may and probably have curtailed the amplitude and duration of the downswings, but this probability does not invalidate the analysis.

Since ΔE is assumed to be equal to $\Delta_r QP$, the behavior of the former quantity would be the same as that of the latter.

The interest rate, unlike the wealth increment, is not determined by the physical factors   The interest rate would seem to be determined in part by financial factors [101] of a somewhat obscure nature, in part by social action.   If the interest rate decreased as saving increased, the diminishment of the profit increment deduced in the text would be reduced or inhibited.   It is necessary, therefore, to consider if such an event is probable.

[99] Estimates of the advance in technology such as those submitted by Brookings Institution in *Productivity, Wages and National Income*, are higher than our estimate partly because the technologically static industries (waiting on table, etc.) are excluded.

[100] Table II, p. 132.

[101] The marginal efficiency of investment, etc.

In former times, the interest rate was left by the social authorities largely to find its own level. In this circumstance, it tended to rise as the demand for money increased and vice versa. Consequently, the interest rate tended to rise during upsurges. A rise in the interest rate would augment the diminishment of the profit increment, deduced in the text,

Latterly, the authorities in the United States have interfered in the determination of the interest rate by measures of various kinds. These have tended to stabilize the interest rate at some level considered low. This procedure, though it would, insofar as it was successful, prevent a rise in the interest rate decreasing the profit increment, would not prevent the decrease in the profit increment to be expected on the grounds cited in the text.

Certain theorists have recommended that society should lower the interest rate by various arbitrary interferences when investment lags. Should such a policy succeed in preventing the diminishment of the profit rate, the reversing of an upsurge might be postponed. However, such a policy not only would not inhibit excess capital formation but would *stimulate excess capital formation*. As a result, the downsurge would probably attain greater dimensions when it finally arrived.

It therefore seems reasonable to suppose that variations in the dimensions of the residual wealth increment and of the interest rate would not be of such a character as to interfere with the relationships deduced in the text.

CHAPTER VI

The Limitations of Price Competition

1. THE FACTORS WHICH INDUCE NONPRODUCTION AND UNEMPLOY-MENT AS DEVELOPED IN THE FOREGOING CHAPTERS WOULD NOT OPERATE IN AN ECONOMY OF PRICE COMPETITION.

THE reader undoubtedly has noticed that price competition industries, such as farming, and the practices which pertain to price competition, such as lowering price when demand is insufficient to purchase the supply, were treated as exceptions to the line of the argument. Similarly, care was taken in many instances to indicate why some relationship did not pertain to price competition, but only to the procedures defined as monopolistic competition. From these exclusions it is evident that our analyses would not apply to an economy of price competition.

It is therefore advisable before going on to consider other corrective measures to ask if nonproduction could be reduced or eliminated by increasing the scope of price competition. First, let us recall briefly its salient characteristics as given in earlier chapters.

In an economy of price competition

1. Production would be conducted by a field of competing concerns varying from the most efficient to the least efficient, all of which would produce to sell at the market price. As a result the market price would determine the quantity produced. (More producers could produce $1.00 wheat than 50¢ wheat.)

2. Each producer would attempt to operate at his most efficient scale, since this scale would promise the highest return should the producer's particular production have no appreciable or observable effect upon price, as in price competition.

3. New enterprisers could feasibly break into a field of effort, because a newcomer would merely have to produce more effi-

ciently than the less efficient producers in order to earn a profit. Business, as a result, would assume the form of a processional, with the dumb, inept, and obstinate being weeded out at one end, and the smart, energetic and ambitious pouring in at the other.

4. A deficiency of demand from no matter what cause would automatically be corrected by a drop in price. Consequently, every producer could count with certainty on being able to sell his production with the result that self-interest would not be served by nonproducing wealth and nonproduction would be unusual. (Should labor operate by price competition, each worker would accept the best obtainable wage, no matter how low, thereby eliminating voluntary unemployment. Should labor operate monopolistically by controlling or differentiating its contribution, workers would presumably refuse to work unless they received their "administered" price or wage, thereby causing more or less unemployment.)

5. Submarginal producers who were forced to close down would shortly close up since intermittent operations would be impractical (for reason 2) and it would not pay to maintain inefficient going concerns in idleness. Consequently, the idle capital which constitutes excess capacity in the existing economy would be torn down, or scrapped, and excess capacity would seldom be appreciable.

6. Since idle capital would be inappreciable, since demand would reflect consumer's desires,[1] and since each producer would operate at his most efficient scale, not only would full production be induced, but also capacity production. For full production would coincide with capacity production in a free economy, were excess capital formation and other uneconomic diversions of effort kept to the technical minimum. Thus, consumer's desires would be maximized, satisfactions being apportioned according to the distribution of income.

7. Since both wages and profits would tend to approach the marginal product of labor, income from these sources would tend to approach each other—as is the case in peacetime America with farmers and their hired hands. A source of inequitable distribution remains, namely, property income. However, society

---

[1] pp. 6 ff.

could reduce a disproportionate income from ownership by graduated income and inheritance taxes, both of which are established in custom and law in the United States.

The market system has been conceived along these ideal lines by many an economist. The fact that nonproduction and other defects are present in fact has often been explained by calling attention to the "imperfections" or flaws in the system, imperfections caused, supposedly by ignorance [2] (failure to recognize self-interest), greed, or laziness.

Reasons will be submitted in this chapter which suggest that price competition has never been instituted, not because of ignorance, greed or laziness, but simply because an economy of price or pure competition is technically infeasible in communities in which technology and the division of labor have reached an advanced stage.

This conclusion is supported though not proved by the seldom faced fact that few legal or administrative difficulties would hinder the institution of price competition in many fields of effort. Should society, or even the social authorities, decide to set up an economy of price competition by outlawing monopolistic competition, a few simple measures would go far toward accomplishing this purpose.

For example, most commodities and distributive services could be standardized and product differentiation, including trademarks, largely eliminated, merely by passing and enforcing certain laws, thereby removing the basis on which one commodity is favored over another and price flexibility curtailed.

Stockholders could be held liable for corporation debt, and the license of all corporations except those designed to perform certain strictly prescribed social functions could be cancelled, thereby making it hazardous to operate large units.

Existing graduated income taxes could be maintained. (Were corporations disqualified as above, this measure would give the small enterpriser an advantage over the large enterpriser, and thereby foster and maintain the requisite atomic structure of industry.)

[2] *The Debacle of Liberalism*, Lippmann.

Organization in restraint of trade could be prohibited and the law so worded that the courts would be compelled to enjoin all labor unions (as well as other trade restrainers) which attempted to raise or maintain wages or to define the conditions of work. Such measures were enforced during the early days of the industrial revolution without undue difficulty and doubtless could be enforced again.   They would probably restore wage flexibility.

Social legislation designed to regulate the conditions of work could be repealed.

Price fixing could be forbidden.   The intent of this latter measure would be to restore higgling, which is a requisite of price flexibility especially when continuous markets are impractical. Probably a publicity campaign might be simultaneously undertaken urging consumers to patronize only stores which higgled. Doubtless, the obsolescent art [2a] could be revived.

These fragmentary suggestions could be improved upon with study.   Some of them seem politically feasible, others not so feasible.   But there appears to be no constitutional barrier to the establishment of price competition.

If we are right in maintaining (a) that nonproduction would be unusual in a system of price competition, and (b) that price competition could be instituted in many fields by enforcing measures along the above or more expert lines, it is pertinent to consider whether a system of price competition would work.   Should price competition be technically feasible, or nearly so [3] no further search for a program to eliminate nonproduction would be needed.

On the other hand, should price competition prove to be unworkable, then an inquiry will be in order, to discover whether measures can be devised to release the existing system, in which monopolistic competition plays so large a part, from the restraints on production and distribution inherent in present procedures.

[2a] Karl Polanyi, *The Great Transformation*, Farrar and Rinehart, submits evidence to show that the propensity to higgle is not natural to mankind but was deliberately fostered by believers in the market system.

[3] The standardization of all products would not be possible   The fact that some stores for example would inevitably be more conveniently located than others would mar the "purity" of their competition even though rent differentials served largely to even out the differences.

2. MANY COMMODITIES, INCLUDING THOSE SUBJECT TO DECREASING COSTS AND A LIMITED DEMAND, CANNOT BE PRODUCED AND DISTRIBUTED EFFECTIVELY BY PRICE OR PURE COMPETITION.

Ever since the fallacies of mercantilism were banished from the academies and forced underground by the insight of Quesnay, Smith and their successors, informed opinion has favored open markets and price competition. Not only the schools, but many business men and politicians have expressed faith in the economic Utopia which the free exchange of goods and services by means of flexible prices has been supposed to induce. Yet the area of price competition has apparently not been expanded. In fact, some fields in which price was once determined by bids and offers on the market are now controlled by dominant corporations which administer their prices and regulate their production, and some fields in which products were once standardized and sold by weight and grade are now notable for the confusing multiplicity of differentiated items.

Perhaps this nonrealization is the best evidence of the impracticability of the ideal. However, other reasons can be cited. Let us therefore consider the technical feasibility of an economy of price competition.

Price competition might be extended to include the whole earth; or it might be instituted in an integrated economy protected by geographical, linguistic and political barriers. Though a world-wide system would possess certain advantages as well as disadvantages, they are not needed for this argument because the establishment of a world wide free market by simultaneous action in political infeasible in the foreseeable future. Consequently a world-wide system could not be achieved unless price competition could first be instituted within a national area. Let us therefore consider if price competition could be instituted in a limited area such as that of the United States.

It is true, the domestic economy would under price competition still need to obtain certain supplies more conveniently produced elsewhere by exchanging them for certain supplies which other societies for one reason or another prefer to obtain from the United States. And it might be desirable in conducting this trade to continue protecting American labor from the impact of foreign workers conditioned to exist on less produce, a protection provided today by the tariff.   There is, however, no reason to suppose that this protection could not continue to be so provided, since price competition within a geographical area does not require economic autarchy or free foreign trade.

Other requisites for price competition as was indicated in Chapter II, consist of (1) a large number of buyers and sellers, so that the influence of one buyer or seller, or groups of buyers and sellers, upon price, is negligible, and of (2) a standardized product.   Consequently, two large categories of goods must be excluded from the domain of price competition.

Goods such as postal, railroad and telephone service could not well be produced and distributed by price competition, since the waste involved in providing such goods by a large enough number of competing agencies to insure the influence of no group of them over price, would be conspicuous.

Goods such as styled clothes, custom cookery, tailored machinery, original works of art, professional and artisan services, etc., could not be produced and distributed by price competition, because their nature is such that these products differ to a more or less perceptible degree from each other, giving the purchaser a basis for favoring one article over another.

Should market prices be imposed on goods of this kind, assuming it could be done, one producer could not afford to put in more effort than another.   As a result, the differentiated products would be reduced to some standard norm or driven off the market, despite the "instinct of workmanship" and the "urge to nonconformity."

However, the exclusion of these two kinds of goods and services, important as they are to certain classes of consumers, still leaves the great bulk of goods and services available for price competition, since most raw materials, most partly processed, and many finished goods, can be produced and distributed by many competing agencies (1) and standardized (2).

There are, however, other conditions necessary for price competition.   For example, price competition is not practical unless a good is subject to increasing costs and an indefinitely expansible demand.

It might be asked: How could the condition of decreasing costs exist in a field of price competition in which each enterpriser presumably operated at his most efficient scale and the less efficient were continually being skimmed off by their inability to cover their costs at the price which prevailed? Also, under what circumstances would demand not expand as price was lowered, human needs being infinite?

Let us postpone until the next section the questions of how the conditions could occur and whether they would be likely to occur, and indicate first why price competition would not be feasible under these conditions.

Were a field of effort subject to decreasing costs and a limited demand, producers would be tempted to increase their production until the limited demand was exceeded. Price, as a result, would fall below costs, were price competition in effect. Let us suppose that enough producers dropped out to curtail production until supply was reduced below the demand, and price started to rise.

As price climbed toward the break-even point, confidence would rise in the industry. Producers subject to decreasing costs would be aware, as the break-even point was approached, that their costs would be reduced and their losses eliminated could they increase production. Were the field divided among many independent producers, as it would be in price competition, a number of them would attempt to take advantage of this condition by stepping up production either by increasing plant capacity [4] or otherwise. Should they do so, supply would soon top demand and price would drop off probably before the break even price was attained.

Price might now and again touch the equilibrium price, or at least approach it. But the situation would be such that the mere approach to solvency would stimulate increased production since a producer who was about to break even would be aware that a slightly greater production and the resulting lower per unit costs

[4] Though decreasing costs for the field are being postulated, the producers who had persisted would be operating the plant in place at or about its most efficient scale were price competition in effect. (Chapter II, p. 33.) However, in many fields of effort, per unit costs can be reduced by increasing plant capacity etc., as will be described in the next section. It is these fields which are subject to decreasing costs regardless of the form of competition. See pp. 205 ff.

would enable him to show a profit. His individual production being too small to affect price (by definition), the rational policy for him under the circumstances would be to step up production whenever solvency came within range. Thus, the sanguine nature of man, combined with the expandibility of equipment so conspicuous in contemporary America, would tend to keep production chronically above demand and price habitually below that price at which the cost of production would be recovered.[5]

Furthermore, each time the producers stepped up production and made goods available in quantities greater than the (postulated) limited demand, the market would not take them at any price. The goods presumably would be stored, if they were storable and of such a character that they could not profitably be shipped abroad. These goods hanging over the market ready to be dumped should prices approach their cost of production, would render it even more difficult for the vendors to obtain a price which would permit of solvency.

As a result, industries in which production incurred decreasing cost within the range of demand would operate at a loss, were they subject to price competition. While enterprisers can operate at a loss for considerable periods under contemporary conditions,[6] enterprisers cannot continue to do so indefinitely. Then, too, society is not benefitted by below cost prices and insolvent industries. Society is composed largely of individuals who both produce and consume. When the income from production of such individuals is curtailed, their capacity to consume is curtailed as well. Consequently, society is impoverished.

Finally, below cost operations even when feasible prohibit the allocation of funds to research and experimentation, thereby in-

[5] See Appendix, p. 203 for a geometrical representation of the situation.

[6] In modern industry, capital is usually paid for over a period by means of interest and amortization. In this situation, it often happens that less money is lost by running at a loss than by closing down and scrapping the unpaid capital. In the former case, some payment may often be made on the capital and a possibility exists of paying up on it fully at some future date. Consequently, banks, bondholders, receivers, etc., usually find ways and means of keeping going concerns going even at a loss, and the bankruptcy which is supposed, when excess capacity arises, to reduce the number of competitors and thereby to restore solvency, often fails to eventuate. Instead, excess capacity and operation at a loss may and often do persist. (See Schlichter, *Modern Economic Society*, pp. 302, 303, 305, for fuller discussion of this phenomenon.)

hibiting the most important means by which the societies of the West have raised their standard of living. Had insolvency been general during the past hundred years instead of sporadic, much of the money diverted to research and capital formation would not have been available and the primitive technology of former times might not have been superseded. Thus modern technology has been fostered not so much by price competition as by monopolistic competition and the comparative security resulting from its stabler prices. There is no reason to suppose that the needs of the present and the future will differ from those of the past in this respect.

In short, prices at which demand and supply were equated, would not constitute an equilibrium under price competition in industries subject to decreasing costs within the range of demand (assuming there are such). Rather, such prices would constitute a limiting price, a price which the producers would periodically approach and seldom attain. Since vendors realize a net loss at below cost prices, and since net losses curtail consumption and are otherwise damaging, goods and services could not be produced and distributed effectively by price competition in such industries. Consequently, the institution of price competition in industries subject to decreasing costs and a limited demand is not desirable.

Furthermore, these two conditions as will be indicated in Section 3, are prevalent in the American economy.

APPENDIX TO SECTION 2. THE RELATIONSHIP DESCRIBED IN SECTION 2 IS EXPRESSED IN GEOMETRICAL TERMS.

Let us recall how demand and supply are equated in a field of price competition under conditions of increasing costs and expansible demand, as described in Chapter II. Figure VIII, which consists of the same demand and cost curve as Figure I, illustrates the situation. Cost CC_1 increases as production increases, thereby representing the condition of increasing costs. Demand DD_1 increases indefinitely as price drops, thereby representing an indefinitely expansible demand. The two curves or schedules must cross each other if the good is to be produced. Their point of intersection marks the equilibrium price PA.

As noted in Chapter II, a higher price such as QB would draw producers whose costs were less than QP into production. Presumably, nearly *OF* goods would be produced at price *QP*. But only *OB* goods could be sold at price *QP*. The excess supply would cause price to drop were price competition in effect.

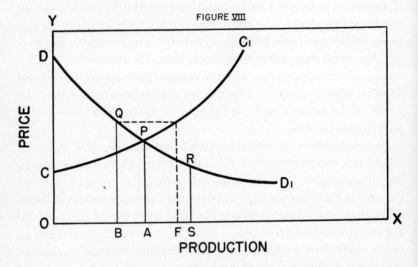

FIGURE VIII

Now let us suppose that the price has reached *RS* on the way down. All producers whose costs were greater than *RS* would now be unable to recover their costs Furthermore, it would do them no good to increase their individual productions. Such a move would raise per unit costs and increase their losses, since increasing costs are being postulated. As a result, operators whose costs were greater than *RS* would for the most part close down, there being no economic alternative. Supply *OS*, which would be demanded at price *RS*, would not be produced. Price therefore would rise. Not until price *PA* was reached would a supply be produced equal to the demand, since producers whose costs were *PA* or more would, *if subject to increasing costs*, have no economic justification for operating until this price could be obtained.

This does not mean that the actual price would come to rest at *PA*. In fact, reasons were suggested why the price would tend to rise above and fall below *PA* were speculation present.[7] But *PA* would mark the equilibrium price, the price which would maximize profit for the industry under conditions of price competition,[8] the price toward which swings in either direction would tend to return.

Now let us suppose the two conditions postulated above do not exist, but that costs, instead of increasing, would fall were production in-

[7] p. 30.
[8] Chamberlin, *op. cit.* p. 19.

creased within the range of demand and that demand was not indefinitely expansible. This situation is illustrated by Figure IX.

Costs, represented by curve CC_1, are lower at each increase in production within the range of the demand, DD_1. Thus CC_1 is drawn to represent the condition of decreasing costs as defined in Chapter II.[9] (Since presumably a most efficient operating rate might exist, costs are represented as rising after OS production. However, this quantity, OS, is represented as being beyond the range of demand.)

Demand, represented by curve DD_1, increases as the price is lowered up to production OE when it ceases to increase. The diagram as drawn represents a situation in which goods in addition to OE goods could not be given away. Thus Figure IX illustrates the negation of the condition of increasing costs and an indefinitely expansible demand represented by Figure VIII.

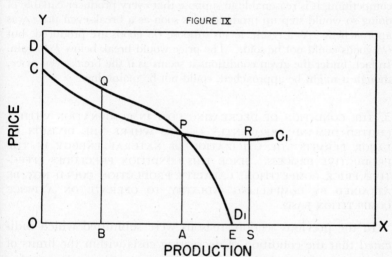

FIGURE IX

The curves as drawn cross at price PA. (The curves might not cross at all, in which case the good presumably would not be produced.) PA therefore indicates the price at which the value of the supply produced would equal the cost of production.

Evidently a price higher than PA, such as QB, would not stand in a market subject to price competition. Every potential producer whose costs were less than QB would start producing. Were the schedules as drawn, goods in greater quantity than OE, the saturation production, would soon be put up for sale. Price would drop precipitously, since the market would be flooded with more goods than it would take at any price.

[9] pp. 30, 49.

Let us suppose that the resulting losses would so discourage the higher cost producers that enough dropped out to permit the redundant supplies to be gradually absorbed. When these had disappeared, price would start to climb.

However, when price approached PA, the price at which supply and demand are equated, certain of the marginal and intramarginal producers would be aware that if they increased production, they would cut their losses and possibly make a profit, since decreasing costs are being postulated within the demand range. In other words, could the producers lower their costs by producing a larger quantity, it would pay them to produce this greater quantity even though they might receive a slightly lower price for it.

Since each producer is acting as if his individual production were too small a fraction of the total to influence price, a condition of price competition, it is reasonable to suppose that every producer capable of doing so would step up production as soon as a break-even price was approached. As a result, let us suppose OS goods are produced, but OS goods could not be sold. The price would break below PA again. In fact, under the given conditions it seems as if the break-even price, though it might be approached, could not be maintained.

3. THE CONDITION OF DECREASING COST IN COMBINATION WITH A LIMITED DEMAND FREQUENTLY OCCURS WHERE THE DIVISION OF LABOR PERMITS THE UTILIZATION OF NATURAL ENERGY IN THE PRODUCTIVE PROCESS. SINCE THIS CONDITION PRECLUDES EFFECTIVE PRICE COMPETITION, CAPACITY PRODUCTION COULD NOT BE ATTAINED BY COMPELLING INDUSTRY TO OPERATE ON A PRICE COMPETITION BASIS.

In the previous section, reasons were submitted which indicated that the condition of decreasing costs within the limits of demand would preclude effective price competition. Decreasing costs, it was brought out in Chapter II, are realized when excess capacity is present, and excess capacity is a normal characteristic of monopolistic competition.[10]

It was also noted that excess capacity would be unlikely to persist in a field of price competition. However, decreasing costs are realized not only when a production increase takes advantage of the excess capacity usually present in monopolistic competition, but also when plant and equipment are expanded in industries utilizing a high proportion of modern machinery and natural

[10] p. 39.

energy. And a plant can nearly always be expanded, regardless of the type of competition, in an economy such as the American, in which manpower, rather than resources or know-how, constitutes the ultimate limit on production. To indicate why plant expansion is likely to lower costs, it will be helpful to recall the reason the so-called law of increasing costs is of limited applicability in the current economy.

As described in Chapter II,[11] a field of effort is subject to increasing costs when certain factors of production are better suited for an operation than other factors. Thus, in agriculture certain pieces of land are more fertile than other pieces. Generally speaking, the better land is drawn into production before the poorer land. As a result, when production of an agricultural commodity is increased, the additional units are likely to cost more than the original units, since poorer land may have had to be utilized in their production. This condition however is exceptional in modern industry for the following reason.

The new technological procedures are distinguished from older procedures by the greater division of labor and the utilization of natural energy. Thus the process from raw material to finished product has been divided into many subprocesses, and certain of these fractional processes have been sufficiently simplified to permit of their performance by power driven machinery which repeats one, or a sequence of motions. In most fields of effort, extraction has thereby been separated from processing and processing from the distribution and sale of the finished goods.

Since one machine is about as good as another of the same kind, the conditions conducive to increased costs are not present in most industrial processes. Furthermore, within limits, two machines are more efficient than one machine, three than two, and so forth, because each increase spreads the cost of buying, selling, management and so forth over more products. Also, the acquisition of an additional machine often increases efficiency per se, because the continuous advance in technology makes it probable that the new machine will be better than the machines already in place. As a result, in power processing, an increase

[11] p. 50.

in capacity and in production [12] is more likely to decrease per unit costs than to increase them, up to a certain point, to be sure, owing to the awkwardness of giants, a limitation that does *not* concern us *here*, since our interest at the moment is in price competition which is predicated on an atomic organization of industry, in which the field is divided among many *small* units.

Because of this potentiality, a processor can usually *reduce his per capita unit costs by expanding his plant*, especially if he is a small processor, as *he would be* were price competition in effect.[13]   In other words, most small processors, who utilize machines and natural energy are subject to decreasing costs, even should they be operating at the most efficient scale with the equipment in place, because of this ability to expand their capacity at no appreciable increase in overhead.

Furthermore, the demand for many producers' goods and intermediate goods is not unlimited.   This probability was implied in Chapter IV [14] where the fact that demand was relatively inelastic for many goods and services was brought out.   The demand for tools, steel shapes, machines, cans, containers, etc., is not only inelastic in that a drop in price increases demand but slightly because the demand for such goods depends upon the demand for some finished good; but also it is limited, at any given moment, for any given national income.   Only a certain number of tools of a specialized purpose can be used effectively for a given production regardless of price.   It follows therefore, that only a certain number could be sold [15] in an economy of price competition even though the price should be dropped nearly to that of

---

[12] The fact that a machine, pushed beyond a certain point by giving it additional tenders, or a man by giving him additional machines to tend, are subject to increasing costs, *is not* being questioned.

[13] Plant expansion would not always be necessary.   Costs might also be reduced by establishing a night shift, by buying supplies in larger quantities, or even by changing the layout of the plant.   In fact, when the exploitation of a natural resource is not in question, the concept of "a most efficient scale of production" has not much meaning unless the plant is considered "frozen."

[14] p. 111.

[15] Were over-all demand in excess of over-all supply (Case IV, etc.) tools in addition to the economic increment could be sold in an economy of monopolistic competition, since excess capital formation would be stimulated as described in Chapters II and IV.   However, in price competition, excess capital formation would be unusual for the reasons noted.   Consequently, demand for extra tools and equipment would be limited roughly to need as stated above.

metal scrap. Similarly, the demand for containers, nails, and a multiplicity of other materials and articles, goods which are not valued for themselves but only in connection with some other good or service, the demand for which latter governs the demand for the former, is limited at a given income level regardless of price. Such goods and services, as well as the producer goods and cheaper consumer goods cited in Chapter IV, have fairly well defined saturation points [16] at every given income level which are not likely to be exceeded.

This aspect of the situation may be summed up as follows:

Owing to the division of processing into many subprocesses, the majority of goods may be called intermediate goods since they consist of goods in process between their primary stage, known as raw material, and their finished stage, known as finished goods. Raw materials, to a large extent, are subject to increasing costs. Finished goods may be subject to unlimited demand. But the intermediate goods, goods falling between raw material and finished products, are usually subject neither to increasing costs (if the possibility of plant expansion be included), nor to unlimited demand. On the contrary, an increase in the production of these goods within the limits of the effective demand can usually be accomplished at a lower per unit cost, and the quantity of these goods which the market can absorb is usually limited by the demand for the finished good. As a result, the great class of goods we are calling intermediate are usually subject to decreasing costs within the limits of demand.

But these characteristics are the negation of the condition of increasing costs and an indefinitely expansible demand, which were shown, in the last section, to be necessary for effective price competition. Consequently, our list of goods and services which

---

[16] Many expensive consumer goods as well as the cheaper consumer goods, producer goods and intermediate goods cited in Chapter IV probably have saturation points. Thus a production of automobiles can be conceived which would so crowd the roads that the diminishing pleasure from driving would establish what would amount to a saturation point. And roads, too, have a conceivable saturation point. However, this probability is not needed for the argument. Even though the demand for most consumer goods is conceived of as unlimited, there are so many semi-processed, intermediate and supplementary goods as well as tools and machines, the demand for which is limited by the production of the finished product and whose sale would not increase beyond a certain point at any price, that our generalization seems valid.

are *not* suitable for price competition, a list which already includes the public utilities and personal services, the arts, handicrafts, styled goods, and certain raw materials which are available in very great quantities (such as coal), must be expanded to include many intermediate and supplementary goods, such as steel shapes, containers, etc., and specialized tools. Evidently the scope of price competition in the contemporary economy is strictly circumscribed. It is therefore reasonable to conclude that capacity production could not be attained by compelling industry to operate on a price competition basis.

4. THE HISTORICAL RECORD SUPPORTS THE THEORETICAL CONSIDERATIONS WHICH SUGGEST THAT CAPACITY PRODUCTION AND FULL EMPLOYMENT ARE MORE LIKELY TO BE ATTAINED BY RELEASING MONOPOLISTIC COMPETITION TO REALIZE ITS POTENTIALITIES, THAN BY INSTITUTING SOME OTHER METHOD OF PRODUCING AND DISTRIBUTING WEALTH.

Reasons were submitted in the last section to explain why most goods and services could not be produced and distributed effectively by price competition procedures. Our conclusion is strongly supported by the experience of industry. Historically few vendors with the exception of farmers and possibly junkmen have been able to engage in price competition for sustained periods. And even the farmers who are subject to increasing costs and an unlimited demand, insofar as anyone is, in communities conversant with modern technology, find it difficult in peacetimes, to recover their production costs.

In nearly all other industries, monopolistic competition prevails. When it is difficult to differentiate the product, as with crude petroleum, copper, tin, etc., other controls are devised. When these break down, as they have done periodically in the raw material field (with the exception of aluminum, nickel, and a few other tightly owned resources) below cost prices have resulted. The profit and loss columns of the copper, steel, oil and other extractive industries during spells of price competition bear out this statement.

Not only extractors but many processors have at one time or another relinquished the attempt to administer their prices and limit their production and have engaged in price competition for a short period. The result, it appears, has always been disastrous. Although a scrutiny of the historical record is outside the scope of this study, it may be appropriate to recall a few of the industries in which price competition has been tried out, a list which the reader can no doubt supplement from his own experience. Thus photo engravers, malleable iron foundries, sugar refiners, whiskey distillers, wire nail fabricators, leather tanners and the ladies' garment trade have competed at one time or another by way of price competition. In every case, the experiment proved disastrous. When prices were cut in order to obtain business, costs could not be recovered. Labor was sweated. Insolvency was frequent when not habitual. Eventually price competition was superseded by some form of control over price and production. Either the employers got together, or labor, or the government intervened to assist in the control of production and prices.[17]

In the last century, when this difficulty was encountered, price stabilization was the popular remedy. But it was discovered that price stabilization alone, that is to say, the maintaining by agreement of a price higher than the price that would be established by price competition, was more likely to intensify the difficulty than otherwise, because new plants were rapidly installed with the result that the market again was hopelessly flooded. To prevent this consummation, production had to be controlled as well as price. But production and price control constitute monopolistic competition.

The record indicates that the various industries which engaged in price competition at one time or another were unable to operate effectively and that no industries have continued to engage in price competition, excepting those few subject to increasing costs within the range of demand.

If our reasoning has been valid and the facts essentially correct in broad outline, the development and extension of modern monopolistic competition would seem not to have been the result of a "misunderstanding of *laissez-faire* and of the classical econo-

---

[17] The government, for example, assisted the bituminous coal mining industry even before the war to maintain some control over price and production.

mists" as Walter Lippmann [18] blithely puts it.   On the contrary, the development would seem to have been the result of the struggle to survive on the part of many thousands of enterprisers engaged in production and distribution.   Price competition was supplanted as the ideal toward which society should move in order to realize the maximum freedom, wealth and security, when the enterpriser ran up against the practical impossibility of making full use of the potentialities of the new technology while harrassed by the uncertain, erratic and extravagant rule of the free (i.e. unadministered) market.

An economy of price competition might be possible for some primitive society in which the division of labor was inchoate. Should each worker, farmer, hunter, woodworker and metal worker carry through from raw material to finished product, then nearly every finishing process, like most extractive processes would be subject to increasing costs and an indefinitely extensible demand.   In this situation, the rule of the market might serve to allocate effort economically.   However, as soon as the division of labor had separated processing from extraction, and as soon as the harnessing of natural energy had made parts of the production process to some extent independent of labor skill, certain processors would find themselves capable on the one hand of processing more material than the extractors made available, and more material than society demanded at cost or above cost prices. Consequently, guilds, labor unions, trade marks, and other measures would be (and actually were) devised in most societies in order to enable groups of processors faced by this difficulty to operate effectively.

It is curious that Adam Smith, who is probably more responsible than other theorists for converting the informed to the elegance of a free market economy, should also have heralded the advantages of the division of labor.   Apparently his famous pin factory would rapidly multiply under price competition until the market was flooded with pins, because each manager of a competing plant, aware that per unit costs would be lower the more pins were turned out, would be impelled to increase his

[18] *op. cit.* pp. 203, 223.

facilities. The demand for pins is not unlimited.[19] Price therefore would drop below costs were the price and production controls of monopolistic competition not in effect. However, insolvency would not hold production down to demand, because
whenever solvency was approached, some of the enterprisers,
aware of the potential saving to be achieved by stepping up production, would proceed to do so. Thus, the pin industry would
seem to be a good example of the situation described in the last
section, which would preclude effective operations under price
competition.

Probably monopolistic competition is the basic procedure for
the production and distribution of wealth in communities which
have reached the trading level. Its roots go back beyond the
time when Solomon and Hiram exchanged cedars for horses at a
price. Price competition and monopoly appear to be variations
of this basic procedure, of utility in special circumstances, but
unsuitable for general application, although many dreamers
believe that an economy consisting entirely of one or other
extreme would preclude nonproduction and unemployment.
In our day theorists on the political left usually advocate pure
monopoly—over-all planning and control by representatives of
the working class (Marxian Socialists), by engineers (techno-
crats), or by a strictly conditioned more or less arbitrarily chosen
elite (Fascists). Dreamers on the right tend to advocate price
competition and a free world market (Mr. Hull and other political and academic spokesmen). It is questionable which alternative is the more Utopian. The infeasibility of pure monopoly
is indicated not only by the logical considerations cited in Chapter I, but also by the experience of the Soviet Union. Competent
social authorities in Russia have been attempting to institute
Socialism for twenty years. And though they have achieved
wonders in modernizing the nation's technological plant, they
have not been able to escape the necessity of utilizing the market
mechanism for pricing, and the profit criterion for allocating
effort, instruments which are inherent features of market com-

---

[19] If only one economy made pins by the division of labor, the export of pins
might relieve this situation. If many economies made pins efficiently, this escape,
however, would not be open.

petition and which would be redundant in a pure monopoly such
as the proposed planned economy of the socialists.

No such clear-cut trial has been made of price competition.
However, the social authorities in England and elsewhere have
frequently proclaimed its tenets.   Nevertheless, they have faltered before taking the relatively simple steps needed to institute
it.   Apparently price competition is even more Utopian than
monopoly, since it apparently cannot even be approached in the
actual world.

However this may be, the theoretical considerations and the
historical evidence indicate that it would be futile to attempt to
achieve capacity production by extending the scope of price
competition.   Such an attempt, our analysis suggests, would lead
to general insolvency and frustration.   Some other means of
eliminating or reducing nonproduction is required.   Let us
therefore consider what measures would enable the existing
glomerate system to realize in peacetimes its technological potentialities.

CHAPTER VII
Full and Capacity Production

1. THE SCOPE OF NONPRODUCTION WOULD BE REDUCED WERE THE EQUILIBRIUM PRODUCTION RAISED AS PRODUCTION INCREASED.

IT was indicated in the preceding chapter that capacity production could not be achieved either by precluding monopolistic interferences in the free play of price or by over-all planning. Since both the pure or unmixed systems are impractical, capacity production will have to be achieved by a mixed system like the existing one. However, before defining the problem in these terms, let us first consider a possibility that has a particular appeal because of the extraordinary success of limited or partial planning in transforming the United States into a great if not the greatest military power.

The Controlled Materials Plan plus the several hundred Material and Limitation Orders of the WPB, plus the price stabilizing and rationing of the OPA, the wage stabilization measures of the WMC, WLB, etc., the rationing, allocating and conserving of the WFA, ODT, PAW, etc., the exporting of FEA, etc., and the deficit spending of the Army, Navy, and Maritime Commission, have enabled society to increase production from some hundred billion dollars worth of goods and services to nearly two hundred billion, with eleven million men removed from the labor force. It is therefore reasonable to ask if similar measures would not enable society in a time of peace to provide a plentitude of both wealth and jobs.

The answer to this question was implicit in Chapter I. Certainly an over-all planning board with war powers and an open-end check book could secure full production.[1] But such a board could neither attain nor maintain capacity production. Limited planning for war was feasible in part because the relatively economic prices and wages of peace were largely frozen for the

[1] Full production was defined as the production of full employment. Capacity production was defined as that full production which maximized satisfactions.

213

duration, thereby making it possible to assemble data against which to check each proposed action. When more landing craft or other item was needed, the requisite facilities, components, materials and manpower were computed, and the impact of the landing craft increase was appraised in terms of its effects on other programs. Thus, schedules could be increased and decreased without incurring important unforeseen consequences. The effect of each action on price was not involved. As a result, the touchstone question, would this or that action hurt or help the war effort, could be answered with reasonable confidence that errors would not invalidate the conclusion.

If, however, prices and wages had been free to make cyclic and structural adjustments, the envisagement of the effect of an individual action would have been rendered difficult, and the envisagement of the effect of the various actions in combination would have been impossible. Since the relatively smaller diversion of effort of the first World War resulted in an inflationary price rise and other maladjustments despite partial controls, it is probable that the recent greater effort would have had even more serious consequences if the price structure had not been largely crystallized.

Consequently a peace drive along the lines of the recent war effort could not be conducted successfully without freezing prices and wages. But if the price and wage structure were frozen, assuming this action to be feasible in times of peace, the parametric function of price [2] would be arrested. As a result, the basis for economic decisions would be gradually undermined, actions would become increasingly haphazard, and over-all efficiency would drop until the advantages of full production would be outweighed by the disadvantages of inefficient production. Sooner or later the standard of living would fall below that of neighboring societies and a modern variety of the Chinese Wall might have to be erected in order to inhibit invidious comparisons.

However, a limited peacetime objective could be attained by over-all planning without freezing prices and wages, just as highways, waterworks, and even vast interstate projects such as that

[2] p. 7.

of the Tennessee Valley Authority are today planned and exe-
cuted. Such projects are feasible, as was noted in Chapter I,[3]
because the authorities are able to estimate relative costs by
using the prices and wage rates provided by the surrounding
economy of competitive enterprise. Thus it might be possible
to abate destitution by diverting materials, facilities, and labor
not utilized by the competitive economy to the production of a
budget of needed goods and services which would then be ra-
tioned or otherwise distributed to the underprivileged outside of
regular channels.[4]

However, such a policy like the free corn and circus policy of
ancient Rome and recent relief measures would evade rather than
resolve the issue. To dull the brutal edge of destitution by a
system of bountiful rationing would be a confession of failure,
desirable to be sure, if part of society *must* be consigned to
desuetude, but defeat none the less. Should there be no corrective measures, then a resort to palliatives, even if they compromised the American ideal of self-reliance, would be in order.
But nothing in the analysis suggests that nonproduction is
inevitable although the discussion indicated that nonproduction
is an inherent characteristic of recent peacetime procedures.

The analysis suggests that the problem may be divided into two
parts. First, a means will have to be devised to achieve full

[3] p. 13.

[4] The writer devised, and believed in a partial rationing plan along these lines for
several year (*The Plan of Plenty*, Continental Committee, 1933). Providable goods
were to be separated from scarce goods. It was proposed to provide the former universally by plan and to leave the balance to be produced and distributed by the
usual market procedures. However, the arbitrary nature of the division between
providable and scarce goods was eventually faced. Since the division was arbitrary,
it could not be commanded by consumers' demand but would have to be imposed
from above. This objection, though serious, would not be conclusive, since a consensus exists in regard to the kinds and quantity of most basic goods requisite for the
countenanced living standard—a consensus which could be used for making the
division. However, the removal of a large section of the economy from the market
and the handling of it according to an imposed schedule would interfere with the
parametric function of price with the result cited so frequently in these pages.

Nevertheless, it seemed to the writer that a partially planned procedure which
insured full production would be less wasteful and more satisfactory to most of the
population than a market procedure such as that of the recent peacetime economy,
which failed to utilize one-half to one-third of the available resources. The question
became academic when further study showed that full production and a market
economy were *not* incompatible.

production. In the second place, some method of controlling the ratio of capital formation to consumer goods production is required because excess capital would be formed, as the historical data as well as our theoretical deductions indicate, whenever production surpassed the equilibrium production level, unless measures were taken to prevent it. Not only is excess capital uneconomic, thereby inhibiting capacity production, but also excess capital reduces profits, increases interest, and results eventually, as the discussion in Chater V indicated, in a production downsurge.

Perhaps the nature of the problem can be made clearer by translating it into the terms of Figure VII.[5] Actual production ranges, in the current economy, between the limits set by full production, F, and a production such as A, below the equilibrium production, B. It cannot exceed full production and seldom remains for long below the equilibrium production. Thus the scope of nonproduction would be reduced were the equilibrium production moved up on the scale of production as production was increased, and the cyclic swings minimized. To increase production without moving up the position of the equilibrium production not only would fail to maximize consumer satisfactions $(GQP_f < GQP_J)$, but also would entail excess capital formation with the result that a downsurge would ensue sooner or later.

On the other hand, were the equilibrium production moved up until it approached full production, the analysis suggests that the economy would be stabilized at a high income level and actual production would be likely to approximate capacity production.

It is evident that the equilibrium production would increase on a production upsurge, could capital formation be contained within certain limits. However, were the volume of capital formation contained as production increased, consumer goods production would have to be augmented by an equivalent volume in order to utilize the resources thus made available.

From this brief resume of the situation, it appears that three adjustments, controls, or interferences, are needed to achieve

[5] p. 170.

capacity production and thereby to release the economy to fulfill its potentialities.

The requisite interferences consist of:

1. An adjustment by which production could be increased or maintained.

2. An adjustment by which private capital formation could be kept from exceeding certain limits on production upsurges.

3. An adjustment by which consumer goods production could be increased in relation to over-all production at higher production levels.

2. PRODUCTION COULD BE INCREASED WHEN SHORT OF FULL BY SPENDING NEW MONEY ON PUBLIC WORKS OR OTHER OUTLETS WHICH DID NOT COMPETE WITH THE PRODUCTS OF PRIVATE ENTERPRISE. HOWEVER, THE UTILITY OF THE MEASURE WOULD BE LIMITED.

The first of the three indicated interferences or controls might not be necessary. For example, should corrective measures be undertaken at a time production was full, Adjustments 2 and 3 might achieve capacity production without other assistance. However, so long as production remains full, as it is at the moment (1944) when this passage is written and there is no unemployment problem, little likelihood exists that procedures which strain traditional concepts will be tried out. It is therefore unreasonable to expect that much will be done about nonproduction until the cancellation of war contracts; or until the cessation of reconversion and reconstruction some years later permits the money supply to be stabilized, with the result that production drops off for the reasons cited in Chapters II to V. Once the decline gets under way, it is likely to develop rapidly.[6] When this occurs, drastic measures to increase production will no doubt be entertained. Iconoclasts have their opportunity when traditionalists are in retreat. It will therefore be assumed that the indicated measures will be applied, if at all, at a time of nonproduction. Thus, a means to increase production, listed in the last section as Adjustment 1, is a requisite of a program designed to achieve capacity production.

[6] Case II, p. 68.

Production could be increased directly by authoritative decree, as shipbuilding, aluminum production, etc. were increased during the war. But the operating rate of private concerns cannot be regulated directly by social fiat unless society assumes liability for the result of such fiats. Such an assumption would involve partial control over profits, wages, prices, and other factors, and the constraint of that free play of price by which economic factors are interpreted and economic decisions made possible, an unsatisfactory proposition for the reasons given in the last section.

Production, however, could be increased indirectly by increasing the effective demand for goods and services. Since in monopolistic competition, enterprisers tend to gear production to the demand evoked at the administered price, an increase in the effective demand for any or all goods and services would lead, as we have seen,[7] to increased production were production less than full.

In Chapter III, several ways in which demand might be increased to release a wealth increment, were scrutinized. It was decided that a wealth increment made available by an advance in efficiency might be released by a drop in price (Case I), by a rise in wages (Case III), or by the creation and spending of new money (Case IV).

However, our concern in this chapter is not with releasing a wealth increment made available by the advance in efficiency, but with the production of wealth in *addition* to the wealth increment made available by the advance in efficiency, because only by inducing the production of additional wealth can employment be increased and full production approached.

Neither a price drop nor a wage increase unaccompanied by other measures may be counted on to increase employment because lower prices or higher wages reduce over-all net profit [8] *cet. par*, as is evident from the formula. Since private capital formation varies directly with profit expectancy, a drop in price

---

[7] In Chapter IV Section 5, p. 122 and appendix, the reaction of the individual field when faced by an increased demand, was considered. The same conditions holds good were all fields affected.

[8] Although it would be difficult to increase over-all net profit by raising prices or reducing wages for the reasons cited in Chapter III, p. 75, the reverse operation is quite feasible and of frequent occurrence.

or a rise in wages would be more likely to curtail production (due to the reduction in profit expectancy and capital formation) than to increase it, despite the fact that either event would increase wages in relation to profits. However, the increased demand resulting from the tendency of wage earners to withhold a smaller proportion of their income than enterprisers, would probably be more than balanced by the diminished demand resulting from the decreased employment consequent on reduced profits and reduced capital formation.[9] Thus the total of wages would be reduced by disemployment more than it would be increased by the higher rate per hour worked, and over-all demand and production would be lowered.

The creation and spending of new money does not encounter this difficulty.[9a] On the contrary, an injection of new money would be likely to increase profit expectancy as well as the effective demand for consumer goods as indicated in our discussion of Case IV (p. 88). It seems therefore that production could be increased at a time it was short of full by the creation and spending of new money.[10]

This supposition is supported by the record. Chart 1 (p. 126) shows that the production increases between the years 1921 and 1944 were accompanied, by an increase of the money supply. It is notable, however, that new money was not created in order to increase demand and thereby to stimulate wealth production, although in nearly every case it did just this. New money,

[9] The data support this deduction. Though real wages per *hour* increased in 1921, the reduction in profit and in production, reduced total wages below that of the previous year. In general, total wages rise and fall with net over-all profit, though occasionally, as in the post-war deflation, real wages per hour have risen and profits have dropped because of special circumstances. Tables III and VI, pp. 133 and 135.

[9a] An increase in Federal spending paid for by increased taxes might also increase the national income. Such an increase however might be nullified by decreased private investment. For a discussion of the possibilities refer to *Income Generating Effects of a Balanced Budget.* Henry C. Wallich. The Quarterly Journal of Economics. Nov. 1944.

[10] Subject to the qualifications discussed in Chapter V. The discussion indicated that a new money injection would not increase employment in the consumer goods industries unless its dimensions were greater than the value of the residual wealth increment, *cet. par.* Thus, money injections of less than one billion dollars more or less might not increase net employment since such a quantity might be used up in releasing the residual wealth increment.

rather, was created either to float new capital, purchase assets, etc. (as in the 1920's) or to assist going concerns and individuals (as in the 1930's), or to prepare for or wage war (as in the 1940's.) The fact that spending new money stimulates wealth creation (when nonproduction exists) has until recently been largely overlooked.

It has already been indicated (p. 4) that new money spending need not be halted by a lack of money, since new money can be created and spent up to the limit set by product capacity; that is to say, inflation does not result from money creation so long as demand is not increased by the spending of the new money more than supply is increased by the creation of additional wealth. In fact, were demand increased (at a time of nonproduction and unemployment) by the deliberate spending of old [11] and new money on public works or other outlets which did not interfere with the interests of private business,[12] the history of recent decades as well as the logic of this analysis indicates that *production would rise.*

Furthermore, it seems reasonable to suppose that a procedure such as money creation, evolved by the efforts, trials and tribulations of business men over a period of time, a procedure which has often stepped up demand and production in the past, is more likely to prove effective for the purpose than a procedure based on some new-born idea logically deduced.   Let us therefore recall briefly the effect of injecting new money into the spending stream, in order to determine to what extent this device could be used deliberately to increase demand, production, and employment at a time when production was less than full.

1. The cost of commodities, the production of which was subject to price competition, might rise.   For the cost of such commodities may increase to some extent as production is increased.[13] These commodities consist largely of certain farm products.

2. The cost of the commodities, the production of which was

[11] As indicated on p. 145, available old money (withholdings) has to be borrowed and spent before it is feasible to create and spend new money.

[12] Should money be spent on goods for the market, private production might be reduced, thereby preventing the sought-for increase in over-all demand and production.

[13] p. 49.

subject to monopolistic competition or regulated monopoly, would fall as the increased demand permitted a greater percentage of the existing plant to be utilized.

3. The lower cost of processing and servicing would more than neutralize the slightly higher cost of producing certain raw materials because the value added in processing, plus the value of the nonpersonal services (subject by and large to decreasing costs), is many times as great as the value of the raw materials subject to increasing costs.[14] Consequently, the economies of increased production would be appreciably greater than the additional increment of cost in the early stage of the upsurge as the existing plant was increasingly better utilized.

4. Since competitors in monopolistic competition tend to maintain their price and increase their production when the demand for their product rises,[15] at least in the early stages of an upsurge, the spending of new money would result in an appreciable increase in production and only a slight increase in price. As a result, the price of finished products and the cost of living would be increased but slightly, if at all, in the first stages of an upsurge.

5. Greater profits would be realized, as the logic of Case IV indicated. Even the farmers would enjoy greater profits and more farmers would make ends meet as prices and consumption rose. In the case of processors, whole industries would enjoy surplus profits, as equipment that had been idle was put to work at no increase in fixed costs and prices failed to reflect the lower costs.

6. The bargaining power of labor would be strengthened as the unemployed were gradually absorbed. However, in the early stage of the movement, wage increases would be confined, probably, to small, skilled, scarce categories because of the pressure, actual or potential of the unemployed, and the average wage might even fall slightly should the price level rise. Total wages, however, would increase as employment increased.

These effects deduced from the relations described in recent chapters correspond closely to the actual event, as the data cited

[14] p. 52. Also see Flow Sheet, *Chart of Plenty*, or NSPPC report, and compare Column 1 (raw materials) with the other columns (which give the value of goods during several stages of their processing).

[15] p. 123.

in Chapter IV suggests. The statistics indicate that the several production upsurges in recent years, all of which were accompanied by the spending of new money, were marked in their early stages by slightly higher prices for raw materials, a stable or slightly rising price level, increased profits, and a steady real wage level. There is no reason to suppose that the creation and spending of new money at a time of nonproduction, if adopted as a deliberate economic policy, would have dissimilar effects.

However, these results are to be expected *only* in the first stage of a production upsurge.

As the upsurge developed, surplus profits would stimulate private capital formation. For this purpose, new money created, borrowed and spent by private going concerns would be available. This new money would be in addition to the money spent by society on public works. Should the upsurge be permitted to take its course, i.e. should society intervene only to the extent indicated above, capital formation in our system of monopolistic competition would shortly be increased disproportionately (Chapter V, Section 2) just as would occur had the upsurge come about by the private spending of new money (as in the 1920's) Instead of production being increased more than plant capacity, the first result of new money spending on public works, etc., capacity would be increased more than production.

But costs per unit product (effect 2, above) would fall as production increased *only* if plant capacity were constant or increasing less than production. Thus the effects noted above could be counted upon to occur only during the initial phase of a production upsurge instigated by new money spending. Later, as plant capacity was increased more than production and the market was subdivided, overhead per unit costs would rise, profit expectancy would be diminished and a downsurge in production touched off. The possibility of obtaining higher wages (effect 5, above) due to the higher marginal product of the initial stage of the movement might evaporate before higher wages were obtained. Despite the upsurge and the feeling of prosperity induced thereby, the standard of living of the population might, as a result, be increased only by the increased family income resulting from the greater employment and by the fraction of the profit increment spent on consumer goods.

In short, before the increased efficiency of the higher production resulted in appreciably higher wages and living standards, surplus profits would stimulate excess capital formation.   As a result, the tendency of overhead costs to fall as production rose would first be halted and then reversed, thereby inhibiting the increase in the standard of living that otherwise would be possible.

To sum of the gist of the discussion:

The authorities could touch off an upsurge in production by spending new money (in excess of the value of the wealth increment made available by the increase in efficiency) on public works or other products which did not compete with the products of private enterprise at a time of unemployment and non-production.

The increment of demand and production would result largely in increased income for the re-employed and in surplus profits.

Because of the nature of monopolistic competition surplus profits would stimulate private capital formation in excess of the capital formation required to maintain a plant capable of satisfying the demand for consumer goods.   At some point in the movement, profit expectancy would be diminished by the resulting subdividing of the market, and demand and production would be reduced by the arrest of private capital formation.

Thus the increase of demand and production by the spending of new money on public works would not by itself solve our problem.   As was maintained on general grounds in the opening section, in order to achieve capacity production, the equilibrium production, as well as production, would have to be increased, i.e. moved up the scale of production.[16]

It may therefore be concluded that Adjustment 1—the spending of new money on public works—though it could be used to increase production at a time when unemployment existed, would not be safe unless supplemented by other measures. However, its deleterious effects would follow the initial stimulating effect of the money injection by a considerable *time lag*. Adjustment 1 therefore would seem a satisfactory instrument to

[16] p. 170, Figure VII.

touch off a production upsurge even though it could not be counted upon to achieve capacity production or even to sustain a higher production level.

3. CAPITAL FORMATION AND THE WITHHOLDING OF INCOME COULD BE LIMITED BY VARYING CERTAIN TAXES. HOWEVER, TAXATION WOULD NOT BE AN EFFECTIVE INSTRUMENT FOR INCREASING THE PROPENSITY TO CONSUME.

Our next step is to decide how best to limit capital formation (Adjustment 2) without interfering with the freedom of price on the market.   A method is suggested by the fact, noted in Chapter V,[17] that private capital formation varies directly with profit expectancy, cet. par.   Profit expectancy can be raised or lowered by adjusting certain taxes without interfering directly with prices, wages, or production.   Thus, society recently increased profits and profit expectancy by lowering the tax on corporation profits. Perhaps this instrument, now largely justified as a means to raise revenue, could be used in combination with new money spending (Adjustment 1) to obtain a profit expectancy sufficient to induce that capital formation required to maintain an optimum plant. Such a procedure would possess the supplementary and not unimportant advantage of conforming to a line of action (profit taxes) the propriety of which has been accepted by public opinion.   Let us therefore consider its feasibility.

The statistical problem does not seem difficult because there would be no need to discover an exact adjustment.   When capital formation increased plant capacity appreciably faster than production was increasing, taxes could be raised and vice versa. Once full production was approximated, a small adjustment one way or the other would probably be sufficient to reverse the trend whenever capital tended to rise above or fall below that plant which best serviced the demands being made upon it.   Should the dimensions of the optimum plant be disputed, the authorities could play safe by accepting the more generous estimate.[18]

[17] Footnote, p. 145.

[18] Some excess capital would always be desirable as insurance against war and natural catastrophy and some capital formation in addition to that needed for replacement would always be useful in order to provide scope for trying out improved procedures.

In short, taxes on corporation profits could be lowered to stimulate private capital formation when private capital formation was below the optimum volume, and profit taxes could be raised to forestall or reduce the formation of excess capital when private capital formation was in excess of the optimum volume. By these adjustments, a capital plant, capable of efficiently filling the demands made upon it at full production [19] could be maintained.

However, if society allocated the money recaptured by taxation to reducing its debt, production might turn downward since the resulting reduction in the volume of money might [20] reduce demand below the available supply. Such a result could be avoided by spending the recaptured money on additional public works [21] (additional to those being paid for by the money increments of Adjustment 1), so that over-all demand would be sustained even though profit expectancy were reduced.

A further possibility needs to be taken into account. Withheld money (*SE* in the formula) as well as new money is used for private capital formation. The proportion of income that is withheld increases as the individual's income increases. [22] Though increasing the tax on corporation profit would reduce the withholdings of corporations and diminish the withholdings of those individuals whose income accrued largely from dividends, this factor might not balance the increased withholding resulting, as production rose, from the increased income of the community. In short, withholdings would be likely to rise faster than consumer spending, and might approach or even surpass the quantity required to pay for the desired capital formation, notwith-

[19] It is assumed that the staff responsible for interpreting statistics could take into account new inventions and changes in taste which at certain times might hasten obsolescence and thereby increase temporarily the optimum replacement rate for capital. Since the different industries do not move forward together but independently, thereby softening the impact of individual advances, the need for such corrections might be infrequent.

[20] If $GE + SE + \Delta E = (Q + \Delta_r Q)P$, and a ΔE_2 were subtracted by taxation, the equation would be unbalanced. However, were the receipts put back into the spending stream by spending them on public works or otherwise, the balance would not be disturbed.

[21] This procedure would result in an indefinite expansion of public works. A means to hold down public works to the desired volume is considered in Sections 5 and 6.

[22] Assumption III, p. 187.

standing the fact that corporation profit and presumably dividends would be held down by the profit tax.

Should the cost of the desired capital formation be less than the quantity of withheld money, some withheld money, possibly an appreciable quantity, would have nowhere to go. When this occurs, as it often does in the contemporary economy, such money may be applied to the repayment of private debt, either by the individual owner, or by the banker with whom the owner leaves it, if the bank is in debt.[23] In either event, the excess money is withdrawn from the spending stream and demand is reduced by the quantity of withdrawn and cancelled money, multiplied by what would have been its velocity.

It is evident that a production upsurge could be checked by such an occurrence. Consequently, a further interference or adjustment is needed, one similar in method to the adjustment just cited. Not only would it be necessary to use the instrument of taxation to hold profit expectancy within the desired limit, but also another form of taxation would be required in order to keep withholdings (SE) to that quantity required to provide [24] the

[23] In the ordinary course of events, a bank which has surplus funds (i.e. owns more money than it owes) and accepts a deposit for which it has no prospective borrower, or other similar outlet, either buys long term or short term securities, thereby transferring "the spending of the money" to the seller. Thus, in the 1920's, such money was usually put out at call.

However, in the 1930's, the interest rate dropped so low on short term money, that the return was sometimes considered not worth the risk. In this situation, the bank might deposit the money in a larger bank to credit its "due from banks" account. Eventually, if not loaned out along the way, most of these deposits would come to rest in a Federal Reserve Bank.

In some years, these idle deposits increased. When this happens, the quantity of money is not reduced by the "withholding," but over-all effective demand is reduced just as if the money were cancelled. The event would appear in the national balance sheet as a decrease in the velocity of money and would have to be taken into account, as noted in the appendix to Chapter III, pp. 92–94.

It is our thought (in contradistinction to that of the Keynsian school) that the above occurrence is a symptom of the physical unbalance under discussion (excess capital) rather than its cause. Could excess capital formation and its reverse, deficient consumer goods buying power, be eliminated, deposits would, as a matter of course, always have somewhere to go. Since banks and other receivers of "withheld funds" are in business to make money, such institutions would put such money to work expeditiously. Attacking the problem from the money end is subject to the difficulties noted in the above mentioned appendix.

[24] It might be desired to keep withholdings somewhat short of the capital formation induced by profit expectancy so that the gap would be bridged by new money spending (the new money needed to release the residual wealth increment). The

requisite capital formation. Since withholdings, as was indicated in Chapter V, are a function of income disparity, the greater the disparity, the greater the proportion withheld, the graduated income tax of today, which reduces income disparity, might be used to achieve the desired income disparity—the disparity which induced the withholding required to pay for the requisite private capital formation.

Were income taxes used as suggested above to secure an income distribution which induced a net withholding equal to the cost of maintaining the optimum capital plant, it might be asked if a tax on corporation profits, designed to secure that profit expectancy which induced an optimum capital formation, would be necessary.

It is evident that even if income taxes secured the desired withholding, the adjustment of profit expectancy would be necessary because withholdings do not govern investments in the contemporary economy. Thus debts would be repaid, and the effective demand would fall short of the available supply were profit expectancy less than the profit expectancy which caused the total of withheld money to be invested. On the other hand, should profit expectancy exceed the profit expectancy which induced the total of withheld money to be invested, additional money would be created and allocated to additional capital formation. In either case, profit taxes would be needed: in the first case to increase profit expectancy and thereby to stimulate private capital formation; in the second case to reduce profit expectancy and thereby to discourage capital formation in excess of the desired amount.

advisability of doing this would depend on the relation of taxation to public works. Should taxation fully cover the cost of the desired public works, then the requisite new money spending could be induced by leaving the above mentioned gap. Should, however, taxation fall short of the cost of the public works program, as would be likely during the initial stages of an upsurge when Adjustment 1 was being exerted to reduce unemployment, then withholdings sufficient to cover the cost of the total private capital formation would be advisable. In this situation, the government would spend the requisite new money as indicated in our discussion of Adjustment 1.

For the sake of simplicity, this complication will not be referred to in the text. It will be assumed in this section that withholdings should be equal to private capital formation.

Although the above adjustments may sound complicated, they are in some ways more logical than contemporary procedures in which the dimensions of income and profit taxes are in part decided by compromising the views of opposing pressure groups. If our analysis is valid, the dimensions of these taxes should not be subject to debate but to statistical determination, on the basis of the economic considerations suggested above quite regardless of the relative strengths of political or class organizations.

Adjustment 2, then, would include not only a profit tax designed to secure an optimum capital formation, but also a graduated income and inheritance tax so that the income disparity which induced the withholding needed to pay for the desired capital formation might be approximated.

An exact determination of the dimensions of these taxes would not be necessary as noted above, since errors of judgment or execution could gradually be reduced by subsequent adjustments and the optimum tax rates gradually approached.

It may also be relevant to note that the adjustments suggested above work both ways. Should, for example, capacity production be sought at the termination of hostilities, both profit and income taxes might have to be drastically curtailed. At the moment of writing this passage (July 1944), existing profit taxes probably restrict profit expectancy more than would be needed at the onset of peace to secure an optimum capital formation, and existing income taxes might reduce withholdings below the quantity needed to pay for the capital formation required to sustain full production. The desired quantitative relations can only be guessed at while the war lasts. However, when the economy had been reconverted to peacetime pursuits, the statistical indices will indicate perhaps in an alarming manner whether the taxes in question are too high or too low. Adjustments could be made accordingly.

Were these taxes adjusted as suggested above, the fraction of the total effort made available by full production and not required for capital formation, desired government expenditure, or to meet the demand for consumer goods, would be recovered by society and allocated to public works of a non-competitive character. As a result, demand would continue to command the supply made available, and production would not be curtailed. But public works and public debt would increase indefinitely.

In order to avoid this result, a further adjustment will be suggested in the sections which follow, an adjustment designed to reroute the income (which otherwise would be spent on unwanted public works) into consumer spendings. Let us postpone its consideration, however, to make one further comment upon the two adjustments considered above.

Adjustments 1 and 2 could be combined as suggested to achieve full production. In fact, this possibility was mentioned in Chapter V, when the effect of paying for public works with created money was considered.[25] Since it is an alternative solution to the one which is in process of formulation, it was called Solution II. Its feasibility has been demonstrated by the experience of Germany and Japan.

Thus the German government successfully reduced nonproduction and unemployment even before the war by spending new money on munitions and other public works. It recovered the increased profits resulting from the new money spending and the more efficient plant utilization in large part by taxation and more or less forced loans. Since it desired to maximize the diversion of effort to public works, it held down and, it is reported, even reduced the income of some workers by controlling wages, and limited the rise in farmers' and other enterprisers' income by controlling prices. By these means, the increased profit resulting from the better plant utilization was largely sluiced into direct and indirect preparation for war. Nevertheless, the feasibility of using money creation and taxation to achieve full production was demonstrated.

It is evident that Solution II would not be satisfactory to the American people. Even though wages and prices were left free to find their economic level and consumer goods production was expanded to meet the resulting increase in demand, much of the benefit of the production increase would be translated into public works. Only if the American people turned imperialist and set out to conquer an additional segment of the earth's surface, or

[25] p. 177.

decided to build monuments of a stupendous size, would they accept the diversion of so large a share of their income to this outlet. Also, Solution II has certain troublesome features. Its execution might involve the unlimited creation and spending of new money. Although no physical limit stops money creation, as was indicated in Chapter I, and injecting money into the spending stream does not cause inflation so long as a demand is not increased more than the supply, the growth of internal debt in time might cause fiscal difficulties.[26] Furthermore, Solution II would fail to achieve *capacity production* or to maximize consumer satisfactions. Not only would effort which might be used to raise the living standard be diverted into less desirable constructions, but the heavy restrictive taxes would inhibit to some extent the flux and flow of the market place which, by its ceaseless turmoil, subjects a multiplicity of products to trial before public opinion, thereby continually evolving new forms and ways of living.

The inadequacy of taxation and money creation unsupplemented by other measures to accomplish the results desired is because taxation can be used to reduce or hold down an income category but cannot be used at full employment to raise an income category except by combining it with a subsidy or other form of charity. And charity is an undesirable means of distributing income except to the unemployed or disabled, and is likely to demoralize even the unemployed if the recaptured money is distributed as relief, or paid out for so-called "made work." Thus, taxation in combination with new money creation and public works might be utilized to attain full employment and to hold down excess private capital formation and excess withholdings. It would not, however, increase the demand for consumer goods and thereby the living standard above the demand and standard of full employment.[27] Some measure, therefore, in addition to new money spending (Adjustment 1) and tax adjustments (Adjustment 2) is called for—a measure capable of raising lower incomes as higher incomes are held down by the two taxes.

[26] This aspect of the problem is considered on pp. 255 ff.
[27] GQP_F in Figure VII, p. 170, $GQP_F < GQP_J$.

4. THE PROPENSITY TO CONSUME COULD NOT BE INCREASED BY IMPOSING LOWER PRICES WITHOUT ARRESTING THE FREE PLAY OF PRICE ON THE MARKET.

Capacity production, it was indicated in the last section, could not be achieved by spending new money and restricting capital formation since these measures, even though they achieved full employment and an optimum capital plant, might result in undesired public works and an indefinitely increasing public debt. Society therefore would be deprived of satisfactions which it was physically and technically equipped to gratify unless a further adjustment was made. To derive the full benefit from full employment, consumer goods production would have to be increased as capital formation was restrained so that public works could be held to that quota desired for their own sake.

Because of the dependence of production upon demand in fields of monopolistic competition, consumer goods production would be increased were the propensity to consume, i.e. the ratio of consumer goods demand to withholdings,[28] increased. Let us therefore consider what adjustment would accomplish this end.

Either lower prices or higher wages would increase the propensity to consume since both events enhance the income of the poor who spend more, in relation to that of the rich who withhold more. The first of these possibilities is advocated by many economic schools and political factions. Brookings Institution as well as the New Deal, laissez-faire economists as well as over-all planners, free traders, consumer and producer cooperators, socialists, single taxers, and many of the great industrialists favor lower prices. Even those groups organized to raise prices, such as farmer organizations, favor lower prices for everything but farm produce, and organized labor favors lower prices for everything but manhours. Seldom is such unanimity to be observed over a controversial issue. Yet little is done about lowering the price level beyond the writing of books, the making of speeches, and the passing of resolutions.

It is true lower prices are usually put forward as a means to enable the population to purchase more goods with the same

[28] The ratio GE/SE.

money, on the supposition that increased buying power would induce increased consumption and production. The improbability of accomplishing this result by price reductions unsupplemented by other measures was brought out in earlier sections. Not only would lower prices *per se* narrow the profit margin thereby curtailing capital formation and over-all production [29] but lower prices *per se* would force high cost producers out of production [30] in fields of price competition, and would entail losses [31] in fields of monopolistic competition. In short, lower prices *per se* would be likely to do more harm than good, although particular price reductions, as was brought out in Chapter II, would be of value in special situations. [32]

However, our present objective is narrower than the general purpose cited above, and does not incur the difficulties referred to. It is proposed to increase production by Adjustment 1. As production rose and excess capital was brought into use, per unit costs would fall. [33] Instead of diverting the potential increase of profit not required for private capital formation, into public works by way of taxes (Adjustment 2), a means is sought to divert this increase and perhaps an additional quantity [34] to the underlying population so that the demand for consumer goods would be increased in relation to withholdings.

Were mathematics the sole consideration, this limited objective could be attained by lowering prices. For example, should Adjustment 1 step up the demand for motor cars from 4 to 5 million cars, and should the higher production rate permit each car to be produced for $100 less on the average, the motor car companies could reduce their prices by this amount without loss. However, the procedure would be complicated owing to the fact that the public might choose to increase their purchases of certain manufacturers' cars and pass by the cars of other manufacturers. Furthermore, the operation would necessitate the separate calculation of the prospective cost reduction of every process and the

[29] p. 218.

[30] p. 32.

[31] p. 42.

[32] pp. 57 ff., 234.

[33] pp. 49 ff.

[34] The problem of determining the amount of the requisite diversion is considered on pp. 238 ff.

freezing of every price. If the controls were effected by a social authority [35] and no alternative is apparent, the impracticability of this approach is evident. Even the price freezing orders of the war period had to be supplemented by subsidies, priorities, material allocations, component scheduling, and hundreds of other administrative devices in order to keep production on a not too uneven keel and the economy more or less pointed to the indicated objectives. Despite war powers, shortages and surpluses succeeded each other with a dizzy rapidity. With production goals unknown, or variously estimated, the administrative problem would be even more complicated. However, the basic objection would be the arrest of the parametric function of price, with the disastrous result stressed in earlier chapters. Like centralized planning, centralized pricing does not appear to be a feasible solution.

The imposition of an over-all price cut, though easier to estimate, would also be unworkable since it could not be imposed without freezing prices, and the prices thus arrived at would be proportioned to the reduction in costs only by accident.

The authorities could intervene to lower prices by still another method. Instead of attempting direct action, they could take measures such as those suggested in Chapter VI to compel price competition. But over-all price competition is infeasible as the discussion of Chapter VI indicated. And an increase in the area in which price competition prevailed would be likely to throw additional industries into the desperate straits experienced by the farmers in the 1930's.

Since exhortation and persuasion have failed to induce lower prices, and since no method of attaining this end other than the infeasible measures suggested above comes to mind, it appears probable that the desired increase in the propensity to consume

[35] The word "social" instead of political will be used to qualify "authorities" because of the nature of the decisions which the authorities in question would be called upon to make. A nonpartisan, nonelective body akin to the Interstate Commerce Commission would be desirable because elected officials are seldom free to make decisions regardless of the views of their constituents and pressure groups. It is evident that decisions should be decided on the basis of the objective factors. Consequently, a scientific approach would be advisable and such an approach could be best approximated by an appointed committee.

will have to be achieved by some other procedure than by compelling lower prices.

Perhaps our dismissal of social interference with pricing should be qualified by recalling certain situations in which interference seems warranted.

The existing economic system consists, as was noted, in part of monopolistic competition, in part of price competition, and in part of regulated monopoly. It is generally recognized, that the regulated monopolies occasionally or frequently curtail their profits by holding prices above the price which maximizes returns. In any case, the prices set by many regulated monopolies are regularly reviewed and sometimes lowered by social boards. The procedure is difficult owing to the intangible nature of many costs (amortization, etc.) and does not operate any too well. However, the imperfect nature of the procedure does not lead to serious consequences, since too high prices in time induce their own correction. Thus, when the railroads hold their rates too high, motor bus competition is encouraged. When the utilities hold their rates too high, the construction of municipal power plants is stimulated. Presumably a price as economic as most other prices is arrived at eventually by the regulated monopolies in one way or another.

However, monopoly, at least imperfect monopoly, exists in other branches of industry in which prices are not reviewed by social boards. The best known example is the aluminum industry, in which 90 per cent of the industry used to be controlled by one company. It is possible, that in some years the price of aluminum has been held higher than that price which would maximize profits. The result has been social loss, since a lower price would have increased the production and consumption of aluminum without damaging the industry or curtailing the income of the enterpriser. Although this situation has been frequently corrected by the aluminum executives waking to the fact that more money could be made at a lower price, the correction may sometimes be delayed overlong. And it is probable that many less important products, particularly in the class of semi-finished and producer goods, are subject to the same probability.[36]

[36] p. 59.

It would seem that in these situations, Federal and anti-trust prosecution (which amounts to an interference in pricing) or at least the threat of anti-trust prosecution, would carry a salutary effect.

Except for the situations noted above and such similar situations as may occur in the future, it seems advisable therefore to continue to permit prices to be established by the competition of vendors on the market as described in Chapter II, so that price could continue to reflect changes in efficiency and in the demand for particular products, and the economy would continue to maintain its ability to allocate scarce resources economically.

5. THE PROPENSITY TO CONSUME COULD BE INCREASED BY RAISING THE MINIMUM WAGE WITHOUT ARRESTING THE FREE PLAY OF PRICE ON THE MARKET.

It was suggested in the last section that a rise in wages as well as a drop in prices would decrease income disparity and thereby increase the propensity to consume.[37]   However, wage fixing is subject to some of the same objections as price fixing.   For example, should the authorities, with the help of the labor unions, or otherwise, attempt to release the wealth increments made available by individual efficiency advances by raising the wages of the workers directly involved, prices, as was indicated in Chapter III [38] would be prevented from reflecting changes in technology. On the other hand, if a general wage increase was compelled by law or union pressure, wages would have to be crystallized and their parametric function arrested.   The uneconomic result of freezing any prices, even wages, has been sufficiently emphasized.

Should wages be raised by the social authorities putting the unemployed to work at wages higher [39] than the wage current in the industries to which they belonged, certain difficulties would be avoided.   Employers would be forced to pay higher wages not by a minimum wage law but because they could not obtain workers at a lower wage.   They are conditioned to support this event, since wages have often been forced up by labor shortages.

[37] The ratio *GE/SE*.
[38] p. 70.
[39] The effect of raising the wage of the less competent is considered on pp. 259 ff.

And a deliberately induced shortage would not arrest the freedom of wages and other prices to reflect economic factors, because raising wages by hiring the unemployed at higher than current wages would allow some scope for bargaining. Presumably wages would rise above the levels thus established by the authorities in those industries which responded most to the increased over-all demand. Wages in the lagging industries would, on the other hand, tend to cling close to the minimum.

However, this procedure would in practice be difficult if not impossible to execute. In any case, it would be wasteful. It would devolve upon the social authorities to hire the various categories of labor in quantities fixed not by the requirements of the public works program (on which the new money was being spent) but by the dimensions of the various labor surpluses. Thus, shipbuilders would have to be put to work at higher than shipbuilding wages, regardless of the possibility that they would never again be needed for building ships. Were it possible to devise a public works program which would utilize the various categories of surplus labor in their existing dimensions by selecting public works with this end in view, the result would be the perpetuation of the maladjustments existing in the labor supply, a consummation costly to society and hard on the individual whose particular skill was no longer needed. Even though full employment at higher wages were obtained by this means, the worker at "made" work would be unable to escape the demoralization associated with futile functioning.

Raising the wage of the lowest paid wage workers escapes most of these difficulties.[40] Such a raise could be accomplished either by law or by hiring the unemployed at a wage higher than the lowest current wage. Since it is being assumed that all or nearly all of the unemployed are to be hired by society in any case, this being the essence of Adjustment 1, there would be little point in raising the minimum wage by law. Hiring the unemployed at wages higher than the current minimum would effec-

[40] Because of regional differences, the imposing of a uniform minimum wage would be impractical in one step. Probably regional differentials would work better, differentials which might gradually be reduced as the prosperity induced by full employment, made itself felt in the backward areas.

tively raise the minimum wage of everyone in the low wage brackets except the few who would prefer to work for private employers at a wage less than that which they could obtain from the government. These few could do as they liked without appreciable effect on the economy. Thus the waste and emotion of the elaborate compliance procedure involved in raising wages by law could be avoided. Furthermore, raising wages by raising the wages only of the lowest paid group *would not interfere* with the ability of particular wages (excepting the minimum) to reflect economic factors. As a result, the parametric function of price would be undisturbed.

A further advantage inheres in this procedure. The purpose of the wage increase is to augment the propensity to consume. An increase in any current wage would augment this propensity because recipients of less than $4,600 a year withhold a smaller proportion of their income than the average. Those receiving $3,000 a year, for example, save some 1% only of their income.[41] Those receiving $1,500 a year *or less* save little or nothing out of their incomes. An increase from $2,500 a year to, for example, $3,000 a year would have less effect on the propensity to consume than an increase from $1,000 a year to $1,500 a year. Thus, an increase in the minimum wage affecting only the non- and minus-withholders [42] would result in nearly the whole of the increase being spent on consumer goods and services; and a five billion dollar increase of the minimum wage would result in nearly a five billion dollar increase in spending and no appreciable increase in withholding. Consequently, an increase in the minimum wage would increase the propensity to consume more effectively than any other possible wage increase.

It therefore seems probable that raising the wage of the lowest paid category of labor would be an effective means of supplementing a money spending and taxation program so that such a program would not only eliminate unemployment but also would increase the demand for consumer goods in relation to withholdings, that is to say, the propensity to consume. Let us, therefore, consider the procedure with care.

[41] *America's Capacity to Consume*, Brookings Institution, p. 262.
[42] A few million individuals, i.e., minus withholders, spend more than they earn by accepting charity in one way or another.

Were the propensity to consume increased by raising the minimum wage, it would probably be desirable to increase costs by
raising wages more than costs were reduced by the increased
efficiency of the higher production levels.   The reason is that the
wage increase, to achieve the desired purpose, would have to
augment the demand for consumer goods by approximately that
amount which otherwise would be diverted to excess withholdings as production was stepped up from x-level to full, an amount
larger than the cost reductions resulting from the increased efficiency of the higher production level because withholdings continue to increase as income increases while the cost reductions
realized from increased production tend to level off as production
approaches full.   The dimensions of the differential are suggested by our war experience.   Savings plus taxation are expected to total 100 billion dollars out of a prospective gross
national production of 200 billion in the fiscal year 1945 if the
war continues.[43]   We may assume that 200 billion 1945 dollars
represents the approximate value of full production.[44]   This total
consists of some 100 billion dollars worth of civilian products and
some 100 billion dollars worth of war products.   The civilian
products will be paid for largely by consumer spending.   The
war products will be paid for in part by money collected by taxation—some 23 billion; in part by money withheld by the population—some 36.5 billion; [45] in part by created money—some 40
billion, more or less.

When the war ends and reconversion is completed, 100 billion
dollars will *not* be needed for government expenditures and private capital formation.   Fifty billion is nearer the probable figure.   Consequently, should full production be maintained, some

[43] *Report of the Budget Director*, August 2, 1944.

[44] Although 11 million men have been removed from productive labor, it is
doubtful if more than 200 billion 1945 dollars worth of goods and services could be
produced in peacetime because over 12 billion dollars worth of overtime as well as
the services of some millions of women, old men, etc. who would retire were hostilities terminated, have contributed to creating the total.   The gross national product
for 1950 with 2 million unemployed is estimated by Hagen & Kirkpatrick ("The
American Economic Review," Sept. 1944) at 195 billion 1944 dollars.   This estimate may be slightly low because no allowance is made for the diversion of workers
from selling to manufacturing, for an increase of real income from better homes
and other by-products of sustained full production.

[45] *Current Business*, Department of Commerce, September 1944.

50 billion dollars worth of effort more or less would have to be spent on undesired public works [46] (Adjustment 1) unless the demand for consumer goods could be raised from $100 to nearly $150 billion, and withholdings, taxes, and money creation reduced from $100 to $50 billion.

It is true that the above rough estimate somewhat over-states the enormity of the problem. Withholdings are inordinately high because of wartime pressures. Consumer goods demand is curtailed in many lines because of shortages. The operation, that is to say, the increase in the propensity to consume, would not have to be effected in one year. (The nation will probably spend considerable sums on the reconstruction and the equipping of foreign economies for several years after the war). Nevertheless, the conclusion is inescapable that if society is to take full advantage of its product capacity, its individual members will have to increase their consumption of goods and services to an unprecedented degree, or reconcile themselves to public works, excess exports, etc. comparable in amount to recent wartime expenditures.[47]

This conclusion is also indicated on other grounds. For example, the correlation of steel production and the national income [48] for the period 1919 to 1940 indicates that some 140 million tons of ingot steel would be demanded at a national income of $160 billion (which very roughly is equivalent to a gross national product of $200 billion). Steel capacity today is about 90 million tons. Consequently, full production would apparently require a 55 per cent increase in steel capacity to meet the resulting demand for steel should the relationship of capital formation to consumer goods production of recent decades hold good in the future.

However, were capital formation held down to plant maintenance (defined to include improvements), then 90 million tons of steel with some help from the increased supply of aluminum now available, appears to be ample since the capital formation of 1929 (which more than maintained the 1929 plant) plus the consumer

[46] Or excess exports, inventory increases, etc.
[47] The recent pamphlet "National Budgets for Full Employment," National Planning Assn., is a statistical study of the gap suggested above.
[48] Chart, p. 98, *Business Week*, July 24, 1944.

durables, etc. of that year took less than 57 million tons of steel ingots. It therefore is probable that existing steel capacity would be adequate for full production should the propensity to consume be increased and capital formation held down, as suggested in this chapter.

Likewise, the capacity to produce consumer goods and services promises to be adequate to meet the prospective demand. Data on this subject are neither up to date nor complete. However, the N.S.P.P.C.[49] estimated the budget which would be demanded were poverty eliminated, on the assumption that the lowest income groups would purchase goods and services in about the same proportions as do the relatively well-to-do, were they able to do so. Then it checked this budget against the national resources and product capacity of 1934. It concluded that the American economy, by putting unemployed men, machines, and knowledge to work, could have provided a liberal diet for everyone instead of the subsistence diet to which so many were then constrained, two to three times as much new clothing as that obtained in 1929, and a new car per family every five years.

Furthermore, within six to ten years of full production, every family according to this study, could have been provided with a modern, well equipped dwelling unit or its equivalent, adequate medical care and an enormous increase of its educational and recreational facilities, all this to be accomplished without curtailing the consumption of those who in 1929 had been consuming more, or reducing the effort allocated in 1929 to capital formation. In short, every American family might have enjoyed within a few years (to allow for building houses, training doctors, teachers, etc.) a minimum income of goods and services worth some four thousand 1929 dollars.

Thirty-four million families at $4,000 a year each, amounts to 136 billion dollars to which must be added some 10 or 20 billion dollars worth of goods and services for the additional consumption of those earning more than $4,000 a year. Consumer goods and services to provide such a budget could nearly have been produced in the 1930's according to the study being quoted. Since then, capacity has been expanded more than the popula-

[49] *op. cit.*

tion. It appears, therefore, that the 150 billion dollars worth of consumer goods and services, which the war record suggests would have to be demanded if full employment were to be sustained without war or other undesired public outlay, is not far from the value [50] of the budget which would be demanded were some $4,000 a year the minimum family income.

It is proposed to achieve this minimum family income by gradually raising the minimum wage to some $2,500 a year,[51] the raise to be accomplished by engaging such unemployed as exist and persist [52] on public works. Obviously the increase need not be made in one step. First, the unemployed could be largely absorbed. When the economy had adjusted itself to full employment, the wage could be raised. But a wage increase, as noted above, increases costs. Increased costs at full production result in lower profits or higher prices. Before rounding out our program by adopting this proposal as Adjustment 3, it is necessary to consider the effect of this latter condition.

A reduction in over-all net profit would be infeasible because it is planned to limit profit by Adjustment 2 to that quantity which induced an optimum capital formation. A supplementary cut, it is evident would obstruct this adjustment. Also, a reduction in profit achieved by raising the minimum wage [53] would force marginal producers out of business, thereby interfering with the accomplishment of capacity production. Furthermore, it would be difficult and sometimes impossible to compel a private concern to absorb higher costs without controlling prices, etc. Since price control has been judged impractical on other grounds, the possibility of translating the increased costs of the higher wage into lower profits, need not be considered further.

The alternative to lower profits is to permit the price of those products whose costs had increased to find their level according to the method of price or monopolistic competition, whichever

[50] The price levels of 1929 and 1945 are not far enough apart to invalidate this judgment.

[51] If each two families averages three gainfully employed, a wage of $2,500 provides a family income just short of $4,000. Some supplementary income may be assumed.

[52] Employment by private industry would increase as production increased in response to the money spending of Adjustment 1.

[53] A reduction in profit achieved by graduated taxation would not force anyone out of business because of its incidence.

the case might be.   This course would result in a rise in the price
level which would have to be taken into account by the administrators of Adjustment 3, since it would to some extent neutralize
the increase in wages.   However, a small price rise that would
neutralize only a small part of the wage increase does not constitute an irremediable objection for the following reason.

Prices would not rise evenly throughout industry.   On the
contrary, raising the minimum wage would increase the operating cost of low wage scale industries only.   But stepping up production by spending new money on public works (Adjustment 1)
would reduce the overhead cost of those operations which previously had possessed excess plant capacity.   Evidently, the industries whose costs were increased by the higher minimum wage
would not be the same as the industries whose costs were lowered
by the increase in production since high wages, excess plant
capacity and the condition of decreasing costs are found largely
in the industries practicing monopolistic competition; and low
wages, little or no excess plant capacity and increasing costs are
found largely in the industries approaching price competition.
Thus the first class would experience a reduction in overhead
costs without incurring an increase in operating costs and vice
versa.   Since free prices are being postulated, the industries
whose costs were raised by the increase in wages would seek and
doubtless obtain higher prices and the industries whose costs
were lowered by the step-up in production would not lower their
prices.   It is necessary to determine whether these complications
render the proposed adjustment unserviceable.   Let us therefore
risk being repetitive by recalling what would happen in the actual
economy were the minimum wage raised.

As noted above, the low-wage, low-profit industries, which include the price competition industries, such as farming, would be
faced by higher per unit operating costs.   The price of their
products would therefore rise, and the demand for certain of their
products *might* [54] fall despite the concurrent increase in over-all

[54] Increasing the income of the poorest families would result in a sharp increase
in the demand for the more expensive foodstuffs as the war experience and certain
studies now in process indicate.   Consequently the net effect on the demand for
farm products subject to two opposite forces, would in many cases be inconsiderable.

demand due to the new money spending. In any case, the demand for the products whose price was increased would not rise as much as the demand for the other products whose price would not increase.

This result, however, is not contrary to the public interest. Demand is always falling for one product or another, even as the demand for other products is rising. It is a phase of the evolutionary process by which better (qualitatively) or cheaper products (i.e., products requiring a smaller man-hour input) supersede poorer or more costly products. The fact that an increase in the price of the lowest labor category would expedite one phase of this process is a point in its favor.

For example, should raspberry cultivation continue to require a high (unskilled) man-hour input, the raising of the cost of the lowest paid workers would necessitate a higher price for raspberries. As a result, the demand for raspberries might fall in relation to the demand for other fruits. But this is as it should be. Either some other fruit would acquire a part of the former raspberry demand or a new raspberry would be developed which could be picked and packed more quickly. *There is no justification for the production of commodities, the demand for which depends on a fraction of society living at a level lower than that technically feasible for all competent members* [55] *of the community.* The economic basis for this value judgment is implicit in our analysis.

Providing all men who want work with a job at a wage higher than the current minimum wage would permit the higher wage industries engaged in monopolistic competition to realize surplus profits. These industries would realize a reduction in overhead costs due to their increased operating rate, and no increase in operating costs, since their workers would not be affected by the rise in the minimum wage. And the increase in costs of certain of their raw material supplies, would, as noted elsewhere, amount in most cases to less than the reduction in overhead costs.

Since price maintenance and production control prevail in

[55] An increase in efficiency does not require an increase in competency. Sometimes it has an opposite effect. Nevertheless some members of the community would not be competent enough to earn the minimum wage. These would have to be taken care of in other ways as they are today. The problem is considered on p. 259.

monopolistic competition, the price of the products of these industries would probably not be lowered by the full amount of the
saving in net cost.   Instead, surplus profits would be realized as
production was stepped up.

However, increased profits, too, are in the public interest.
Higher profits are in themselves good.   Like higher wages, they
enable people to increase their consumption of goods, their living
standard, and their satisfaction.   Thus the fact that certain profits, like certain wages, would be increased, may be considered
advantageous unless the greater profit should result, as it has in
the production upsurges of recent decades, in excess capital
formation.   But as full production was approached, Adjustment
2 would be used to discourage excess capital formation by holding
down these surplus profits.

Furthermore, should the program under discussion be inaugu-
rated, as would be probable, during a depression—during, that
is to say, a period in which net private capital formation had
come to, or nearly come to, a halt—higher profits would be
needed in order to stimulate private capital formation.   At such
a time, plant renovation is usually required and new processes,
etc. are usually waiting to be installed.   The renewal of private
capital formation would relieve the public authorities from the
necessity of finding work for *all* the unemployed.   If, as the
unemployed were being enlisted on public works, the demand for
additional workers on the part of private interests also surged
forward, full employment would evidently be attained more
quickly and more easily than if the total reemployment were
accomplished by the public agency.

Thus, raising the minimum wage at a time production was
being stepped up by new money spending, would raise wages
and prices in the price competition industries and production
and profits in the monopolistic competition industries (and in
the regulated monopolies).   It would thereby reduce the gap between low wages and high wages and divert an increasing proportion of the total effort into the high wage, high profit, high marginal product industries.

Concretely, farm and other low-priced labor would receive
more pay, the employers being compensated by higher prices.

At the same time, more men would find scope for functioning in manufacturing and building (high wage activities when employment is year-long), educational work, recreation, therapy, and other specialized activities held down to relatively small proportions in peace years because a great section of the population have incomes so low, from unemployment, low wages, and low profits, that they are deprived of providable goods and services.

Eventually, as prices and wages rose in the low marginal product activities (the price index rising slightly) and production increased especially in the high marginal product activities the gap between the marginal product of the various activities would narrow and income disparity would be reduced.

But this is the very result the procedure was designed to achieve. Perhaps another aspect of the situation will bring out more clearly why so happy a consequence may be expected.

Income disparity may be due to (a) the accumulation of enterpriser and property income in a few hands, (b) surplus profits and lagging wages, and (c) the spread between the wages and profits in the low marginal product industries and the wages and profits in the high marginal product industries.

The first source, though important in the 1920's, has since been reduced by losses and taxation. It is probable that a further increase in income taxes is not needed to induce a withholding equal to the quantity required for capital formation and public works at full employment. In fact, existing taxes would probably prove excessive by the above criterion in a peace economy.

The second source is inappreciable during depressions, even negative at the nadir of the business cycle. Furthermore, if corporation taxes were so adjusted that capital formation approximated the optimum capital formation, a further increase in profit taxes would result in a deficient capital formation. Consequently, profit taxation could not be utilized to decrease income disparity. In fact, profit taxation might have to be reduced from present levels (1944) for profit expectancy again to induce the requisite private capital formation.

It has been indicated that consumer spending would be too low and withholding too high at full employment with wages equal to the present marginal product of labor, were excess capital held within desired limits. Since taxing higher incomes and inhibiting surplus profit would not correct the difficulty for the reasons noted [56] income disparity due to source (c) would have to be reduced.

In the hypothetic economy of the theorists, this disparity is supposed [57] to be held within narrow limits automatically, that is to say, the marginal product of the various activities is supposed to approach a common norm by the reasonable reactions of free individuals. Men engaged in activities whose marginal product is low are supposed to desert them for fields of activities whose marginal product is high. In fact, such a process has been observed and commented upon for many decades. For example, workers have been drifting from the farms to the mills. Were this factor effective, such income disparity as existed would be due in large part to source (a) or (b).

In the actual economy the force which persuades individuals to desert fields of low pay in order to better their condition has been rendered more or less impotent by unemployment. As noted previously, a job may be left with impunity only if other jobs are available. And for many years in the Twentieth Century and in every year between 1929 and 1941, jobs have been far fewer in number than job seekers. As a result, the disparity between wages in the various fields of effort has become very wide, far wider than the relative scarcities of the various skills or the relative attractiveness of the various jobs would justify.

We are seeking to decrease income disparity so that the propensity to consume may be increased. Adjustment 3 would seem the most suitable device to accomplish this purpose because it appears to be the only method by which wage disparity could be diminished without arresting the free play of price on the market.

Furthermore, Adjustment 3 would not increase wages appreciably in relation to profits but would increase wages in relation to total income. Consequently, raising the minimum wage would not interfere with Adjustment 2 by which an economic capital formation and a withholding consonant with the capital

[56] pp. 224 ff.
[57] p. 8.

formation would be induced by varying profit and income taxes.

In short an increase in the minimum wage would seem to be a feasible device to decrease income disparity and increase the propensity to consume.

6. TO CORRELATE THE THREE ADJUSTMENTS EFFECTIVELY WOULD REQUIRE THAT PART OF THE PUBLIC WORKS PROGRAM (ADJUSTMENT 1) SHOULD BE ELASTIC.

An interesting aspect of the proposed solution is the fact that the *three adjustments under discussion have already been instituted.* New money has been spent on public works, capital formation has been discouraged by graduated taxation, savings have been curtailed by the income tax, and a minimum wage has been established by law and by public relief. The institution of these measures has not led to disaster. On the contrary, conditions seem to have been bettered by them. That is to say, wealth creation increased in the years when new money was spent on public works. The capital plant was maintained before the war, despite the profit tax, at a level capable of more than satisfying the demands made upon it. Withholdings in peace years were more than ample to pay for the capital despite the graduated income tax. Consumer buying power rose when the minimum wage was instituted, apparently without depriving other members of the community of butter, eggs, or other desired commodities.

It is therefore reasonable to conclude that the measures in themselves are workable, i.e. that new money spending, graduated taxation and the establishment of a minimum wage, are feasible operations. Difficulties need be looked for not in the measures themselves but in their extension and coordination.

It is true the measures have not been coordinated to reduce nonproduction. In fact they have not been coordinated. Our proposed solution departs from current usage chiefly in that it proposes to administer certain existing social controls to reduce unemployment, to limit excess capital formation, and to raise the standard of living.

It remains to suggest how these controls might be coordinated so that these goals would be realized.

As suggested in the first section, a blueprint or five year plan would not be necessary, and might even cause difficulties. One reason is that the end sought consists of a balance or relationship and not of a predetermined quantitative goal. It is true that a quantity is involved, that is to say, the optimum budget of goods and services which could be produced. But this quantity would not be known in advance, because the effect of stepping up production upon technology and demand is unforeseeable, though, to be sure, it could be guessed at.

Should the United States choose to raise the standard of living of the underprivileged by authoritative rationing, presumably a plan could be drawn up as was noted above (p. 214) which would utilize the dispensable manpower, resources and equipment to provide a budgeted quota of goods and services. This procedure, however, even if successful in eliminating unnecessary poverty would be incapable of translating the myriad desires, ambitions, capacities, fancies, inspirations, etc., of millions of people into goods, services, jobs, vanities, victories, defeats, etc.— a translation which constitutes an essential aspect of that variously defined ideal sometimes called democracy. This would seem to be the ideological objection to a system of bountiful rationing.

The technical objection need merely be recalled. As brought out in Chapter II and elsewhere, however effective a planned procedure might be in the first place, it would run into trouble by its inability to translate changing desires and scarcities into appropriate prices and production schedules, with the result that sooner or later the touchstone by which resources are economically utilized would lose its effectiveness.

We have therefore foregone the master plan approach and propose instead to obtain capacity production by manipulating the three adjustments or controls described in the foregoing sections by an empirical trial and error method.

Let us suppose that in some point in time a political administration has been empowered to coordinate these adjustments. If we assume conditions resembling the conditions of 1938 [58] such

---

[58] Should the controls be instituted at the termination of hostilities, the problem would be simpler since employment would not have to be increased but merely maintained.

an administration might inaugurate the program by initiating a program of public works so large that several million men would be required to accomplish it. At the same time the social authority charged with the administration of the three adjustments would probably be well advised to reduce corporation taxes. The primary objective would be to stimulate profit expectancy and the flow of privately borrowed money into capital formation. But a secondary objective of nearly as great importance would be realized. Business men, despite their wartime experience, are probably still conditioned to suppose that public spending of created money is dangerous, and private spending of created money the fulcrum of prosperity. (Our analysis suggests that the reverse is nearer the truth, since public spending on public works does not increase the capacity of the productive plant directly and therefore is less likely to result in excess capital than private borrowing and spending.) Consequently, the increase of private profit resulting from lower taxes would tend to bolster their confidence and good will, both of which would be reduced, past experience indicates, by public spending. And confidence and good will would facilitate the realization of the objectives.

In any case, the two measures, the public works and lower taxes, would undoubtedly touch off an upsurge of production, if the quantity of new money created and spent was greater than the value of the residual wealth increment released by the advance in efficiency. As a result, the unemployed would be gradually absorbed in gainful, constructive occupations.

The increment of wealth created by the production upsurge would consist in part of private capital formation, in part of consumer goods production, in part of public works. The public authority or board would not know in advance the dimensions of the three increments which would result from its measures but the board could observe and tabulate the respective increases by means of periodic reports, etc. nearly as fast as they occurred.

Soon after the upward movement had gained momentum, the optimum capital formation would be exceeded. Thereafter capital would be formed in excess of that quantity needed to replace outworn and obsolescent equipment, to introduce improved procedures and products, and to take care of the increased demand.

As a result the full productive plant would no longer be required in order to provide the consumer goods and services being demanded. This condition would be indicated by the production and capacity figures of the automobile, steel, lumber, and other key industries. Instead of waiting until the dividing of the market, the increase in unit costs and the decrease in profits brought about liquidation in the stock market and an arrest of private capital formation, the board might immediately increase corporation taxes and step up the minimum wage.

This action would doubtless precipitate the stock market break. However, should the workers who were disemployed by the indirect effects of this event, be rehired on public works at the increased minimum wage, over-all demand would be increased by the new money spending and the higher labor costs neutralized by the increased efficiency of the higher operating rate. As a result, the stock market liquidation would dry up, and the upsurge be revived.

The proposed method of exerting the three adjustments or interferences could be likened to entering a harbor under sail. Instead of steering for the harbor's mouth as would be the case were steam the motor force, or were the procedure planned in advance, the attainment of capacity production would require a series of back and forth, tacking movements none of which would be pointed for the goal, but all of which, by correcting unbalances as they showed themselves, would gradually bring the economy closer to the optimum relations.

By coordinating the three controls in some such fashion, full production, it is believed, could be gradually approached. When attained, further tax adjustments would be in order, an adjustment of profit taxes in order that capital formation would come to approximate the economic or optimum volume, and an adjustment of income taxes to bring withholdings close to that amount needed to pay for the desired capital formation. Should these tax adjustments cause a further slump, the slack would be taken up as before by an increment of public works at higher pay. Eventually an equilibrium adjustment is contemplated, at which wages would be high enough to induce a demand for consumer goods sufficient to maintain full employment even though capital formation was just sufficient to maintain and improve the plant and public works consisted *only of those works desired for their own sake*. When this condition was reached, the amplitude of the swings between more and less private capital formation would have become quite narrow and the residual public works program would be covered in *whole* or *large part* by *taxation*.[59]

Furthermore, when the optimum ratio between production and plant was approximated, taxes and the minimum wage would no longer have to be increased simultaneously. Thereafter, full production could be maintained and capacity production approximated by stepping up the minimum wage *pari passu* with the increase in efficiency, and by adjusting corporation taxes slightly upward and downward in order to stimulate or discourage private capital formation as the need might be. Thereafter, consumer goods demand would be increased by creating and spending money only as productivity [60] increased, the swings between more or less private capital formation (known as prosperity and depression) being held within narrow limits.

Even after capacity production had been approximated, no freezing of prices, wages, or profits would be desirable. On the contrary, it might be helpful to foster their liquidity by leaving scope as suggested above for small upsurges and downsurges at a high production level, since variation in the profit margin stimulates price and other adjustments thereby keeping the several industries and the concerns within the industries on their figurative toes in order to maintain their relative positions. Also the interpretation of changes in technology and in consumer taste by appropriate price adjustments would be abetted by such minor disturbances.[61]

[59] This suggestion is amplified on p. 256.

[60] Footnote p. 256 defines more fully the desirable increase in the volume of money.

[61] Other reasons for leaving some slack for cyclic movements could be cited. For example downsurges foster the liquidity of labor and management thereby facilitating the search of individuals for suitable jobs and of jobs for suitable individuals. Also depressions force the liquidation of dead wood concerns, a disagreeable but useful operation best performed by an impersonal agent such as the market. However no reason is apparent why the scope of such cyclic movements should be permitted to extend beyond that small amplitude in which the benefits are maximized and the bad effects minimized.

In short, it is contemplated that structural changes would continue to be translated into price and wage adjustments despite the minimization of cyclic movements, so that the economy would maintain its flexibility and its ability to allocate scarce resources economically.

It is evident that Adjustment 1 would be faciliated by a public works program of usefulness and elasticity.   At present (1944) a great public works program is being accomplished on created money, though its economic as distinct from its military utility is but dimly realized.   At other times, the usual outlets for public spending—river, soil and forest control, public building, highways, warships, etc.—might fulfill requirements especially in the later stages when the public works would be limited to those desired for their own sake.   However, such projects lack the elasticity needed for the early stages of the program, owing to their large scale and long span.

It might therefore be advisable for society to supplement the customary outlets for public works by taking over city planning and low cost housing at least temporarily.   Many volumes have been written citing the aesthetic, cultural, and technological advantages of so doing.   Such considerations are outside the scope of this argument.   It is, however, relevant to note that an extension of planned procedures to include low cost housing would not interfere with the parametric function of price, since the materials involved could be produced, as they are today, by market procedures, and the finished product, low cost dwelling units, etc., are not today produced privately by market procedures.[62]   Consequently, a program of public housing would involve no important institutional innovations but would require merely that run-down properties and land should be acquired by purchase or condemnation proceedings, instead of permitting them to be cut up by private interests or depreciated by neglect.

The attribute of low cost housing projects which relates to our problem is its elasticity.   Society can get along with better or worse housing without imperilling critically the individual's abil-

[62] Low cost housing is obtained in peacetimes largely by way of obsolescence. The poor wait until the houses of the better-to-do run down, or the character of a neighborhood depreciates, for habitations which they can afford.

ity to survive. Housing differs thereby from staple food provisioning, the upper and lower limits of which are relatively close together, and from military protection, reforestation, etc., the optimum dimensions of which are established by considerations other than the need for public works. Housing, however, can be improved indefinitely and continue to increase satisfactions at a rate which diminishes but slightly. As a result, the inclusion of low cost housing among other public works would permit the expansion and contraction of the spending program (Adjustment 1) as required.

Housing has another advantage over other spending outlets. The skills required for housing, city planning, etc., are so various that nearly every skill possessed by disemployed workers could be used to advantage and little retraining would be necessary in order to fit most individuals for some form of useful effort in this field. In short, the need for some form of public works which could be increased and curtailed widely and sporadically might best be met by adding low cost housing to the other outlets for public expenditures.

The considerations sketched in above merely ruffle the surface of the problem. However, this chapter, as was noted elsewhere, is supplementary to the analysis. No attempt therefore will be made to answer all the probable objections, although the next section is appended to fill in some of the more conspicuous gaps.

7. MONEY, DEBT, PRICES, WAGES, FOREIGN TRADE, AND SELLING EXPENSES ARE CONSIDERED IN CONNECTION WITH THE PROGRAM.

In general, it is proposed that society coordinate certain quantities which in the past have not been coordinated because of the explicit or implicit belief that optimum relations would be automatically approximated by the reflex interactions of economic factors. Thus, it is proposed to achieve an effective demand sufficient to require full employment by spending new money on public works (Adjustment 1). Demand has not been sustained at this level, presumably because it was erroneously believed that in a competitive system price would drop whenever demand was deficient in a particular field, thereby precluding a serious demand deficiency.

Similarly, it is proposed to limit the capital plant (Adjustment 2) to dimensions suited to accomplish the work asked of it. Such an adjustment has not been attempted, probably because it was supposed either that there could not be too much capital [63] or that variations in profit expectancy would induce an optimum allocation of effort between capital formation and consumer goods production. The tendency of monopolistic competition to form excess capital has not been taken fully into account.

It is also proposed to limit withholdings (Adjustments 2 and 3) to that quantity needed to pay for the requisite capital formation. Such a limitation has not been attempted, probably because it was supposed either that too much money could not be withheld from consumer goods purchases or that automatic variations in the interest rate would induce optimum savings. Finally, it is proposed to secure the propensity to consume (Adjustment 3) needed to maintain full employment (without diverting more effort to capital formation or public works than is desired) by raising the minimum wage. Until recently, the minimum wage was left to find its own level, possibly because it was supposed that the natural striving of individuals to better themselves would maximize real wages (which would be the case were employment full) or because it was supposed that a low wage merely meant that some would obtain more of the good things of life if others obtained less (which also would be the case were production full).

Despite society's reluctance to interfere in the above relationships, the control measures themselves have been instituted, for one reason or another, at least to some extent, as was noted earlier. Consequently, doubt in respect to them will probably center in most readers' minds not so much on the extension and coordination of the controls as on the effect of their coordination on debt, prices, wages, and foreign trade. Let us consider each in turn.

[63] Also capital, the means of production, is often not distinguished from that form of effort which serves the consumer directly, such as bridges, roads, monuments, etc. —structures which can be multiplied indefinitely without losing utility. Although the multiplication of these latter structures is subject, like everything else, to the law of diminishing utility, the means of production not only are subject to diminishing utility, but also lose their utility when redundant.

MONEY AND DEBT

The money aspect of Adjustment 1 has been touched upon several times. It has been brought out that so long as new money spending does not create an effective demand greater than the supply provided, the creation and spending of money does not result in inflation. Furthermore, the feasibility of achieving full production by spending money in excess of that withdrawn from the spending stream was indicated in 1942 when the unemployed (and additional millions enticed from civilian life) were quickly absorbed by activities paid for largely by created money. However, when debit money [64] is used for the spending, as during the war years, the operation leaves a residue of debt which has to be paid back or carried into the future. This feature of the operation has caused and is causing concern, although there is no reason to suppose that a further increase in the public debt would have more serious consequences than the last increase in the public debt. In other words, it would be difficult to prove that an internal debt of 350 billion dollars would be disastrous, when an internal debt of 300 billion evidently is not. Also, an increase of such magnitude would probably not be necessary to achieve full employment. On the contrary, less would be required were corrective action initiated when employment had fallen only a short distance.

Much of the concern is due to a misapprehension in regard to the nature of internal debt. Clearly a national *internal* debt cannot be compared to a private debt, since the American people owe the money to themselves. Thus every interest payment or refunding operation is a two-way transaction in which money is transferred from one set of pockets to another. Should the weight of the debt bear too heavily on any particular segment of the population, it would be due to an incorrect tax incidence, since it is evident that even a ten billion interest load cannot weigh heavily on a society which not only meets the interest but also receives it. However, debt could become embarrassing were it to increase indefinitely and were it to be concentrated among a few holders. Such an eventuality need not be antici-

[64] Conceivably currency or even a commodity money such as gold could be used for this purpose. Probably debit money is to be preferred, since it is easiest to control.

pated from the program under consideration, since the money spending feature would be needed only to achieve full employment.   Thereafter, Adjustments 2 and 3 could be used to maintain an equilibrium adjustment lacking the unbalanced features of the 1929 adjustment.   Full production with capital formation and consumer spending in economic proportions and with the annual wealth increment released by new money spending in combination with a gradually rising minimum wage should be self-perpetuating.   The minor forward and back movements resulting from seasonal unemployment, changes in consumer taste, and similar events, could be corrected when needed by equally minor changes in the tax rates.

Also, it might be feasible at full production to recapture by taxation more money than was needed for desired public works and government running expenses.   This unneeded money could then be applied to reducing the public debt, were precautions taken not to reduce demand thereby below the level of supply. Because of the difficulty involved in money cancellation when new money creation would be needed to release the residual wealth increment, and because the criteria for determining the optimum dimensions of the public debt, a problem studied by Hamilton and other Treasurers, are uncertain, the writer would be inclined once full production was attained, not to reduce the debt but to increase it thereafter, as suggested in Section 6, by the increments of new money (borrowed either by private industry or the government) needed to release the residual wealth increments made available annually by the advance of efficiency.   By so doing, *money and debt would increase only as product capacity and income increased*, and by a lesser amount.[65]

[65] The residual wealth increment by definition is less than the wealth increment made available by the advance in efficiency.   However the volume of money should probably increase "at a rate approximating the sum of the average annual rate of growth in population, trend of production per capita (efficiency) and the trend of increased use of money as a store of value."   Warburton, "Normal Production, etc." *op. cit.* p. 234.   If interested in the relation of the increment of income released by the new money spending and the increment of interest required to carry the increased debt, reference can be made to an article by Evsey D. Domar in the *American Economic Review*, December 1944, p. 798, "The Burden of the Debt and the National Income."   It appears that the debt increment can easily be carried if the wealth increment resulting from the efficiency advance is released, as postulated, by the new money increment.

PRICES

Though the suggested adjustments would not make any essential change in current pricing procedures, Adjustment 2 has a bearing upon the profits and prices of monopolistic competition, the consideration of which may help to bring out a somewhat obscure feature of the proposal.

In monopolistic competition, it was indicated in Chapter II, profits are assumedly held to a minimum by the ingress of new competitors and the resulting subdividing of the market whenever increased efficiency or other cause lowers the cost of production. It is proposed under the program to increase demand at some moment in time by spending new money on public works, thereby inducing an increase in production. An increase in production reduces per unit costs in fields of monopolistic competition, thereby increasing profits. Instead of permitting this increase to stimulate the ingress of newcomers without limit, it is proposed to recapture part of the excess profits by taxation, and thus hold down private capital formation to some desired volume. (So far the proposal parallels the actual events of the early war years.) However, such a diversion of funds would result in public works far in excess of those desired for their own sake in peace times, since the increased profits of industry would largely be diverted to the state which would spend them. (Solution II.) In order to shift the unneeded fraction of the increment from the state to the people, it is therefore proposed to raise the minimum wage, an adjustment which would increase certain costs and raise certain prices. The limit to the process would be that income distribution at which withholdings were just sufficient to pay for the requisite capital formation with taxes sufficient to cover government expenses, including desired public works.

Thus Adjustments 2 and 3 are designed to sluice effort, which in the past either went into excess capital formation or was unexerted [66] into the production of consumer goods and services, thereby raising the living standard.

In the discussion, no mention was made of the possibility that Adjustment 2, which is supposed to capture some of the excess

[66] In good years excess capital would be formed, in bad years the effort would not be exerted.

profit made available by Adjustment 1, might be hindered or nullified by enterprisers passing the profit taxes on to the public by means of higher prices. Such a reaction would, it is evident, defeat the purpose of the adjustment, since it would prevent profit expectancy from being reduced and excess capital formation from being limited. However, this eventuality need not be anticipated because a profit tax does not fall evenly on all producers. Instead, the tax would vary with the individual firm's profit declining to zero in the case of marginal producers. Consequently, *no* particular price increase would cover the new tax, the event differing thereby from an industry-wide wage increase, which because of its even application is likely to induce a compensatory industry-wide price increase.

Should the members of the industry get together and raise prices notwithstanding, conspiracy would be indicated. Consequently, the threat of prosecution under the Anti-Trust Law would serve usually as noted in Section IV to prevent this development, as it serves to prevent uncalled-for price rises in the current economy.

Another feature of a profit tax needs to be considered. It is evident that a graduated profit tax tends to smooth out the effect of differences in efficiency, since the efficient would be penalized more than the inefficient. This result could have dangerous consequences, because the standard of living is a function of efficiency, and an arrest in its advance would inhibit further increases in the living standard. Thus profit taxes on the 1944 scale might be disastrous, since they level down profits until the difference between the highest and the lowest is relatively narrow. However, Adjustment 3, the increase in the minimum wage, would raise costs indirectly as well as directly thereby neutralizing in part the cost reduction resulting from the higher rate of production. As a result taxes lower than 1944 taxes would probably serve to hold capital formation to the desired volume without weakening appreciably the inducement to produce at the lowest possible cost.

Though the actual dimensions of the profit and income taxes could best be established by experimental, or trial and error steps toward the desired quantitative relationships, the considerations cited above indicate that profit taxes should not be raised to a level which interfered with the incentive to produce efficiently.

In general, the over-all pricing problem of the individual enterpriser would be simplified by the proposed adjustments. Price administration today is complicated because account must be taken of the possibility of a drastic fall in demand and production. Thus steel used to be priced to cover costs at a 60% or 70% operating rate, on the assumption that production was likely to vary between 20% and 100%. Should the proposed adjustments achieve their purpose, demand would never fall below 80% of the demand of full production and could be counted upon to rise as efficiency and the population increased. As price administrators, in their competitive striving to entice a greater share of the market, took this changed condition into account, price calculations would be refined and prices gradually lowered. Thus the program may be expected to increase the living standard not only by increasing employment, raising the minimum wage, and reducing excess capital formation, but also by effecting a downward revision in certain prices.

WAGES

As the minimum wage rose, other wage adjustments would not be prohibited. Probably, the saving due to the sustained higher production rate, instead of being translated into lower prices as suggested above, would be diverted in some industries into higher wages. Such choices could be left to negotiation and other events as they are today.

The establishment of a gradually rising minimum wage does however present a subsidiary problem. Today, with no over-all minimum wage established, many individuals of less than marginal competency make a contribution to society and pass through life without unwonted suffering by accepting a less than usual compensation for their services. Were a job at a certain wage open to them, as it would be under an unmodified Adjustment 1, many such people would be overpaid, that is to say, would be paid more than their labor was worth.

It is no sin to overpay the congenitally incompetent. In fact, contemporary civilization supports the wholly incompetent, the senile, insane, crippled, under-aged, etc., in some fashion or other without asking anything in return. And the statistical data [67] indicate there could be enough staple goods produced to permit every individual to consume what he needed of them. However, paying the incompetent as much as the competent is likely to disrupt the morale of an organization. Consequently, a job for everyone might lessen the effectiveness of the public work's program to which presumably the less competent would largely accrete. This event not only would be costly to society but also might have damaging indirect results because of the infectious character of shared dissatisfactions.

It therefore would be desirable to have several categories of public services: (1) the regular services, (2) the elastic public works organization available to all competent workers (workers, the value of whose output in some field of effort equalled the minimum wage), and (3) other categories to take care of those who did not fit into these frames. Just what such categories should consist of lies outside the scope of this study.[68] Such alternative dispositions would be needed in order that the public works program itself should possess no stigma of charity or overtone of failure, but would constitute merely an institutional procedure like the post office and the forest service, designed to accomplish certain works and to maintain a certain balance between certain economic factors. As such, the morale of those employed in it might even be heightened and their skills increased.

FOREIGN TRADE

The domestic price structure would have to be guarded from the impact of foreign goods, many of which are produced by workers whose standard of living is lower than that of the American, and from the distress selling of overbuilt foreign industries for the following reason.

---

[67] The NSPPC report and our war record.

[68] It would be important, however, that service in these special groups should be less desirable than in groups (1) and (2), so that their enrollment would be held to a minimum. The individual would of course be free to accept private service in preference to the public service categories. No doubt many would prefer as they do today domestic services to public or private impersonal service. However, the existence of an alternative would no doubt force an increase in working standards, that of domestic service as well as others.

Underlying the program suggested in this chapter is a skepticism in respect to the ability of monopolistic competition to hold capital down to economic dimensions. Consequently, Adjustments 2 and 3 are designed to enable society indirectly to limit capital formation. No such limitation over foreign industries is feasible. Consequently, were international trade free, overbuilt foreign industries might be expected to attempt to extricate themselves from awkward situations by dumping part of their produce in other lands. Although such dumping would enable the American buyers to obtain goods for less than their cost, it would also disrupt domestic production, bankrupting business concerns and throwing men out of work. Rather than attempt to devise measures to neutralize each such event, it would be simpler to protect American prices from this kind of foreign competition, especially since the American standard of living and real wage even now range higher than that of economies less endowed with organizational ability and with natural resources.

To protect the American price structure, tariffs have long been used. Probably the existing tariffs [69] with an adjustment here and there as new conditions arose, would serve to accomplish this purpose. In making such adjustments, certain considerations which tend to be overlooked might well be given increased emphasis.

Foreign trade consists essentially of exchanging commodities conveniently produced at home for commodities more conveniently produced elsewhere. Thus America conveniently imports nickel, tin, tea, coffee, leather, etc., and conveniently exports cotton, corn, tobacco, lard and many varieties of manufactured goods as noted in an early chapter. A socially useful foreign trade, as we saw in Chapter I, would not persistently export goods in excess of those imported, since this form of altruism causes painful and unnecessary complications. Also, a society would increase its future living at little sacrifice should it conserve its limited resources, such as the non-recurrent raw materials, by minimizing their export, and use for exports as large a

---

[69] The tariff protects American prices, including the wage, real as well as monetary from the competition of foreigners conditioned as noted above to exist on less produce. Should the American minimum wage be raised as suggested, the need of this protection might be greater.

proportion as possible of its recurrent resources, such as farm products and embodied human skills.[70]   Finally, a society would make itself more secure, could it export commodities such as airplanes and munitions, which are needed for defense and thereby justify the maintenance of a plant capacity for these commodities greater than that called for by the domestic demand. Thus the factors involved in foreign trade transcend the simple criteria of buying cheap and selling dear emphasized by the free traders.

It may therefore be that in the future, more complicated criteria for regulating foreign trade will be utilized.   The controls, however, need not cover the exchange of works of art and handicraft, travel, luxury goods, etc., all of which would seem suitable for unrestricted international barter, though each tariff-enclosed trading unit might find it advisable to take the annual net excess or deficit from this free trade into account when budgeting its exchange of the staples.[71]

SELLING EXPENSES

Nonproduction and excess capital formation are not the only procedures that hold down wealth production, although they are probably the most wasteful.   Of the other wastes that have to do with economic procedures, only one seems important enough for comment.

In defining monopolistic competition, it was noted that the procedure removed competition to a large extent from the sphere of efficiency and transferred it to that of salesmanship.   Instead of profit depending largely upon the relative efficiencies of the competing concerns, as is the case with farmers [72] and other producers subject to price competition, profit has come to depend largely upon the relative success of the vendor in disposing of his goods.   When capacity is greater than production, the usual con-

---

[70] Processed goods usually contain a large quota of human skill.

[71] Should excess capacity be held within narrow limits in other areas, and should the population of India, China & other regions learn how to prevent the population rising with the food supply, tariffs & other international restrictions could be attenuated.

[72] Rent may be assumed to equalize natural advantages, such as soil fertility, etc. as noted in Chapter I.

dition in the existing form of monopolistic competition, a producer whose production approached more closely to his plant capacity than that of another producer, would make the greater profit or the smaller loss, other things being equal. This condition has resulted in an extraordinary increase in the proportion of man-hours assigned to selling,[73]—direct selling, publicity, advertising, etc. Not all of this selling effort appears to be social useful. Should some of the effort now allocated to selling be diverted to production, capacity would be increased.[74]

Though the program as presented does not curtail the waste of duplicate, disutile and nuisance selling directly, it would indirectly reduce the proportion of effort allocated to selling for the following reason.

Raising the minimum wage at a time of increasing production would increase disproportionately, as was noted, the demand for many kinds of consumer goods and services. For example, the demand for educational, recreational and medical services would probably be increased more than the demand for staple foods, clothing, heat, etc. Furthermore, were capital formation held down as demand and production increased, producers after a while would not need to infringe upon each other's share of the market in order to obtain enough orders to operate at or near their most efficient scale. As a result, the importance of salesmanship would diminish and the importance of producing with the fewest man-hours per unit output (efficiency) would increase.

It therefore is reasonable to expect the demand for professional services to increase and the demand for selling services to decrease as the proposed adjustments took effect. As a result, the pay of teachers, doctors, etc. would rise and the pay of salesmen would fall. As time passed, these trends would divert man-hours from selling to producing and servicing. Eventually, selling effort might even come to approximate that proportion of the total effort which is socially useful, a proportion sufficient to introduce new products, to educate prospective consumers in re-

[73] *Recent Social Trends, op. cit.*

[74] When production is less than full, even useless selling effort is better than no effort, since a salesman is better off than a charity ward, and one form of subsidy is no more disagreeable than the other so far as society is concerned.

spect to the character of the various goods, and to render such producer services as are helpful to the consumer.

8. THE GENERAL FEASIBILITY OF THE PROPOSED ADJUSTMENTS IS REVIEWED.

In order to bring out wherein our proposal departs from popular thinking on the subject, a comparison may be helpful. Let us oversimplify the situation by supposing that increased production is usually sought along one of the two following lines which we shall arbitrarily call the "Old Deal" and the "New Deal," since these tags seem to illuminate the contrasted approaches more than they obfuscate them.

According to the Old Deal, employment depends upon production and production upon profit expectancy. Profit is increased by reducing costs, cet. par. Therefore, the Old Deal, when unemployment exists, logically recommends lower real wages in order to increase profits, profit expectancy, and production on the supposition that the family income would be raised more by the increased employment than it would be reduced by the lower wage of the individual workers. Should this result ensue, the underlying population would share with the enterprisers and owners the wealth increment made available by the step-up in production and everybody would be better off. Although the Old Deal has been on the defensive in America because of a dim realization that it is not necessary to cut anybody's pay in order to produce and distribute more wealth, it is still put forward in its original form by some business men, Von Mises (*op. cit.*) and other purists.

According to the New Deal, employment depends upon production and production upon demand, in particular the demand for consumer goods. Therefore, the New Deal recommends raising wages by law, union pressure, etc., and the income of the unemployed by doles and made work in order to increase the demand and production of consumer goods, on the supposition that the enterprisers and owners would share with the workers the wealth increment made available by the step-up in production, since profit rises with turnover, and everybody would be better off.

Our study has indicated the inadequacy of both theses. Lower wages, it was indicated, would not increase profit cet. par. because the reduction in demand resulting from the lowered wage would probably induce a drop in production. The increased overhead costs per unit as production dropped might neutralize or more than neutralize the decreased costs per unit due to the lower wage, profit might be diminished instead of increased, and general impoverishment result.

The New Deal is not quite so vulnerable. However, it too is inadequate as presented above. Were real wages and the dole raised and were no other measures instituted, the payments would come out of owner and enterpriser income. As a result, profit expectancy would be lowered. Capital formation would be reduced and might even be arrested. The expected increase of demand due to the higher wage and charity payments might be neutralized or more than neutralized by the reduction in demand due to the increased unemployment. As over-all production dropped, the workers would share the loss with the owners and enterprisers.

Something like the above sequence may have occurred in France under the Blum regime. The American New Deal has been more fortunate. First for humanitarian and pump-priming reasons (the CWA and relief), later for humanitarian and pressure group reasons (the bonus) and lastly for defense reasons, the wage and dole increases of recent years have sometimes been synchronized with the creation and spending of new money. The new money stepped up production and profit expectancy (Case IV) even as wages were increased. As a result, thrice the New Deal has touched off upsurges in production, in which workers, owners and enterprisers divided the resulting wealth increment.

The fallacy underlying both the Old Deal and the New Deal (as presented above in an oversimplified form) probably stems from Ricardo. As noted in the introduction, he believed that economics had to do with the distribution of wealth rather than with its production, a logical enough thesis were full production automatically induced. If production were always full, then a drop in wages would increase profits and vice versa, as he clearly saw.[75]   And if a drop in wages increased profits, the logic of the Old Deal would be indefeasible, since the increased profits would stimulate capital formation, the new capital was supposed to increase efficiency, and the increased efficiency would enable society to produce more wealth.   Similarly, if production were always full, a rise in wages would increase demand and the production of consumer goods as the New Deal hoped.

However, in a system of monopolistic competition, in which full production is not automatically induced, a drop in wages, as noted above, would be likely directly to reduce demand and thereby production, and a rise in wages would be likely to reduce profits, capital formation, demand and thereby production.

In short, production and the standard of living might not be increased by increasing profit at the expense of wages (Old Deal) or increasing wages at the expense of profit (New Deal) but could be stepped up at a time of unemployment by increasing simultaneously wages, profits and production.

Our analysis, to put it another way, avoids the dilemma of higher wages—lower profits, or lower wages—higher profits, by taking into account that production (Q) is variable.   When consideration is given to the fact that Q in the equation $W + D = QP$ may vary as well as wages and profits, then the supposed conflict between exploiter and exploited disappears, or at least is postponed until full production is realized.

Nevertheless, it is certain that the proposed measures which attempt to take advantage of this possibility would not work out in all respects as anticipated.   The mind cannot foresee all the ramifications of an event in a complicated field.   Fortunately, several critical features of the program have already been subjected to the test of trial.

As was noted in an earlier section, Adjustment 1 has been accomplished not only by the United States but by all the other warring nations.

Adjustment 2 is subject to no such clear cut proof.   Since capital formation varies with profit expectancy and profit expectancy can be reduced by taxing profits, other things being

[75] To Karl Marx belongs the credit for pushing this thesis to its reductio ad absurdum.

equal, the effectiveness of Adjustment 2 depends essentially on whether the balance sought, namely, an optimum relationship between the means of production and consumer goods production, could be achieved by means of so indirect a control.

However, the program would not be compromised by the failure of this phase of the adjustment to achieve its full objective. Thus, if too much effort continued to be allocated to private capital formation, despite the increased tax on profits, per unit cost would not fall to the fullest possible extent and the minimum wage could not be raised as much as it otherwise might be. Neither of these inadequacies would cause unemployment or disrupt other features of the program.

Similarly, it might be doubted that "withholdings" just sufficient to pay for the desired capital formation could be induced by adjusting income taxes and the minimum wage. Again it must be admitted that such an adjustment has not been attempted. However, income distribution is known to affect the propensity to consume. And if the desired "withholdings" were not exactly achieved, a differential in any year would not seriously upset the balance, since the resulting excess or deficiency of withholdings over investments could be neutralized by a compensatory increment or decrement of new money. Thus, if more money was withheld than was invested, society could counteract the deflationary effect of private debt repayment by government spending on public works. And if less money was withheld than was required, the banks would undoubtedly find the necessary funds by creating them, as they frequently do under current procedures. Presumably, such differentials could be reduced over the years as insight into the reactions of the various factors gradually sharpened.

With respect to Adjustment 3, its feasibility was demonstrated during the war. The minimum wage was effectively raised several notches by the shortage of labor caused by the draft and the other demands of the military. There is no reason to suppose that a similar result could not be deliberately accomplished in peacetimes by the indicated measure. Furthermore, the peacetime adjustment would be less drastic and put less pressure on prices than the war time adjustment because there would be no need to absorb more labor by public works than was readily available. As a result, the lower wage industries would not find themselves short of labor, as they did during the war, but merely under pressure to meet the minimum wage. The price of raspberries would undoubtedly rise, as it did during the war, but the supply of raspberries would not necessarily be reduced since pickers could be had at a price.

Thus, the observed behavior of the economy suggests that a program which coordinated new money spending with tax and minimum wage adjustments could induce full production and raise the living standard without infringing upon the freedom of prices and wages to interpret economic factors, nor the freedom of the individual to conduct his life according to his taste and competency. That capacity production also could be approached seems probable.[76] But even should society have to content itself with something less than the maximization of consumer goods, something more in the form of public works than the majority desired, nevertheless the resulting situation would be vastly better than that which prevailed in prewar America, when a large quota of effort was not applied and a fraction of society was unable to function usefully.

---

[76] This statement is qualified in the Conclusion by considering several factors lying outside the realm of economics.

Conclusion

THE statistics and our war record indicate that production in the United States would satisfy the needs and many of the desires of the *entire* population were the economy released to fulfill its potentialities. The analysis suggests that advantage is not taken of this possibility in times of peace because certain inherited inhibitions or taboos lend a sacrosanct character to the institutional entity known as "effective demand." Because of these inhibitions, production, that is to say, work in the world of men and materials, is in practice limited to the effective demand even when demand falls short of requiring full employment and of satisfying essential needs. It was concluded that the situation would be remedied were effective demand maintained at a level approaching the value of the possible supply by coordinating certain existing controls over money, income distribution, and the minimum wage.

I had intended to close the study with this thought. However, conditions outside of the borders of the United States affect and will continue to affect the domestic situation. Unless these outside factors are taken into account, a purely domestic solution might prove inadequate.

At the moment of writing (1944), another great war is approaching its conclusion. Because of the advance in technology and the resulting surplus of effort over that needed for survival, it has been feasible to divert a larger fraction of the national effort to waging war than was previously possible. As a result, recent wars have involved a greater proportion of the population and caused a relatively greater destruction than those of the last century. For the same reason, the ravages of war should be easier to repair than formerly, at any rate, in the regions where the ability to organize has not deteriorated. On the other hand, the ever-widening involvement in the military action is reducing the oases of safety where procreation and cultivation can continue undisturbed. Should the trend persist, the continuity of social development might in time be impaired. The release of atomic energy makes such a result even more probable. For this and other reasons the desirability of eliminating large scale warfare has become widely accepted among the United Nations. In fact, for the moment the problem of avoiding international war has distracted the public's thought from the problem underlying this study, of instituting domestic peace.

Actually, the two problems are intimately related because nonproduction created the climate which fostered the birth and growth of the Fascist-Nazi ideology. Unless nonproduction is held hereafter to smaller dimensions, I believe future conflicts will ensue regardless of the wisdom, ruthlessness or moderation exhibited at the peace table. It is true, many observers do not accept this thesis but maintain that there is something inherent in the German nature which induces this particular set of Central Europeans periodically to make a bid for world hegemony. Despite the eloquence of Vansittart and others less literary, this position seems somewhat fantastic. The similar origins of the Germans, English, Dutch, Northern French, etc., preclude the possibility of appreciable congenital differences. If the German proclivity for conquest is not congenital, but a matter of conditioning, based on some kind of an inferiority complex, then it could disappear as inconspicuously as it came into being. Should this opinion be sound, the destruction of Germany as a modern power would not eradicate the source of contemporary conflict.

Furthermore, if the enemy is not the glomerations of people tied together by language known as Germany and Japan, but rather a streamlined modern version of an ancient escape pattern, which might as well be called Nazism (since the Germans with their disciplined thoroughness have pushed the credo to its most effective and dreadful extreme); then the destruction of Germany not only would not eradicate the disease, but by scattering the germs, might even assist in its spread and growth.

There are always individuals scourged by personal frustration who tend to grasp at dogmatic credos which salve their vanity by placing the blame for their ills, real or imagined, on someone else, and which assuage their sense of inadequacy by giving them parts in a collective drive for power. Nazism, despite its peculiarly abhorrent variations, is probably a collective form of this well recognized reaction. The superstitions and hatreds on which it feeds stagnate in the cesspools of society among the abnormal and maladjusted when community life is healthy and the energetic find outlets for their drives and ambitions. They spread quickly, however, when the young and ambitious are baffled through no fault of their own by a situation which cannot be surmounted. Owing to nonproduction, such a situation became widespread among technically advanced societies in the early 1930's.

The assumption that the tendency to Nazism is not a national or racial characteristic but the product of an economic impasse is based on empirical as well as theoretical considerations. During the nadir of the depression, every country had its Nazi movements, some clearly inspired by the German example, others with roots smelling of their native soil. This condition was brought conspicuously to my attention during a speaking tour in 1933 when I visited a sampling of popular, so-called radical conventions. Among groups which traditionally favored the extension and intensification of the Democratic process, speeches could be heard favoring direct action, a march on Washington, the hanging of politicians, bankers, Jews, foreigners. Suspicion was rife. Conspiracy was charged. Could the ferment have been channelled against a set of enemies, as it had been in Germany, the urge to direct action might have been organized into a mass movement. In the United States, no one was able, during the short period, to bring the variegated animi into a unified frame, possibly because the political administration by fast, decisive action diverted a large proportion of the potential adherents into constructive channels, a service sometimes forgotten in later years.

It is not hard to understand why sustained nonproduction should lead to this development. In fact, were it not for the preference of most people for well-trodden paths, a more immediate reaction might be expected. Destitution is never easy to support. But mankind has been conditioned through the ages to do without needed goods when the cause is natural; such as drought, flood and pestilence. Even the suffering caused by war is accepted by many as part of the nature of things. But to go hungry when there is plenty of food, shabby when the textile

mills are idle, and ill-housed when millions of would-be builders
are unemployed, requires a different kind of forbearance. Since
the cause of such irrational conjunctions is obscure, an evil agent
is sought. Since no one gains by nonproduction, those with
peculiar antipathies have scope to persuade others of the potency
of their personal devils.

Admittedly revolutionary currents, some with high-sounding
ideals as well as predatory urges, have eddied beneath the surface
of society in all epochs, ready to surge to the top whenever conditions warranted. The peculiar aspect of our particular moment
is not that subversive movements exist, but that the subversive
movements when they gain power are able to fulfill certain of
their promises. This condition is unusual. Most past revolts,
even when initially successful, faltered once the immediate booty
was divided, because thereafter there was less to share than there
had been. But this result does not necessarily follow in our time.
Any group which put the unemployed to work on seizing power
would have more wealth to divide than the superseded authorities who had been supporting men in idleness. This self-evident
truism was grasped by Hitler and cleverly utilized.

He was able to take advantage of the situation so effectively
because of a further possibility. It was noted in the last chapter
that demand could be maintained at a level commanding full
production by certain measures other than those selected. In
particular, an alternative program called Solution II was indicated. It differed from the preferred program in that new
money and money recovered by taxation in excess of that needed
for government running expenses would continue to be spent on
public works, without attempting to divert an appreciable fraction of it to the consumer by raising wages, lowering prices or
otherwise. Consequently, the fraction diverted to public works
would increase as efficiency advanced and a smaller proportion
of the total income was required for the more or less stabilized
cost of living. A ruling clique adopting Solution II would thus
be able not only to eliminate unemployment but also would
shortly be in a position to make a bid for world power if their
potential rivals persisted in non-employing men and non-produc-

ing wealth. Such a clique might in due course attempt to make good on their foreign as well as their domestic boasts.

Not only would such a program be practical, as events have demonstrated, but also it would outrage traditional concepts less the proposal outlined on these pages. Both programs, it is true, violate the widely held belief that governments, like individuals, should pay as they go. However, it is conventional to disregard this convention in emergencies. In order to obtain consent for government deficit spending, it is necessary merely to discover or to create an emergency. A Nazi racketeer can satisfy this condition more easily than a duly elected political authority, because the strength of the former is the result in large part of his having convinced his following before taking power of the existence of an emergency. After power is seized, the sense of emergency can be maintained by manipulating public opinion through the press and otherwise. Thus the Nazi clique encountered little domestic opposition to spending money on armament.

The widespread belief that an unbalanced budget leads shortly to disaster had a curious by-product in the years before the war. Many have wondered why England and France permitted the Nazi government to reconstruct its war machine and to proceed with its widely publicized plan for world domination. The unnatural humility of the Democracies during the critical years of German preparation is usually explained by imputing spinelessness treachery or other weakness. No doubt pacificism too had something to do with it. However, it is often forgotten that many of those in responsible positions whose job it was to be hardheaded were soothed into a policy of appeasement by the conviction that there was nothing to worry about. They believed Germany would go bankrupt before she got very far. Thus the mental confusion which permits physical production to be regulated by a variable institutional entity, *not only enabled the assailants to arm*, but also *to some extent disarmed* the assaulted.

Solution I outrages a further belief which Solution II leaves undisturbed. It is proposed to raise wages at the same time that production is being increased. Although such wage raises are quite usual in practice, the belief that the real wage must fall when production rises, is still firmly held not only by some economists, who have in mind the so-called law [1] of decreasing returns, but also by many of the very business men who resist wage increases less strongly when orders flow in, than when business is bad. It may be because of these considerations that variations of Solution II have been put into effect in many countries, while nothing approximating Solution I has been deliberately attempted, although the three indicated adjustments have been exerted though not coordinated in the United States and elsewhere, as noted in the last chapter.

In any case, secondary powers are likely again to challenge the ascendancy of the democracies by adopting Solution II and thereby diverting that effort not needed for maintaining the standard of living to preparing for and waging war if the democracies persist in non-utilizing a large fraction of their resources. This event, which happened in the 1930's with one set of protagonists, might, if the conditions are repeated, recur in the 1950's with the same or a new set of protagonists. In brief, the Nazis may lose the war and win the world. They are laying plans to bring about just such a denouement. Some of them are said to be going underground, others to be emigrating. Undoubtedly funds have been expatriated. Probably their agents will keep out of the public eye so long as the vast work of restoration maintains a simulacrum of health and a fever of activity. However, should industry again be throttled to meet the curtailed demand of half employed societies when the work of restoration has run its course, Nazi promises of a golden age if the "folk" would only exorcize the demons supposed to be curtailing production for the sake of profit, might again fall on eager ears.

It is therefore reasonable to expect that the practice of nonproduction, which has caused such world-shaking disturbances in the past, is likely to instigate even greater crises in the future, unless mankind by discarding certain economic superstitions liberates technology from the taboos which prevent it from delivering the goods and services it stands ready to provide.

It is not being maintained that such a release would remove the possibility of future war. Man is an ingenious animal and doubtless will continue to find things to fight about. But such a release

----

[1] p. 50.

and the resulting welfare would eliminate the main and unanswerable source of contemporary dissatisfaction, loosely called "want in the midst of plenty." Even more important, the release of production would reduce the advantage that a society adopting Solution II now has over the democracies. Should the United Nations by way of Solution I or otherwise, learn how to keep their human and other resources usefully functioning, it is hard to see how their position could be successfully challenged, at any rate for a long time. It is true that a society diverting all effort to military preparation, except the minimum needed to maintain its population's morale, would be stronger in a military way than a society with equal resources diverting all surplus effort to increasing its living standard. However, the United States, the British Empire and the Soviet Union have greater resources than other national units, which gives them a margin of safety. Furthermore, no nation is likely in the near future to adopt Solution I in its absolute form. On the contrary, the democracies are certain to maintain considerable excess capital for some time to come and to divert an appreciable fraction of their effort to military weapons of one kind and another. Thus the elimination of nonproduction would render war unlikely not so much because it would make the peace-preferring societies invulnerable, as because it would remove the main source of social unrest. In short political gangsters would lose their most powerful weapon should the full employment of our human resources provide the goods and leisure, which every technically advanced society could furnish all its members without taking anything, except involuntary unemployment, away from anyone.

The above argument, however, is negative, a reason why the United States cannot afford again to nonproduce in a big way. Reasons just as cogent can be marshalled on the positive side. Most of them have become hackneyed by repetition. Perhaps by presenting the primary advantage from an odd angle, its significance can be focussed.

Thorstein Veblen, writing before the days of persistent large scale nonproduction, supposed that the increment of wealth and time made available by the increase in efficiency accrued largely to the propertied, enterpriser, and other elite classes who devised or adopted various forms of "conspicuous waste" in order to use it up.   Thus he supposed that the wealth increment which might have gone to raising the living standard of the underlying population was translated largely into surplus clothes, conveyances, golf courses, hunting lodges, paintings, music and the thousand other items indulged in by those with time (leisure) on their hands.

The foregoing analysis suggests that these so-called "wastes" have been insufficient under present conditions to utilize all the energy made available by the advance in efficiency.   Society, in order to hold supply down to an inadequate demand, has had also to engage in large scale nonproduction.   Our proposed adjustments are designed to remove this necessity by increasing the buying power of the underlying population.   If the program should succeed in accomplishing this purpose, it would permit nearly everyone, instead of fractional elites, to indulge at least in a small way in what Veblen called "conspicuous waste."   Thus the successful accomplishment of the program not only would eliminate the waste of nonproduction and of excess capital formation but also might increase slightly the so-called "conspicuous wastes" that had formerly been confined largely to the pecunious classes.

However, the term "conspicuous waste" would seem deliberately invidious.[2]   The activities of the elite might just as well be described as "the amenities of civilization," a value judgment neither more nor less valid than Veblen's.

The gist of the matter is that the successful accomplishment of the program would enable the whole population, instead of a small fraction thereof, to indulge in certain supplementary activities which are not essential to physical survival.   These activities might be called "conspicuous wastes," "the amenities of civilization," or by some other name which seemed more suitable to the person using it.   In any case, the satisfaction of essential needs, with something left over for the less essential satisfactions, might result in disaster, or might provide the foundation of a new and better way of life.   This double-barreled potentiality may be

---

[2] Veblen calls the term "technical," on the assumption, that all consumption above that necessary for physical survival may be considered a "waste."   Though "technical," the term is none-the-less "invidious."

inferred from the record of the many "leisure classes" that have been thrown up in the past by the various more advanced civilizations. Some of these have wrecked themselves with what might be called "indulgences," some created works of various kinds which added zest to the days of those coming after. A more widespread leisure and command over commodities might have results just as diverse as the highly concentrated leisures of other periods.

Thus the release of production, now that technology has advanced to a point where favored societies could fully provide for their physical needs, would face all of society instead of a fraction thereof with the question of what to do with the energy not required for physical survival. No whole society has ever been faced with this question, though small classes in many communities have had a look at it. The answer, however, is the responsibility of artists, teachers and philosophers rather than economists.

One aspect of it, however, concerns every one. In a very real sense, the United States is dedicated by its founders to individual freedom. Probably no great society has gone farther toward achieving this ideal. Notwithstanding this triumph, large segments of the population have of late been deprived in effect of the exercise of freedom by the yoke of unemployment. Could the monopolistic competitors which pace the economy be released from the arbitrary limitations which now erratically and unnecessarily curtail their output, not only would everyone be privileged to function as a matter of course, but the competent would receive in return a satisfactory living with spots of leisure, and sometimes a great deal more. In such a society each individual would have scope to exercise his constitutional liberties. Thus the dream of a free society which has sustained successive generations of Americans, would be brought appreciably nearer realization.

Index I

REFERENCES

279

Index II

DEFINITIONS AND CONCEPTS